SAGE was founded in 1965 by Sara Miller McCune to support the dissemination of usable knowledge by publishing innovative and high-quality research and teaching content. Today, we publish over 900 journals, including those of more than 400 learned societies, more than 800 new books per year, and a growing range of library products including archives, data, case studies, reports, and video. SAGE remains majority-owned by our founder, and after Sara's lifetime will become owned by a charitable trust that secures our continued independence.

Los Angeles | London | New Delhi | Singapore | Washington DC | Melbourne

RENDEZVOUS WITH HINDI CINEMA

Thank you for choosing a SAGE product!
If you have any comment, observation or feedback,
I would like to personally hear from you.

Please write to me at **contactceo@sagepub.in**

Vivek Mehra, Managing Director and CEO, SAGE India.

Bulk Sales

SAGE India offers special discounts
for purchase of books in bulk.
We also make available special imprints
and excerpts from our books on demand.

For orders and enquiries, write to us at

Marketing Department
SAGE Publications India Pvt Ltd
B1/I-1, Mohan Cooperative Industrial Area
Mathura Road, Post Bag 7
New Delhi 110044, India

E-mail us at **marketing@sagepub.in**

Subscribe to our mailing list
Write to **marketing@sagepub.in**

This book is also available as an e-book.

RENDEZVOUS WITH HINDI CINEMA

Ophélie Wiel

Los Angeles | London | New Delhi
Singapore | Washington DC | Melbourne

Copyright © Ophélie Wiel, 2019

All rights reserved. No part of this book may be reproduced or utilized in any form or by any means, electronic or mechanical, including photocopying, recording, or by any information storage or retrieval system, without permission in writing from the publisher.

First published in 2019 by

SAGE Publications India Pvt Ltd
B1/I-1 Mohan Cooperative Industrial Area
Mathura Road, New Delhi 110 044, India
www.sagepub.in

YODA Press
79 Gulmohar Enclave
New Delhi 110049
www.yodapress.co.in

SAGE Publications Inc
2455 Teller Road
Thousand Oaks, California 91320, USA

SAGE Publications Ltd
1 Oliver's Yard, 55 City Road
London EC1Y 1SP, United Kingdom

SAGE Publications Asia-Pacific Pte Ltd
18 Cross Street #10-10/11/12
China Square Central
Singapore 048423

Published by Vivek Mehra for SAGE Publications India Pvt Ltd. Typeset in 10.5/13pt Bembo Regular by Fidus Design Pvt. Ltd, Chandigarh.

Library of Congress Cataloging-in-Publication Data Available

ISBN: 978-93-532-8655-2 (PB)

SAGE Yoda Team: Amrita Dutta, Vandana Gupta, Arpita Das, Ishita Gupta and Tanya Singh

CONTENTS

Foreword by Shabana Azmi	vii
Introduction	ix

Part 1: From Single-Screen Theatres to Multiplexes: The Indian Divide — 1

Jyothi Kapur Das, Ex-Producer for Viacom18 Motion Pictures	5
Avtar Panesar, Vice-President of International Operations at Yash Raj Films	19
Nazir Hossein, Exhibitor, Owner of Liberty Cinema	37

Part 2: The 'Bollywood' Show — 53

Atul Mongia, Casting Director	55
Sneha Khanwalkar, Music Composer	73
Manoshi Nath and Rushi Sharma, Costume Designers	93
Anjum Rajabali, Scriptwriter	109

Part 3: A New Generation in Mumbai — 119

Dibakar Banerjee, Director and Producer	123
Mayank Shekhar, Film Critic	143

Part 4: Women in the Hindi Film Industry   163

The Female Technicians of Hindi Cinema   167

Namrata Rao, Editor   167

Neha Parti Matiyani, Director of Photography   183

The Young Actresses of Hindi Cinema   201

Kalki Koechlin, Actress   201

Richa Chadha, Actress   217

Part 5: Censorship and Sexuality: The Taboos of Hindi Cinema   233

Pankaja Thakur, Ex-CEO of the Central Board of Film Certification (CBFC)   237

Onir, Director   251

Sridhar Rangayan, Director of the LGBT Film Festival 'Kashish' in Mumbai   271

Part 6: The Forgotten Genres: Animation and Documentary   289

Gitanjali Rao, Director   291

Nishtha Jain, Documentary Filmmaker   307

Conclusion   323

Acknowledgements   325

About the Author   327

FOREWORD

Ophélie Wiel's book is one that was waiting to happen. After so many books on celebrity actors and directors, and iconic film biographies, we needed books that take a more incisive look at the behind-the-scenes aspects of the splendid community that I am part of, the Indian film industry. Of course, Ophélie's book looks at the film industry in Mumbai, but many of the themes and trends she draws attention to in the book would be true of film communities and industries in other parts of India as well. This is a book that is written with a genuine commitment to let the interviewee's voice be heard clearly, without losing the candour of an informed outsider's eye. Ophélie comes from a country renowned for its film expertise and history, and she is also armed with an education in the field. However, her delight in Bombay cinema is unabated even as it cannot shake her from being a sharp interviewer.

One of the most empowering facts to emerge from this book, personally for me, and I suspect for many fans of Bombay cinema, is how women are finally making their presence felt on screen, behind the camera and on the floors. They are finally beginning to call the shots and inspire what could be a deluge of women professionals in filmmaking in the years to come. Women are speaking out loud, making their demands known, and beginning to bring a new aesthetic and sensibility to our films. And it's not soft power anymore, they are laughing their way to the banks doing all this now!

One of the most important and earliest things that I learnt being a part of the film community was that a film is not made by one person, it is made by a village, if you like. So many people invest their time, effort and energy into creating life and light and sound and magic by way of a film. This book will remind every reader and fan of the industry of this fact, even as it adds another page in making our audiences more aware about the process of filmmaking, the stupendous challenges therein, and how with every film that gets made, the determination to overcome those challenges again and again.

   I congratulate Ophélie Wiel on this important book which will add an important chapter to the growing corpus of writing on Indian cinema, a corpus that needs to grow ever more, each year.

Shabana Azmi

INTRODUCTION

It is a well-known fact that Indian Cinema is too diverse to be limited to the Bombay Film Industry, poorly named as Bollywood (a term we will use in this book, however, just for easy reference). Having said that, since I live in Mumbai, and because my knowledge of Hindi Cinema is vaster than that of Telugu, Tamil or other regional cinemas, it quickly became obvious to me that this fascinating city should remain, for now, the focus of my research.

The reader should thus be aware that the interviews published in this book focus on the international capital of Indian Cinema, so to speak, and may perhaps be of less interest to a Bengali film enthusiast. But despite its focus, it does not alienate itself from the other cinemas of India. After all, the Indian sub-continent is almost as big as Europe, and in being so, is home to as many cinemas as there are languages. However, many similarities still exist between one state and another—as much as Renoir's work cannot be completely dissociated from Rosselini's. Hence, our insisting, a little too often, on the differences between the Dravidian South India and the Indo-European North India, is a bit unfair given that most people who live in these regions define themselves as Indians before anything else.

What is interesting about this book is that it is a compilation of conversations with the very people who work in the Bombay film industry and therefore, both partake in and contribute to Hindi cinema. Technicians, actors, directors, film critics, individuals who, by being behind or in front of the camera, have chosen film as their profession. Despite how passionately I feel for this country, where

I have lived for the last seven years, it cannot be denied that I watch its cinema with European eyes, and I will probably never be able to escape the codes that I grew up with. Not to imply that the point-of-view of a foreigner would have less value, but the specificity of Indian cinema is such that one should appreciate in this book the fact that the industry is perceived here mostly through the eyes of those who make it.

These interviews were not completely planned or predetermined. They were the result of unexpected meetings and opportunities, and while going through them later I discovered that in more than half the interviews, what emerged were very powerful female voices. Though I had not consciously evoked these voices, I am proud to think that perhaps this is, in a way, India's answer for how poorly it comes across to the rest of the world in regards to the condition of its women.

A large number of the people I interviewed also knew each other, having worked together on several occasions. They constitute this group of film-buffs who dream of changing the face of Hindi cinema and whose work I discovered fourteen years ago with my first visit to India. These are exciting times for the Bombay film industry and I am grateful to be one of their prime witnesses.

PART 1

FROM SINGLE-SCREEN THEATRES TO MULTIPLEXES: THE INDIAN DIVIDE

The Indian film industry is a lot like the country itself, in an amusing sort of way, famous for its 'organized chaos'. One finds it difficult to get reliable data, as almost every film is declared a hit even before the second day of its release. It is best to be content with estimates: India has the biggest film industry in the world in terms of volume, ahead of Nigeria and United States. It produces around one thousand films per year, inclusive of all regions (Tamil and Telugu industries being the most prolific), and between two hundred and three hundred films for the Hindi film industry alone. Three billion tickets are sold per year (about eight million a day), with some superhits such as *Sholay* or *Dilwale Dulhania Le Jayenge* running in theatres for years (five for *Sholay*, nineteen for *Dilwale Dulhania Le Jayenge*). Though these numbers are astounding, they need to be put into perspective. India's biggest blockbuster of 2013 for instance, *Dhoom:3*, made about thirty-one million euros at the Indian box-office in ten days, while its American competition, *Iron-Man 3*, made a revenue of three hundred million euros in the same period. Of course, one should also assess these numbers keeping in mind international box-office, as well as the different standards of living between India and the United States. While Indian cinema rules the southern parts of the world, the fact remains that Hollywood is the worldwide leader in terms of revenues.

Since its humble beginnings in 1913, the Indian film industry has turned what was imaginable only in dreams into a reality so attractive that every day more and more individuals are drawn towards it. From the 1930s to the 1960s was the era of powerful studios, a model also used in Hollywood. Then came a period in which anyone would become a producer and films were financed from the most unlikely and unconventional sources. By the 1980s, the mafia got involved because financing a film was the most convenient way of money-laundering.

As a consequence, one of Indian cinema's main problems is ineffective channels of production and distribution, resulting in many films being abandoned or, once made, not being distributed. What is more, theatres in India (from mobile cinemas and rundown private viewing rooms to multiplexes) are neither sufficient in number nor spread out evenly across the country.

Who is to blame? The Indian film industry, for which cinema is not an art but a product? Or the government, whose interest in films never went beyond creating a few film schools (notably, the Film and Television Institute of India in Pune), an outdated film library (the National Film Archive of India in Pune) and financing a few arthouse films for festivals through the NFDC (National Film and Development Corporation)?

The 2000s brought a breath of fresh air, beginning with increasing globalization, and greater competition from Hollywood (though still limited, with less than ten per cent of releases in theatres). Above all, this was a period marked with the arrival of multiplexes and cable television. In Mumbai especially, these factors allowed audiences to claim that they wanted to see something other than the *masala* Bollywood film in theatres. This desire led to the growth of a new Indian cinema that was highly appreciated abroad, but widened the gap between the masses and the Westernized elite within India.

The professionals interviewed in this chapter represent the diversity of the cinema system in Mumbai: one is a producer attached to a TV channel that promotes this new kind of cinema; the second distributes films for Yash Raj, one of the biggest Indian studios and the largest exporter of Bollywood films, and the last owns a traditional theatre which struggles to fit into a new form of film screening. There is a need for relentless work to organize the chaos within the fraternity. Nonetheless, looking from where we are now, the future of Indian cinema may not appear completely positive, but promises to be exciting as some of its biggest changes are expected in the next ten years.

JYOTHI KAPUR DAS
Ex-Producer for Viacom18 Motion Pictures

I enter Viacom18's huge office in Vile Parle, next to the Mumbai Western Express Highway, as a kid would enter Willy Wonka's chocolate factory. Open spaces on all floors, screening rooms, and the huge enthusiastic smile of Producer Jyothi Kapur Das (who has since then become a full-time writer and director, winning a Filmfare Award for her short film *Chutney*) welcome me: before the conversation even started, I am already a satisfied customer, anticipating the good times that await me. I am almost tempted to bring a script with me the next time I am invited.

Founded in 2007 from a match between Viacom (today the fourth biggest media company in the world after Disney, Warner Bros and News Corporation) and the multimedia company Network 18, Viacom18 offers diverse channels for Indian satellite television (MTV, CNBC, CNN and Comedy Central to name a few). Its cinema production company, Viacom18 Motion Pictures, manages the entire assembly line from production to distribution, and owes its celebrity today to some wise choices it made along the way; instead of getting into a somewhat moribund sector (the Bollywood romantic comedy), Viacom18 decided to cater to the disillusioned audience that could not find anything satisfying in the theatres. Hence some almost unexpected successes, such as the highly acclaimed gangster film *Gangs of Wasseypur* [Anurag Kashyap, 2012] or the dramatic satire *Kahaani* [Sujoy Ghosh, 2012].

No one could ever blame Jyothi for delivering a speech formatted by her company. She talks about cinema with such passion and warmth that you start seeing a bright future for Indian cinema with her. She definitely knows how to convince you that smart ideas and original content will always find their way to the producers' hearts. True enough, 2016 started with a bang: two fairly non-traditional Bollywood films, *Airlift* [Raja Krishna Menon] and *Neerja* [Ram Madhvani], catering to the patriotic feelings of the Indian audience, and one regional film in Marathi, *Sairat* [Nagraj Manjule], made their way to the top spots of the Indian box-office. One could not forget though, that in 2015, the Indian film industry also experienced some of its biggest losses, with the most expensive film ever made, *Bombay Velvet* [Anurag Kashyap], not even recovering its costs. Struggling filmmakers are definitely not done denouncing the lack of audacity from studios which are still very much attached to having a star's face on the film poster. Never mind! Let us forget about cynicism for a moment and buy into the famous Indian maxim: 'In India, everything is possible'.

What made you get into films?

I did my editing course at the FTII, which is in Pune. I was editing for a bit, then I switched over to direction where I assisted on very hardcore Bollywood movies. I dropped out to have my babies, because you can't make babies when you're forty but you can still make movies! *(laughs)* Then I was writing scripts and doing what people do when they think they want to make films. I eventually got a call to join a company. I actually turned corporate at forty.

What happens is, when you're a technician, especially if you've come from a film school, you call people who've joined channels or corporate houses 'sell-outs': they sold their soul. They've gone over to the other side. They're the losers; those who can't make films go and make a salary. I, for a change, found it great to find myself in a corporate space, because the infrastructure is available, you can work in a very systematic manner, which I love because I am a very organized person except when I have to grab my kids from school. *(laughs)* When you are a freelancer, you write, you pitch to somebody, you get the money, you produce yourself. You are pretty much overseeing everything. A corporate structure allows you to have people in specific departments, helping you do all the operational stuff when you're keeping creative control.

I've got into corporate a few years ago and I'm loving the fact that I think I am making a difference somewhere, because I am from the other side. When people are coming to pitch, I am a lot easier with them, because I know where they're coming from. I am very realistic about the fact that, as a studio, every pitch that comes to us is not going to get made. But if there's potential in it, I try to help them out by giving them ways and means, and opportunities that I may have heard of, that they wouldn't have access to. I am not doing it completely selflessly: even if they go and make a first film somewhere, and it's a good film, they will remember that I gave them a good deal, and they'll come back with their second film. I am working on the principle that what goes around comes around. *(laughs)*

And I love films of course, I probably watch four-five films on the weekend, because I don't get the time during the week.

Which kind of films?

All kinds. I watch a film like an audience, because I know people are paying money to come into the theatre. It doesn't mean I don't appreciate a niche film, but lately, I am more in touch with resources that are invested into a film and how it ought to be feasible (which is a word that's ruling my life). There is always a voice in my head saying, 'you like it but it's not going to make the money'.

Why did you choose to attend a film school?

It's a good story. Way back in 1984, when I started doing my grade ten, the Indian television brought the University Grants Commission, which had afternoon educational television programmes for kids, across India. It didn't have any of their own content, so they would source out content from abroad. I knew nothing. I was just addicted to watching them because it was interesting and I got a window into different cultures. One day, I was watching one of the shows on *Battleship Potemkin* and the step sequence. I used to keep a little diary in which I would write down anything I found interesting. It made no sense to me, Potemkin or Eisenstein, I barely got the spelling right. But it was there in my diary and I remember seeing that step sequence and thinking 'wow'. When I graduated from my Bachelor of Arts, I went to a school that taught social mass media in Mumbai and they had a full-time course—advertising, film, journalism, television, radio. So you basically had a sample of how everything works, and you could choose later on what you wanted to do. In the film course, we were shown *Battleship Potemkin* and we had a discussion on how Eisenstein used editing film techniques in the step sequence. I flashed back into 1984 and how, as a fourteen year old, I was so kicked by that scene. So next year, I applied for the Institute [FTII] and I got through. Editing was what I chose because I thought that was really what was the most influential thing in the filmmaking process.

But you weren't an editor for too long …

I did some, but when I came out of film school, there weren't too many television channels which were making content, and there wasn't too much work in the corporate film sector or documentary sector. Of course everyone wants to make a film, whether sound recordists, directors of photography, editors, etc. The best way to learn is on the floor, so I just called up a few people and I said I wanted to assist them.

So you switched to direction. Did you make any feature films?

No, I assisted on feature films; I was doing corporate films and ads. Then there was this crazy boom that happened a few years ago in Bollywood, with the corporate houses actually. They basically skewed the entire market. People with smaller films, smaller budgets, somehow just went over the loop. There was a really strong independent film movement which was cut off at that point. There is another one now, but it's more corporate-driven, because even people like Anurag Kashyap, Sudhir Mishra, the stars of independent cinema, do need to hold hands with a corporate house to make sure that what they're doing comes out right and gets the kind of release that they would like. I always use *Gangs of Wasseypur* as an example of how crazy it is that a film with Manoj Bajpayee and Nawaz[uddin Siddiqui], who was completely unknown, can make the kind of money it did.

Where does this new boom come from?

People are going to spend two hundred bucks on a ticket, and about one hundred on their snacks, in the interval. They're spending three hundred bucks per person to come in and watch a film. Unless it's a big Salman Khan film or a Shah Rukh [Khan] film, the audience realizes they are not going to waste their money on stuff that doesn't make them engaged and excited. The word of mouth is out really fast because of the whole technology boom—Facebook, Twitter, social media networking, reviews coming out, radio. Content can really make a difference, even if, of course, we still have a very strong emphasis on whose faces are on the poster. Even actors, even directors are realizing that unless their story is really smart and kick-ass, they're not getting those bums on seats. So they've gotten cleverer, and they've decided to go ahead with projects which make sense even to them. It is all determined by the fact that the audience is not just lying down and playing dead anymore.

Didn't it come also from the fact that most traditional Bollywood romantic comedies started to flop at the box-office?

The writers were writing the same trash, directors were making the same stuff, actors were just repeating themselves in movies, and the audience just said, 'we are not going to watch movies anymore in the theatres, let it come on television.' There are a lot of films from that time, good films also, which suffered. The audience wouldn't know which one was good, which was bad. There were films for which people said, 'I didn't go to see it in the theatre, but when I saw it on TV, I realized it's not bad.' Television is perceived to be a free medium, although it's not—you pay the cable fees. So your tolerance level is a lot higher, you can tolerate more bullshit from a movie.

Viacom18 was created through a fusion between Viacom and Network 18. Was the company born from that boom in the industry?

There was this studio called Studio 18, which produced a lot of big films: *Ghajini* [A. R. Murugadoss, 2008], *Welcome* [Anees Bazmee, 2007]. Because of the changing trend of viewership—because of

MTV, Nick, Comedy Central which were part of the Viacom bouquet—this marriage happened. Viacom is known for a lot of content-driven business. The content has to be really kick-ass, and it also has to be revenue-generating. It's no use doing something that's very eclectic and very niche, if people are not going to watch it. If you do that, you have to be very clever about strategising when you are releasing the product. When we make films that are niche, we do a very limited release, and we keep increasing screens as it goes along if we think it justifies that.

We are the studio who brought *That Girl in Yellow Boots* [Anurag Kashyap, 2010], *Shaitan* [Bejoy Nambiar, 2011], and *Pyaar Ka Punchnama* [Luv Ranjan, 2011] which had four totally unknown new boys. It connected with the audience. When I went to see it, there were people repeating the dialogues, which means they were there before. That's the kind of connect that a producer can hope to get from a studio that believes in the content enough to put it out there, whether or not you have faces attached to it. But the responsibility shared with the producer is to keep costs in a reasonable space so that the studio isn't burdened. If you've blown a lot of money on something you thought was your dream, and it hasn't come back, then the people who counted on your dream happening are now really restricted with their purses. I saw *Barfi!* [Anurag Basu, 2012] in a theatre with tickets that I bought (not try-out shows, not free screenings). What was really exciting for me, first as a film school person, then as a corporate person, was that I was sitting in a Mumbai multiplex, surrounded by ordinary, middle-class people coming in to watch a film and enjoying what is essentially European cinema. You can discuss where it's derived from, where the scenes are copied from, etc. I am not even getting into that. I'm saying when it finally came on-screen, 90 per cent of the people who saw it hadn't seen the Hollywood or the European cinema precedents to it, they were watching a Hindi movie with Ranbir Kapoor, Priyanka Chopra and a new girl. And they enjoyed it, even though it's European in its craft. It's a gamble that paid off, which is something that is so exciting for me.

Bollywood is known to be a very star-driven industry ...

That's true.

But from what you've told me, at least for your company, the script has become more important.

It is. At least at Viacom18. When we come across something that's an exceptionally brilliant script, and we can tell that the director is really passionate, knows his craft, will be giving us a project that is exactly what he is promising, we take an effort to connect him with an actor, to add values to it. We say, 'Viacom likes this, do you want to come on board?' Because even if the actors like the script, they don't want it to be made and languish somewhere, they want to know who is going to release the film. My policy at Viacom usually is to get an actor interested. Because I know how difficult it is for a producer or a director on a set to have an actor who comes in simply because he thinks x, y, z studio is associated with it, or somebody's money is in it. That's demeaning, demoralizing for a producer or a direction team. The actor is a technician on the set; he's just another team member. So if you come back with somebody big, you don't need to talk money, you don't need to talk dates. If they really like what you're doing, we'll make sure your project happens. But they have to like it on the basis of the script, and their conviction that you will be able to follow through. Actors do still rule Bollywood in that sense.

Content-wise, all the producers, all the studios are getting really choosy about what they want to put up there. I had a conversation a couple of days ago with a director who is associated with rom-coms [romantic comedies]. He was saying, 'Listen, if there's something happening with you, it could be a thriller, it could be a drama, I don't have to just do rom-coms all the time.' He has built a whole empire on romantic comedies and his company gets forty-odd scripts a month, just rom-com driven. *Bombay Talkies* [Dibakar Banerjee, Anurag Kashyap, Zoya Akhtar, Karan Johar, 2013] had Karan [Johar], and Zoya [Akhtar] coming out of her comfort zone, Dibakar [Banerjee] with this great story and Anurag's which is so uplifting! [*Bombay Talkies* was a feature film consisting of four short films by four different directors] Each film has a different nuance of how people are looking at films, but I think the biggest thing that *Bombay Talkies* did, as an experiment, was to get these four mainstream directors to put completely new content out there. What Anurag [Kashyap] is associated with is hard-hitting, violent kind of cinema, the cross routes, the greedy, the darker side of life. Yet his short in *Bombay Talkies, Murabba* [*Fruit Preserve*], is sweet, very different from what he does usually. With *Bombay Talkies* we used the directors as stars.

So the script is the foundation, but you still need to use the stars if the director is not someone big.

Yes.

Studios were omnipotent in the 1950s. And then films were made by more or less independent producers ...

Anybody who had money came in and signed the actor, whether the script was written or not. Then a story was written, some dialogues were written. The underworld money came in, so that was all black money. I call these films black and white films. They were produced to lose money. X had got cash, black money from somewhere, and needed to launder it. The easiest way to launder is through films. If the film flopped, it was great news: with the losses, the money had been laundered away.

How do you make a movie that is going to lose money for sure?

You cast your family members! *(laughs)* Then, of course, corporates came in at a certain point with a large amount of money and they were signing people on left, right and centre. Actors, directors were doing three film deals, and there was a lot of money floating around in the market but no content to back it. You signed a director thinking he's made one or two films that were great and he's going to become the next big thing. But he derailed and went off somewhere. So you have court cases. The number of court cases that are floating around in Bollywood is impressive! Now we've reached a kind of real new age, which is a balance between the content and the commerce. The intention is to get known as a studio that makes good, engaging content. It may not be stuff that you've seen before, but why don't you try to see if you like it? These actors may not be actors that you recognize, but they're going to surprise you with some funny lines or some good performances. Or films with actors or directors who just work out-of-the-box, from what they've been known so far to do. For example, when Akshay Kumar was doing all these *Rowdy Rathore* [Prabhudeva, 2012] or *Khiladi 786* [Ashish R. Mogan, 2012], he comes around and does *Special Chabbis* [Neeraj Pandey, 2013] for Viacom, which was a thriller, a period film, in which he had a completely different look. Also, he produced and did a special appearance in *Oh My God!* [Umesh Shukla, 2012], where you have this common man who is an atheist and takes God to court. The director Farhan Akhtar acted in a biopic, *Bhaag Milkha Bhaag* [Rakeysh Omprakash Mehra, 2013]. Priyanka Chopra is playing the main character, a boxer, in the biopic *Mary Kom* [Omung Kumar, 2014]. And of course, we're doing a lot of smaller films, which go from as low as literally a 1.5 crore budget to whatever. We feel that there are different risks that each story carries, so we're taking prudent steps with each genre, each class, each type of films. Every film is judged, which doesn't mean there are only fifteen-crore projects and they cannot go to thirty crores, or cannot go down to three. If a big actor comes into something that we see as a five-six crores film, the values go up, so the investment is more, but the risk is minimized. Or if you have a good music director who is popular, you know you're going to get an audience. Maybe by virtue of having been on the other side, where I've pitched in corporate houses, I always try and make sure—and I think that's something a lot of my colleagues in other corporate houses do now—to keep the turnaround time of refusal very short. If we don't like something, the old-fashioned way is that nobody says, 'no, we are not interested.' At Viacom, when there's a narration, we'll all be sitting at the table together and give an opinion. It's more or less unanimous: everybody has to be really excited, to see potential, and then we go ahead.

How different is your studio system from the studio system of the 1950s?

The earlier studio system, like Bombay Talkies, had actors on payroll.

Like in Hollywood?

Absolutely, the Hollywood model. Whereas now, the studio system helps to streamline the production of a film. It exists to guarantee the financing of a film, to guarantee that your film doesn't run out of funds while you're shooting, to guarantee a distribution if you've made it the way you've promised that you were going to make it. It's a stress-free guarantee. When a studio comes in to partner, it's literally the studios putting in the money and the producers putting in the execution: it's a 50/50 partnership. A producer is free to go work on his next film somewhere else. But I would think that if there's been a good experience with one project, on both sides, then they would be happy working with each other again. That emotional and professional comfort is the binding force now.

Most of the films you have done at Viacom18 were co-productions. What is your exact role in the production of a movie?

The whole creative team will sit when the script is ready and we'll have a lot of interactions with the directors, with the actors—how they are looking at the film and all that. Then you move to the pre-production stage, where we are constantly kept looped in through the executive producer on whatever values are being added—the technicians being signed, for example. We keep a record of the paperwork as well, because budgets are all audited. So we are being very responsible with that, because it's our money.

Do you have a say in the choice of technicians?

We are pretty easy with a lot of stuff. In a *Gangs of Wasseypur* situation, for example, the music would be one of the last concerns. Because the script itself and the performances needed to fall so correctly into place, it was an added bonus that the music was really good. Anurag gave us not only a great film, but also a superb album. If it's a *Tanu Weds Manu* [Anand L. Rai, 2011], which is a wedding movie in a very commercial mainstream space, you do need good music. *Tanu Weds Manu* was an acquisition: the studio came in much later during the shooting to buy the film out, but we got RDB (who is a very big bhangra-pop singer) to do a song. That song is not even in the film—it was just playing in the promotions—but the film just flew because of that song. People came and liked the film, but maybe they wouldn't have come without the song, because the pairing of the film was really unusual.

There are different times when we used our discretion in terms of what's important to the partnership. How much am I giving? How much do I insist on this, how much do I let the team and the director be comfortable? And then maybe you can put forth something. There are certain places in which we as a studio have tie-ups: film stock, film processing lab, or sound processing labs, or VFX studios. We pass on those benefits to our partners.

Our executive producer is there usually throughout the shoot to deal with any problems, any delays in money coming through. When you know there is going to be a really big crowd sequence that's coming up four days later, and you need two thousand, three thousand people in a field that need to be paid and fed at the end of the day, the executive producer will immediately process this. It has to be process-driven, because otherwise, there would be a lot of irregularities. You try to be as prepared as possible to cover all bases. Too many people depend on a good organization. On *Gangs of Wasseypur*, there was an accident: we lost an assistant director in a jeep sequence. Our executive producer was there. She coordinated with the insurance company. In post-production, we are constantly in touch with the team. Our marketing department gets focus groups to come in, take a look, give suggestions, because we're already so close, we lose focus. And then distribution steps in and says, 'I can risk this film to release in so many theatres.' Or, 'there's a biggie coming, I don't want to clash with that.' Or, 'The similar kind of film is coming up, we should wait or release it before that.' All these strategic decisions are taken in conjunction with the producer. When it's a partnership, it literally means a partnership. We keep communicating back and forth with whomever on that side we are talking to.

And what part do you play in this? Do you follow the film from beginning to end?

I used to do that. Now we've got way too many films on the floor. Really too many. Like twenty. They are not all on the floor, but we know they are lined up, they are all signed. I am looking at the first filter of development, making sure whatever content is coming in is good. I am listening to five-six narrations a week. A lot of people come to us with films that they've already put their money in, or edits, or completed films that they want us to acquire. We wouldn't say no to listening to or seeing anything, because you never know what gem is hidden there. Currently I am focusing only on the development of all materials. We've got about three people in development, and the other three are just on production (who go on the sets and check all the edits). I go on the sets occasionally, I check the edits for sure, because that's really my *forte*. There are low-budget films which I feel need a lot of input from us as a team; in those cases I've been there hand-holding throughout. But mostly now I've stayed out of the hardcore production floor. I've moved to the content and all the new films we want to line-up.

Viacom18 also deals with distribution—a crucial problem for films in India.

We would like to think of ourselves as a onestop shopper. You come in with a concept and we could do a development deal with you to develop a script, we could go into production, cast it, get all the values on it. Then you finish your film, we all hope it's not a nasty shock, and we can line it up for distribution. We don't like to come in right at the end, when somebody has made something and we just need to sell it. Then it's only marketing and distribution which put their heads together.

Has it happened that once the film is finished, you realized you can't release it because it's so bad?

Yes. *(laughs)* Not often. It's happened because we operate on leaps of faith. Usually, the faith is sustained. The director delivered what we hoped he would. When we decided not to release a film, it never was because somebody has been incompetent, but because a lot of factors didn't work: the sample that we saw of someone's work has been in a very different space, or a different genre, or a different language, etc., and when they had to deliver in a Hindi-Bollywood space, somehow it just back-fired, and in that case those films haven't released yet.

Is there a lot of money in Bollywood now?

Yes. Indian movies are making a lot of money. Some smaller films are also making a lot of money, which is great. *Kai Po Che!* [Abhishek Kapoor, 2013] did well with newcomers because of the content. Same goes for *Tanu Weds Manu*. It's always a very happy situation across the industry when you know the investment is low and a product has over-delivered. That's a situation that you want to keep replicating. I am very happy—even if it's from another studio—when a small film does well, because that means I can do it too.

So you're optimistic about the future of Indian cinema?

Very.

What about worldwide distribution?

Whenever I go to Berlin, everybody knows Shah Rukh Khan, because they shot *Don 2* [Farhan Akhtar, 2011] there. And *Khabhi Khushi Kabhi Gham* [Karan Johar, 2001] was a big hit on television. But what would really excite me would be if a truly Indian film did well there, like *Gangs of Wasseypur*, which was appreciated abroad by the festival circuit, and did really well in India. It has a very Indian content—it uses a lot of Bollywood references, the language, the milieu. It was not Bengali cinema, very aesthetic, very eclectic, intellectual. It was hardcore. There were abuses. It translated into what audiences find recognizable everywhere—revenge, lust, violence, somebody cheating on his wife. I think the French understood that. *(laughs)*

On which kind of movies do you prefer to work? Mainstream Bollywood or a *Gangs of Wasseypur*?

I watch pretty much everything. I whistle in the theatre! Because I am from film school and because I've been in the industry for twenty years, I know most of the names in the credits, technicians and everyone, so I am whistling right from there. I think most people do that. They go to see a mindless entertainer, keeping their mind at home, so they enjoy it in their own way; and they go to see something they know is going to be challenging. When you already have the pre-conceived attitude with which you go watch a movie, you enjoy every film, hopefully in the way the producer or the director wants you to enjoy it!

AVTAR PANESAR
Vice-President of International Operations at Yash Raj Films

You can't help feeling a little emotional when you enter the offices of Yash Raj Studios—the closest look-alike to Universal that can be found in Mumbai—knowing that you might get a glimpse of Shah Rukh Khan smoking a cigarette between shots, or feel the warmth of Ranveer Singh's seductive smile. As luck wouldn't have it, no shoot of that sort was happening on the day of my interview, but I felt fortunate enough to be welcomed into the sanctuary of decision-making, not far away from the office of 'Adi', as everyone in the industry familiarly calls the powerful head of Yash Raj, Aditya Chopra.

Indeed, Yash Raj Films is one of the most legendary film production companies in Mumbai. Founded in 1970 by Yash Chopra, it produced some truly celebrated films of Hindi cinema: Yash Chopra's films, such as *Kabhi Kabhie* [1976], *Silsila* [1981] or *Veer-Zaara* [2004], but also the work of his son Aditya (now the managing director of the company), *Dilwale Dulhania Le Jayenge* [1995] or *Mohabbatein* [2000] which gave superstar Shah Rukh Khan some of his first major hits. For a long time Yash Raj focused on producing family-oriented movies. In the last few years, however, it has spread to other genres, evidently conscious that the Bollywood machinery has to update itself if it doesn't want to die out. Yash Raj has notably signed a three-film contract with filmmaker Dibakar Banerjee—the second one, *Detective Byomkesh Bakshy!* was released in April 2015.

YRF is also the best-established Indian studio abroad, with offices in London, New York and Dubai. Last but not least, it has recently opened a wing dedicated for web series, Y Films, which produces content that is slightly liberated from the conservative values of its parent company.

Avtar Panesar is one of the pillars of the studio, having worked there for sixteen years, first in London and now in Mumbai. Vice-President of International Affairs for YRF, he is a mine of information when it comes to the growing international space for commercial Bollywood films and on the reactions of NRIs [Non Resident Indians], a somewhat forgotten but truly vital social entity for Indian cinema. Avtar is a smart-looking man who worked his way up the company ladder and is truly passionate about movies. He never lost his serious composure during the interview but, with much-appreciated kindness, confided in me all the YRF secrets he could share.

You've been working for sixteen years at Yash Raj. How did you join the company?

I used to work in the music business, with EMI India. We released all Yash Raj music. The Chopras wanted to open an international arm and office in London. That's when they contacted me, through Aditya Chopra, in 1997.

Were you born in London?

I was born in India but I grew up in London. I just moved to India four years ago.

Did your interest in cinema develop early in life?

I was about ten when I moved to London, and I always loved Indian movies and Indian music. Living in London made it even closer to my heart, perhaps, because I was far from India—as it is with everybody else who lives in these countries: they are more connected to India through cinema than anything else. I was no different. I used to get one pound pocket-money a week. The LP record cost three pounds seventy-five cents, so I would save up for four weeks and I would go to the nearest record shop to buy my record. We had an old radiogram, so I sat there, listened to the songs, opened the LP and just kept looking at the visuals. LPs like *Kabhi Kabhie* [Yash Chopra, 1976], *Laila Majnu* [Harnam Singh Rawail, 1979], *Muqaddar Ka Sikandar* [Prakash Mehra, 1978] had lovely pages with lots of visuals. At about sixteen, I joined the Gramophone Company of India, which is the EMI arm for Indian music. They said the only vacancy they had was in the stock room, so I had to pack boxes. I loved the fact of just handling these LPs that I used to listen to. That's how I started, in the warehouse. Eventually I sort of moved my way up the ladder, and I was the youngest sales manager in that company, which in India and everywhere employed about two thousand people. After that I joined Yash Raj Films, so the music and the film interest have really helped my career.

During your childhood, was it easy to find and watch Indian films in London?

I grew up in London in the 1970s. We had three main cinemas where we lived, and they all showed Hindi films regularly. In fact, growing up we used to go to cinemas, sneak in—we'd watch films any way we could, even if we didn't have money. Of course in the 1980s, when the cinemas closed down, the video piracy took over. Then it was even more widely available.

Was the audience only NRIs? Were British people interested in Hindi movies?

No. No interest whatsoever from non-Indians. When I say non-Indians, I don't mean Pakistanis, for instance. We had cinemas which had a capacity of three thousand five hundred people. I still remember watching *Muqaddar Ka Sikandar* [Prakash Mehra, 1978] with a full-house: three thousand five hundred people and I couldn't find a seat. So I saw the first half-an-hour of the film sitting on the stairs.

Only in Hindi? No subtitles?

Only Hindi. No subtitles. I actually started the subtitles as a policy when I released *Mohabbatein* [Aditya Chopra] back in 2000, in the overseas. So from that day onwards we took a conscious decision that we would always subtitle our films. That was the first subtitled film that actually went out there. Before that, we didn't subtitle films. Even *Dil To Pagal Hai* [Yash Chopra, 1997], the first one that we distributed in this region, wasn't subtitled.

When they hired you at Yash Raj, which brief were you given?

See, the objective is very simple. We as a company have been making films for over twenty-five years. We made *Dilwale Dulhania Le Jayenge* [Aditya Chopra, 1995], which was a huge success everywhere. It's still running in some cinemas in Mumbai, after seventeen years. That makes it the longest running film in Indian cinema history. But the distributors at that time said it didn't do the business that we all perceived it did. If we believed in our films so much, then we felt that we should control our own destiny instead of pointing fingers at somebody else or getting into a mud-slinging match. So I had to set up an office and bring about transparency in the business. To give an example, prior to *Dil To Pagal Hai*, which was in 1997, no film in the United Kingdom had ever officially crossed 300,000 pounds at the box-office. That included *Dilwale Dulhania Le Jayenge* and *Hum Aapke Hain Koun...!* [Sooraj Barjatya, 1994]. But *Dil To Pagal Hai*, on eighteen screens, did a million pounds. So I suspect that our instinct and our belief in our product paid off. We had to prove to ourselves that our films do in fact work abroad.

You were still aiming at the diaspora, right?

Oh, absolutely.

Why not aim at people who were not part of the diaspora?

Let's be honest, our business is driven by the diaspora. Even if there's a non-diaspora audience, it's a minuscule percentage. In the early days, the objective was to build on our key strength. So rather than spread ourselves thin, trying to do everything all at once, we believed that if we had this ready-made market, we should capitalize on that first and lay the foundations which we can build on. There was no point in me reaching out to an audience who perhaps, in those days at least, didn't think much of or didn't respect Indian cinema (and some still don't).

In these sixteen years, have you seen the market growing? Have you seen it expanding to other countries?

Our core audience still remains the Asian sub-continent diaspora. Even the subtitling isn't entirely driven for the non-Indians, but the second, third, even fourth generation Asians who live there, who speak the language but perhaps don't connect with every word. I'll give you an example: my niece, born, brought up there, is eleven years of age. If I don't know a song and ask her which film that song belongs to, she knows. She doesn't speak Hindi, she doesn't write Hindi, she cannot really understand it, but she watches every film there is. Because they're subtitled, she can connect. I didn't study Hindi, but I learned Hindi through watching films and listening to music. What we found was that because of the subtitling, we've driven more people to the cinema, even from the diaspora. So the market grew somehow. The knock-on effect of those young kids who go to school with their non-Indian friends is that in the event that they would call their friends to a cinema, could do so because it's subtitled. As far as new markets are concerned, yes, of course, there's a constant effort on each one of us in the business to push and see if there are new markets that can be opened up. Germany was the first key market that opened, then little bit of France, and Poland. Our films are very popular in Korea and Japan. We did a film in Turkey and in Brazil. These are markets that have subsequently opened, but I can't say they sustain. The only market that really sustained has been Germany.

Do you have an explanation for that? Why Germany?

Germans were very conservative people. I have a German friend and she wasn't allowed to wear jeans, for example, by her parents. Her father wouldn't allow her mother to drive. So if you go back a hundred years, German people were generally very entrenched in tradition. When they see our films, they see a part of themselves also. Because that's what their traditions were like, very rigid. Now that has changed, but they can identify with it to some extent. The other thing is the fact that television in Germany embraced our films. Once it started on television, the common person could just flick channels and see movies for free in the comfort of their living-room, and then if they liked it, they came back to it and would buy the DVD. Because they didn't have to make the effort to leave their house to find out who's this guy, why do I want to see his films. That's what connected, because our films are so starkly different from (a) the kind of films they make, (b) the kind of life they live, and (c) those are just joyous films, happy-ending films largely.

Then why do you think French people don't connect to your films?

There are a lot of French people who do love our cinema, and it's really remarkable. But I like to believe they have a subjective problem with this industry, which is not artistic enough according to them. Anything that doesn't fall in the parameters that they've set for art, isn't art. The other thing is we've not been able to break through to the most commonly reached medium, which is television. We can't reach the French audience in the comfort of their living-rooms so they could experience it and decide for themselves whether they like it or not. If you came to me today and said, 'go buy a ticket and watch some French film, or Italian film', and I have no idea who the star cast or the plot are, I'll be wondering why do I want to do that? I'd rather go watch something that I know, and it's no different for them. But if I've seen something on television, like ... What is the name of that French film that did so well? About those two friends, one is a disabled guy...

The Intouchables?

That's right. Everybody was talking about that film. I made it a point to see it. But if nobody is talking about it, why would I do that? I saw a really beautiful Japanese film in a flight once called *Be With You* [*Ima ai ni yukimasu*, Nobuhiro Doi, 2004]. I loved the film. But if it had been showing at my local cinema, would I have gone to see it? Perhaps not. Because it would have been an effort to do that. Now, if you ever tell me that the actor that starred in that film is in another film coming, I'll probably go watch it. It's really about how convenient we can make it for the audience.

How come the young NRIs are still into Hindi movies when the themes of those movies are so engrained in Indian traditions?

It is down to the individual largely, but I do believe that the environment that they all live in is still very Indian. My brother would be listening to Indian music. His wife would be watching TV soaps. As a family, we talk about cinema, especially in our family because I am in the business. But even beyond that, kids are still finding the same reasons to watch Indian films, which is to connect to India and to know where they come from. That might not be the exact depiction as to where we exactly come from, but for them it's a great way of seeing India. There's no other reason. Nobody makes them watch them. But because watching films is a family event with Indians, you can see three generations all together. The grandparents will be there, the parents will be there, the kids will be there, they are all watching the same film. It's not necessarily the case with Western cinema. Very seldom do you see a family going together to watch a movie.

Africa and Asia are also markets that have been passionate about Hindi cinema for a long time. How do you work with these markets?

When you're away from home, you connect more with home.

So this is still about the diaspora only?

Malaysian people, because they listen to Indian music, watch Indian films. Now a lot of them are originally from India anyway, as are South African and East African people. In Malaysia, for example, there are people who have lived there for four, five, six generations, but they still connect with India through cinema, as it is the case in Indonesia. They might not converse in Hindi at home, but they'll still watch Indian cinema.

You'll find fans of Bollywood in North Africa who are not Indians.

Indian cinema made its way into these places in the 1950s, early 1960s, largely driven by the popularity of stars and music. Also remember because of the cold war between the United States and the USSR, a lot of these countries were allied, their loyalty lay with one or the other. They were not as exposed to American cinema, and if they were, they found that culturally Indian films were closer to them. I went to a Moroccan film festival [the Marrakesh Film Festival] and people would just stop Yash Chopra in the streets and start singing songs to him, because they knew who he was. There is this amazing love that audiences have for Indian cinema in these countries. While it seems inexplicable, it stems from the fact that they are culturally close to us. They enjoy the music. Even though they can't speak the language *per se*, they can understand the songs. I organized a premiere for *Veer-Zaara* [Yash Chopra, 2004] at the Rex Cinema [in Paris]. We went to the Virgin Megastore...

And they had to close the doors because so many people were waiting outside to see Shah Rukh Khan!

I was so proud of our achievement. We were able to put up a big banner and a red carpet outside the Megastore. We couldn't see the carpet and we had to go from the back entrance! It was largely North-Africans who were there.

Are these the markets you are working on?

Absolutely. The problem is whilst there is a huge audience there who loves Indian cinema, they are not the audience who go and buy the tickets. They are the audience who buy a bootleg DVD. It stops those markets from flourishing. So when we go to Pathé or Gaumont

Cinémas [in France] and we say to them, 'there's this big film coming, and we think it will do this'—it doesn't, because although the fans are very loyal to the stars, they are not loyal to the film. If those people came out in numbers and watched these films in cinemas, it would be a very good market.

How are you dealing with piracy?

Unfortunately, the DVD business is over, largely because we can't afford to sell them for the pirates' prices. When this person who makes those [pirated] DVDs in his backyard is getting the film for free, there is no cost involved for him. This pen for example (*he shows me a pen on his desk*): if I get it for nothing, even if I sold it to you for one rupee, it's a great deal. If I sold it for ten paisa, that's still a great deal. But if my cost price is one rupee, the best I can do is giving it to you at one rupee. Any product which is legitimate is going to cost you money. You can't go into a trench war with a pirate and expect to win, because he doesn't play by the rules. Whatever the acquisition prices are, he can undercut you anyway. We've been through all the legal procedures, and unfortunately the laws, anywhere in the world, are really just useless when it comes to piracy. Because governments have other priorities. They'll say drugs are more important, guns are more important. If the pirate knows that his offence is not taken very seriously by the authorities, what can we do?

Does Yash Raj suffer a lot from piracy?

Yes, we spent millions of dollars in the United States, in United Kingdom, in Holland in particular, because we felt that these were the markets where we really needed to establish our business. We lost pretty much everywhere.

How much money does Yash Raj lose because of piracy?

For example, I would be able to sell between 15,000 and 20,000 DVDs of a film in the United Kingdom, and 40 to 60,000 DVDs in the United States on the day of the release. Today those markets can only take between 200 to 400 DVDs. That's the market we lost.

Is there a solution to recover that money?

We were always hoping that VOD and IPTV would be a solution, but it's not replenishing that business. Our target audience is the youth, they are also tech-savvy and they watch these films free online. Nobody really wants to pay for them. Unfortunately, people feel that once the film is made and is available, it's their birthright not to pay for it. And unfortunately again, the authorities fail to protect our rights. As a result, we lost that whole chunk of business, which we can't reinvest back.

Unlike Hollywood, you have this large audience of poverty-stricken people. They don't have access to Internet.

That's when television comes in. We reach them through television.

So that's the main core of business for Yash Raj? Television?

Today, if we didn't have television, I don't think you would see half of the films being made. It is only because television has become a medium to reach this audience and is willing to pay a price in a legitimate way that we are able to do some of the things that we are doing.

How did Bollywood suddenly become famous all over the world in the early 2000s?

Inherently we are a country which is very driven by cinema and music: it forms every part of our lives. For a hundred years that this industry has been going, it's been a very self-sufficient industry. It's never needed the West for money, marketing, distribution, nothing. We've been driven by a bunch of creative people who had an entrepreneurial streak—they would sell their houses or whatever to make the films that they wanted to make. When these people moved abroad, they looked for opportunities to reconnect, whether they lived in Fiji, in America, wherever in the world. It's like Indian restaurants: when you know that you have x number of people in this town and there's no Indian restaurant, there's a pretty good chance that they are going to like Indian food. Local people have taken it upon themselves to say: there are so many people, they all love Indian films but there is no cinema. So they've come in, they got into distribution, or they bought a cinema and they've started importing films. That's how it kind of flourished. What they've done is set up distribution for Indian cinema without going to a studio and asking them to do it because it's driven by the Indians, and therefore it becomes a very community-driven business. No other community in the world has been able to achieve this, so it's quite remarkable. That's how no matter where you go now, there will be Indian films.

Indian films also get better chances at festivals nowadays.

Film festivals are another discussion.

I'm also talking about the recognition of Indian cinema. Now there are Bollywood film studies. People like me are writing about Indian cinema. How come we are now interested in your films when we largely ignored them earlier?

I think it all changed in the 1990s. In the old days, the leading men didn't wear clothes, they wore what you call costumes. There was no way in hell I was going to be seen wearing those clothes that you see in the 1980s films! That identification ability came in the mid-90s after *Dilwale Dulhania Le Jayenge*, because Shah Rukh Khan was wearing torn jeans, loose shirts and a jacket. One year prior to that, in *Hum Aapke Hain Koun...!* Salman [Khan] was wearing these glitzy jackets with lapel sequins on it. Now I wouldn't be wearing that but I wouldn't mind wearing leather jackets. I was twenty-four, twenty-five, and I could identify with the hero of *Dilwale*.... It also meant that there were younger filmmakers who were talking a more universal language, and therefore it was easier for us in the West to swallow that and talk about that cinema. Once the business started to flourish and cinemas started to mushroom, the mainstream press also picked up on that and reported the success and the boom of Indian cinema, which meant that people like yourself who would perhaps normally not hear of it, started reading and thinking, 'What is this all about?'. The other reason is that the festival route started to happen. *Lagaan* [Ashutosh Gowariker, 2001] made it to the Oscars nomination. *Moonsoon Wedding* [Mira Nair, 2001], and *Slumdog Millionaire* [Danny Boyle, 2008] were perceived to be Indian films, although they weren't produced in India. The press got hold of these stories, and because of that, it ignited a certain level of interest from people who perhaps didn't know anything about Indian cinema. That has played a huge role in the awareness that you see today.

When I first came to Bombay in 2005, I was told that Bollywood was an industry which was losing money.

The ratio of hits versus flops has always been the same. If there are about two hundred films that are made here every year, ten per cent would be hits. That's been the norm all the way through. It's never been like ninety per cent would be hits, and ten per cent would not work. It might go to 80-20 if we are lucky. But even if you look at Hollywood, the hit ratio is going to be ninety per cent not working and ten per cent that are. And it's always those 10-15 per cent that keep driving the industry. It's absolutely true, the success ratio is very, very low.

Are there films which are hits abroad and flops here?

In 2002, *Mujhse Dosti Karoge!* [Kunal Kohli, 2003] with Hrithik Roshan, Rani Mukherjee and Kareena Kapoor worked abroad but it didn't work in India. *My Name is Khan* [Karan Johar, 2010] was a bigger hit abroad than it was in India, as was *Kabhi Alvida Naa Kehna* [Karan Johar, 2006]. But generally the business is seventy per cent out of India, thirty per cent out of abroad.

But isn't a film like *Kabhi Alvida Naa Kehna*, which takes place in New York and deals with adultery, mainly made for the audiences living in the United States, for the Indian diaspora?

No filmmaker is going to make a film thinking it's going to do more business abroad. As a filmmaker, you'll always want to cater to your home market first. You do know that this will definitely connect more or better abroad, but I don't think anyone designs a film with that in mind. They design a film to hopefully work everywhere. For example, if you look at a film like *Jab Tak Hai Jaan* [Yash Chopra, 2012], we knew that there was a very good market for it abroad. But we didn't expect for the film to do more business abroad than in India.

What is Yash Raj's strategy when it's producing films like Dibakar Banerjee's, which are known to be non-mainstream films?

The strategy is very simple. We as a company used to make one or two films a year. We scaled to about three films a year from 2002, 2004 and so forth. We then subsequently scaled it to five films a year. We cannot survive if we keep on making the same kind of films that we've made in the past. We need to reinvent ourselves, or from having a hundred per cent hit ratio, our hit ratio will get down to seventy-five per cent. Clearly there will be films that work, some that don't work. But in order for us as a business to continue to grow, we need to have a mix basket of films. We look at ourselves as an entertainment machine, therefore we have to churn out films, which are our product. If we churned out just one kind of product, we would have a very limited base. Because the market is evolving, the viewer is evolving, we need to cater to all kinds of viewers. If McDonalds only sold one kind of burger, only one kind of person would go to McDonalds; but in India they'll sell you vegetarian burgers, chicken burgers, fish burgers. We also like to believe that we can make a difference to even a smaller film, which is what happened when we made a film called *Kabul Express* [Kabir Khan, 2008]. Nobody expected us to make a film like that, but we did, and it worked really well for us. When we put the Yash Raj brand to a small film, it immediately elevates it to the next level and takes it out to different markets. Some of our film fans go to see a film that they perhaps wouldn't have wanted to see. If I was a hardcore Yash Chopra, Aditya Chopra fan and only saw their kind of films, and now they're coming out with this new film, I might say, 'You know what, let's give it a shot.' We are hoping that with Dibakar's kind of films, we will be able to replicate that success.

From what I've understood, there's a problem with the distribution system in India: not enough theatres, and too many films. Are things changing? Are people willing to change them?

Things are changing daily. There are more people coming in the business; there are new screens being opened. Of course, I suspect they are not changing as fast as we would like them to in terms of the number of screens that are available. For example, when there are two big films releasing on the same day, we struggle for screens. It should not be the case for a country of this size, where you sell three billion tickets a year. We should have far more screens. It's unfortunate that it's taking too much time, because the focus for new screens remains the metros, and then the rural India doesn't get any.

Even you, the biggest studio in India, are struggling to get screens?

Fortunately, we never had problems getting theatres. When we released *Dhoom:3*, we didn't have a problem getting screens. [*Ek Tha*] *Tiger* [Kabir Khan, 2012] released in two thousand seven hundred screens without any problem. But everybody is targeting the same screens. So if somebody wants to come in the same date as *Dhoom:3*, where will they play his film?

Since the screens are already booked ...

... by us.

What would be your answer to independent filmmakers who complain about the studio system which prevents independent films from being screened in theatres?

I don't disagree with it, but the problem doesn't lie with the studios. The problem lies largely with the exhibitors. The exhibitors decide what's going to work for them and who they're going to give the screen to. If the exhibitor says, 'I've got five to eight screens', he only allocates screens based on bums on seats. He only cares about how many seats he can fill. So if tomorrow I went to him with a small film, for instance *My Brother... Nikhil* [Onir, 2005, cf. interview] that we released, he might not accept it. Part of the problem is low seat capacity. The second problem is, with all due respect—I have a lot of friends who make these kind of films—there's no art-house cinema circuit in India. So why make these films for the Indian audience? Make your art-house films and take them abroad, because that's where they are going to work. If you go to multiplexes with an art-house film, they are not going to play your films. When you make these films and you take them to the same place where mainstream films are going to sell, why would they give your film a preference? That's not their business model. Their business model is to play a film where they make a quick buck. Art-house cinema needs to be nurtured; it has its separate audience. So when you make an art-house film, you can't hold it against the studios. You have to address the issue to the exhibitors, because their business model doesn't allow them to play art-house films.

But the studios are so big you cannot fight them.

Same thing in America. American indie filmmakers say the same thing.

But it seems it's easier in France or in the United States to make an independent film.

True, it's easy to make an indie film. It's just more difficult to sell it!

How many theatres are missing in India?

I think you need to double the capacity right now.

How do you distribute your films all over India, like in Tamil Nadu for instance, which has its own industry?

The key films are dubbed into Tamil, Telugu or Malayalam. I think the biggest crossover is happening in India, where even the North Indians are watching South Indian films and vice versa. That's a very healthy trend.

Films like *Jab Tak Hai Jaan* are working in Tamil Nadu?

Whenever we have dubbed our films, they've done really well. But it's a kind of cinema that works. *Dhoom:2* worked there, so we'll give them a *Dhoom:3*. Not every film was translated.

How do you feel about the future of Indian cinema? In India, and abroad?

It's bright, it's evolving. The beautiful thing is we are able to make different kinds of films, which was not the case in the 1970s or 1980s. There are a lot of new filmmakers coming with a very different point of view, making different kinds of films, also in various languages. Every regional cinema is flourishing in its own right as well. Be it Tamil, Telugu, which historically has been very successful, but Punjabi films have been taking off now in a big way. I'd like to see Bengali cinema doing better, because Bengali cinema is historically a creative hub, but I think it's a very positive sign that every kind of cinema is working. From a business standpoint alone, because we have these screens that are opening up slowly and we are frequenting cinemas more regularly than we used to, I'd like to see the ticket prices go up on an average because now only the multiplex ticket prices are high. If you average it all, if it's three billion tickets sold, it's only one dollar per ticket. That's where we lag behind. This will change hopefully as the business grows, and as the income level grows. As far as national market only is concerned, it's always been on an upward evolution for a while. I hope it continues. The only challenge I feel is always going to be to keep our youth in the international market with us, as film fans. And I hope it won't prove too difficult by the time they get to sixth, seventh or eighth generation out of India. Will they still speak the language, will they want to be connected to India?

India is seen as a growing economy, and might become a superpower in fifty years from now, along with China. So can Bollywood beat Hollywood also?

Never say never! I think the world is going to globalize completely and we can all find our share of the pie. But whether we will take over is a little premature to say; we probably need to make our presence be felt more. Hollywood has a huge advantage. It has the advantage of language. Hollywood has always dominated the English-speaking world and whichever way we go, and whoever the so-called superpower is, the English-speaking world will always be dominant. Even the Chinese are importing people to teach them English, and in India English is frankly the main language, so unless we start making films along those lines, perhaps not. Unless people start speaking Hindi all over the world. Or Chinese. The power doesn't come necessarily with the kind of films we make; the power comes from the language. And that's what the biggest challenge is. British cinema has always been fabulous. Even today, when they make British films, they're fabulous films. But they can never compete with Hollywood, because they're speaking the same language, and no matter how good the film they make is, because of the spectacular films Hollywood comes up with, Hollywood has a global appeal. The budgets that they are able to put towards those films have given them the edge.

Yash Chopra passed away recently. How does Yash Raj, the company he created, survive without him?

Any company, be it Ford, Disney or Yash Raj, as long as the basic ethos is in place, will carry that vision on. The torch has to be passed on. It is why from making one film every year, we've moved to five films a year. The vision cannot be carried by remaining in your comfort zone. You need to come out of it, and that's what we've done. Right now, fortunately, the head of the company is Yash Chopra's son, who is as talented, perhaps even more visionary than the father. I believe the company is in very safe hands. Going forward, I think the vision for the company is to grow, but also remain true to the basic ethos and be a creative hub.

NAZIR HOSSEIN
Exhibitor, Owner of Liberty Cinema

Is there still space and time for nostalgia in a world where watching movies has just become a part of a package, between eating overpriced sandwiches in a food court, rushing for sales in a mall, stuffing yourself with popcorn and checking-in on Facebook while the movie is on? Much like Paris, Mumbai still displays a few of its old, lovely theatres, which somehow survived, probably because cinema-going is still the only entertainment for many Indians. Entering one of them is like travelling in a time machine: you feel as if you could smell the past.

In the twentieth century the theatres in India, especially in big cities like Mumbai, were gigantic, architecturally-impressive single-screen spaces, built almost like temples. Liberty Cinema, created after the Second World War, is a splendid example of Art Deco architecture and a lost era of old-fashioned cinema halls: plush red velvet curtains, fully-carpeted floors, deliciously uncomfortable wooden chairs, and an understated atmosphere with black-and-white photographs on the walls that whisper stories of another time. A time when films would remain in theatres for months, while audiences would come to watch them several times, cheer at the hero, boo at the villain, and experience cinema as Mia Farrow in *The Purple Rose of Cairo* dreamed it, the best way to escape your bleak life.

Located in South Mumbai, the Liberty suffered, as most single-screen theatres such as Metro, Regal and Eros did, from the rise of multiplexes which began to boom ten years ago in the urban Indian cities. Liberty's owner, Nazir Hossein, a dynamic and charming man in his eighties, welcomed me into his office, tucked away in a loop of never-ending corridors. He explained how changing trends led him to transform his theatre which, though legendary, had been abandoned by the crowds. Interestingly enough, he showed no bitterness; this is a man who always knew how to adapt, from his early youth spent in the car business to being forced by fate into taking over his father's business years later.

As always, when two different generations are lost in a long conversation about the past, tales of the Golden Age that will never come back worked their magic.

Liberty Cinema was founded by your father ...

Not founded, it was *built* by him. The family business, if I go back to my grandfather, was cotton. My grandfather was the chief cotton selector for a group which represented almost all the mills that existed in Bombay at that time. When the ownership passed from one generation to the other, the young generation was more interested in wine, women and songs, and they destroyed the company. My grandfather invested all of his earnings in the business, which were quite considerable at that time, so he died a very disappointed man. My father was trained in cotton. He was sent to Hong Kong, Macao, and goodness knows where else to learn about cotton. And he was not interested. He was interested in cinema. So he started by showing pictures at the Bandra Gymkhana. He used to show 16 mm pictures on Sundays, or Saturdays.

When exactly was that?

I would say it was in the 1920s. It was 16mm at that time, he told me, probably silent movies and then moving on, in the 1930s to perhaps, sound. He then made his money in World War II. He began by putting up cinemas where the Allied Forces were stationed: Bombay, Pune, Nasik, etc. This entire area was a major allied base for the fighting that took place in the East. So wherever the armies were stationed and there were a large number of people stationed for the Eastern fighting, he put up cinemas.

Was he showing English movies?

Yes. I mean, at that time, the Allied Forces were not interested in Hindi films. *(laughs)* By the time the war ended, he found himself with forty-five cinemas. Some were in tents—tent cinemas exist even today in India—some were proper structures, some were tin sheds. When the war ended, my father found that he was not able to control these businesses. Because you have no means to ensure that the money you've received for the tickets goes into the bank, if you are that spread. And communication in those days was not what it is today. So he felt that it was not such a good idea to have so many cinemas, and he thought it best to get rid of them and create one, which is where we are today. Hindi cinema needed a cinema that was outstanding for the products that were being made. Nothing existed, except cinemas on Lamington Road. At that time we had the Eros, the Regal, the Metro, the Empire, the Excelsior, and they were all showing English films. Nobody was showing Hindi.

Why is that?

The audience was at that time more English-oriented.

Even Indians?

Oh, yes, absolutely.

So Liberty Cinemas was designed to show only Hindi.

Yes, and it started with *Andaz* [Mehboob Khan, 1949], on the 21st of March 1949.

What can you tell us about the architecture of this theatre?

It is the Art Deco form of art, it's an excellent example of it.

Why did your father choose the Art Deco architecture?

The first architect for this cinema was a man called Riddley Abbott, an Englishman. This was immediately after World War II. The hole in the ground started in 1947. In a war, there cannot be development of architecture. People are too busy killing one another, and destroying the rest of it. So the architecture that was prevalent at that time after World War II was the architecture that was prevalent before World War II, which was Art Deco. Our whole air-conditioning plant is a fantastic design. It came from carriers in America and was so big that when the basement was completed, the building had to be built on top of the plant. Now that plant doesn't exist anymore because it was ozone-unfriendly and I destroyed it a few years ago. But it's only to give you an example of the care that went into the construction of this cinema. Riddley Abbott went on a holiday with his wife when the first floor had been built. Unfortunately, the plane crashed and both of them died. So my father carried on with an Indian architect called John Fernandes. He finished the drawings—I don't know exactly what John Fernandes' role was, I don't know exactly what Abbott did. But the theatre was finished with John Fernandes. And the interior, which is really an excellent work of Art Deco, was done by my father himself (Habib Hossein) and the Indian architect at that time, Waman Namjoshi. After gaining experience with the Liberty, Namjoshi went on to build the Maratha Mandir, and then the Raj Mandir in Jaipur. How much of the inspiration for those came from him or from my father, I am not able to say. But I expect a large percentage of it came from my father.

You said there were no theatres showing Hindi films...

No, I said there were no top-grade cinemas showing Hindi films.

The Indian elite wouldn't go watch Hindi films because they despised it.

I wouldn't say despise. It is a wrong word because Hindi cinema was just being born. We got our independence in 1947. The audience for Hindi movies was not the elite audience.

It was the less educated people who watched Hindi movies.

That's right.

So top-grade cinemas wouldn't show Hindi movies because they didn't want this audience to come to their theatres.

Permit me to read a little bit of the introduction of the brochure that was published in 1949 for the opening of the Liberty. *With the opening of the Liberty, a major milestone is passed in the history of showmanship in India. It marks the beginning of the showman's consciousness of his product. It is a statement to the Indian people that no theatre could be too good for them and no screen too good for Indian pictures.* It answers the question beautifully. *To the Indian pictures-goers and producers who complained the finest facilities were being used to show foreign products, the Liberty comes as the first promise of a brighter future in the shape of an ultramodern, air-conditioned, luxury cinema dedicated to the showing of the best Indian films. It stands as a pledge from the Indian exhibitor that he will stand by the Indian film industry first. An industry that has suffered so many post-war reverses and has so often lacked adequate support.* I don't think I have to read more. *(laughs)*

So was it a success?

Oh yeah. In those days a picture was considered to be a hit if it ran for twenty-five weeks. The method of marketing was quite different at that time, in the sense that a picture would open at the Liberty and maybe four or five cinemas in Bombay. If it was a hit at the Liberty, the price in the rest of the territories in India went up. It meant the success or the failure of the movie.

What was considered the best of Hindi films?

Well you had *Andaaz*, Mehboob Khan, Raj Kapoor, R. Kardar, V. Shantaram. So when you're talking about the best of Hindi films, you're talking about movies made by people who were stars in their field. If a picture ran for twenty-five weeks, we needed only two pictures a year for goodness' sake! *(laughs)*

Isn't it a problem? You were showing two pictures a year and there were so many films being made per year ...

There were not so many top-rate products in 1949. Most of them came here, and as I said, there was a crying need for more cinemas at that time. My father went on to build the Naaz, which was at Lamington Road and is a disaster today. He sold it subsequently; it was not up to the standards of Liberty. He couldn't repeat what he had achieved once.

But then even if there are only four or five top-rate films a year, how do you choose the two that are going to run in the theatre?

I really can't answer that, I was too young at that time. And I was not involved in my father's picture business because we couldn't see eye-to-eye on many issues. I was more into automobiles.

You were not into films because your father was, or because you didn't like watching movies?

No, I liked watching movies, but we were both strong people and we agreed to disagree. That's the best way of putting it. He looked up to cinema, and I went in automobiles, opened a little garage, started repairing motorcars.

Was he disappointed with you, like your grandfather was disappointed with him?

I presume so. But I moved back to cinema before my father passed away. He was quite relieved that he was leaving his precious Liberty in good hands.

Did you eventually develop an interest in movies?

The saying in English goes, 'There's more than one way to skin a cat'. Perhaps it's an apt statement. His way was fine. At that time when Hindi cinema was born, he was a major figure in the exhibition of Hindi cinema. But it was not my way. My way was different, which also worked.

When did you take over?

You can say that I started really in the late 1960s.

How did the Liberty follow the changes of Hindi cinema? There were more movies being made.

We were getting the best products because we were an outstanding cinema. We still are. Unfortunately, before my father died in the early 1970s, he gave the cinema to some friends of his to run because he still felt that my interest was not that deep in cinema. And they made a mess of this place in the sense that they were interested in making money and not in maintaining. Carpets were torn, the seats were not in good shape, and after my father passed away, we landed up in court. The Indian system of jurisprudence takes forever. They had a twenty-year agreement. I think I started fighting with them in their third or fourth year, and in their twentieth year, I got it back. The first thing I did was to restore this place to its original beauty. And then came a family called the Barjatyas. The Barjatya family's father and my father were really close friends. They came to see me and said, 'We like your cinema very much, we like the work that you've been doing. We made a film called *Hum Aapke Hain Koun...!* and we'd like to exhibit it here, but you'll have to change the sound system.' I said, 'Yes, I agree with you, but it will cost me twenty lakhs, and what happens to me if your picture fails?' So they said, 'If our picture fails, we'll buy the equipment from you for the price you paid for it.' I said, 'Done!' *(laughs)* It didn't take long because the film was a hit. It started again with six cinemas in Bombay, which ran full. By the time the picture hit, it was showing in twenty-five cinemas in Bombay. At the Liberty, which was a 1,886-seats cinema, we ran three full shows a day for forty-four weeks and we ran the picture for one hundred and twenty-five weeks.

Does that mean you were not showing another movie for almost two and a half years?

Nothing else! And I did a rough calculation: about twenty million people saw it.

Does it mean that people came back to see it?

Back, and back, and back. The most famous example is perhaps our greatest painter, M. F. Husain. He fell for the actress Madhuri Dixit in that film and he said he came to see it fifty times. He would get so carried away by the music that he would start dancing in the aisle and the people sitting behind him would naturally get agitated. So I told him, 'Look, I have a box, it's a private box, it's got five seats, you can sit and watch or you can dance in the box, don't disturb anybody that way.' He said, 'No, I'll buy a ticket, I'll sit with the people and if I want to dance, I'll bloody well dance.'

People dancing and singing during screenings—did that happen in Liberty cinema?

Oh yeah, of course! Absolutely! Flowers, money, the whole bloody lot! *(laughs)*

How do you explain that?

I never tried, so I'll hazard a guess. In the old days, you had stage shows. And how did you appreciate the act? You would throw money on the stage. It was an old habit and of course when the stage became a screen, old habits die hard.

But it doesn't happen anymore?

No, those habits are gone. Money remains in the pockets now. *(laughs)*

Do you regret it?

No, it's the changing of time. When a film was running here for twenty-five weeks, the first few weeks we'd have black market ticketing going on in a very big way. In fact, the true barometer was the price of the ticket in the black market. If that price was high, the picture was a success.

It must have been really high for *Hum Aapke Hain Koun...!*

Yes, it was high because it was released only in six cinemas, but I don't think it was as high as in the 1950s or 1960s.

Why was it running only in six theatres?

This was a marketing technique. Different people had different methods to distribute their products. The Barjatyas had a lot of faith in their product and they felt that they would create the demand first and then move to other territories, cinemas in Bombay and so on, which is the exact opposite of what is happening today. You take a picture now, a good Hindi product, on the assumption that it's showing in Liberty, in Metro which is now a multiplex, in Sterling, which is now a multiplex, in Inox, which is now a multiplex (I am talking only South Bombay), in Eros, in Regal, in Empire. Everyone is showing the same picture now, which is one of the reasons why we stopped screenings unless we have a good deal.

Most cinemas have turned into multiplexes ...

Not most, we do have cinemas that are single-screens ... Eros, Regal, Empire, Excelsior ...

Then let's say some of them have turned into multiplexes, but you haven't. Why?

Because this is a superb creation. Multiplexes destroy that creation and I wasn't interested. I was interested in retaining the charm of this cinema and the ambience that it has. Nose is above water, I can't say I am making a lot of money. The move towards stage shows and the rest of it is to survive.

Are you scared for the future of Liberty Cinema?

No, because we've done live shows, music shows. Quite honestly, I was petrified initially because sometimes the acoustics for a live performance are not the same as the acoustics required for a cinema.

As it turned out, the acoustics are excellent, and it is not my saying, this was told to me by the people who were performing on stage. With that being the case, I am not afraid of surviving anymore. Now it's a question of more and more activities coming along, us promoting this as more as a theatre that also shows cinema.

Could you tell me more about the big hits of Liberty Cinema?

There were so many pictures that were a big success, and I've chosen *Hum Aapke Hain Koun…!* because Liberty was going down as a cinema at the time, and it was the first super hit after I managed to get it back. It would be my biggest success. But you can't equate in time, because the value of the rupee changes. When we started this cinema, we had four classes and our cheapest class was ten and a half annas, which is sixteen annas to a rupee. So ten and a half annas was less than a rupee, which is unheard of in today's age. And our highest ticket was three rupees, which today is one hundred thirty rupees. So the cost of seeing movies has changed.

Anybody could come to the Liberty?

Of course, we had four classes. In the old days, the people dressed up to go to the movies. They went to the dress circle. And then you had the balcony, which was a little cheaper, again upstairs. The ten-and-a-half annas seats were just three rows, right in front, so you had to look up. The screen at that time was very small, when my father built it, because that was the technology at that time. And as time progressed, the screen became larger and larger, which means it came more and more forward, and now it is as big as it can be without me destroying the cinema. I can't make it any bigger.

Was it always open to anybody?

Always. Now, because of the fact that we are moving more into stage shows, the lower class seats became my highest price ticket. I've extended the stage because I wanted an orchestra on the stage.

So there are fewer seats?

Yes. We had 1,196; we have now 1,150. It's still a hell of a lot. But for a stage show, we use only downstairs, 728 seats. The upstairs is for a cinema, not for a stage.

When you were still showing films, you never screened a film that was not in Hindi?

No, we had a period when we were showing English pictures, but English pictures have never done well in this cinema.

And what about regional cinema?

Yes, we showed regional cinema also, but again that did not do well. Now, I am looking at the possibility of doing stage shows on weekends and regional cinema on weekdays.

Which kind of cinema?

What you call 'European Cinema', you should be familiar with that.

Why did you have to transform your cinema? I guess single-screen theatres faced the competition of multiplexes.

As far as Liberty is concerned, we are not very well-located. We are in a lane, not on the main road. If you're familiar with South Bombay, you're familiar with Eros. Eros faces the terminus of Churchgate Station. So the walking audience in Eros is much higher than here. If we are showing the same picture at the same time, and I am doing a turnover of x, Eros would do two-and-a-half times x, because of the walking audience. Regal, which is the Southern-most cinema in Bombay, between Colaba and Cuffe Parade, would do two times x. We're next to a very big hospital. People going out of the hospital are not usually in the mood to go to the movies. *(laughs)* So my walking audience is almost non-existent. That was one of the reasons. And yes, of course, the government in its infinite wisdom decided, when the multiplex era began, to give the multiplexes a tax-holiday for five years, when our entertainment tax in Maharashtra is forty-five per cent.

Forty-five per cent of the price of the ticket?

Yes. It's based on my turnover. The calculation is somewhat complicated, there's no point going into all that, but if you buy a one hundred rupees ticket, forty-five rupees go to the government. There are other taxes—a show tax, a property tax—so by the time you're finished, fifty-one per cent of your ticket price is going to the government. The multiplexes got a five-year tax holiday. The reason given was that they were a tourist attraction.

How many tourists go to see Hindi movies?!

I am telling you what the government said, I am not saying I agree with them. Today we've got too many screens and not enough products, because in South Bombay you have the Metro, which has become a multiplex, the Sterling, the Inox...

Producers and distributors would say the exact opposite, that there are not enough screens and too many movies.

But all you have to do is buy a newspaper! I don't know about India—I am just talking South Bombay. Every cinema is showing the same picture. How is it going to work?

What has changed in the twenty-first century, for you, for Indian cinema?

Basically it was the policy of the government when multiplexes were born to give them a tax-holiday for five years, for them to exist for a minimum of ten years. Taxes are abnormally high here and based on the ticket price, with the result that the total tax on a one-hundred rupee ticket would be approximately fifty-one per cent. The balance of forty-nine per cent has to be shared between the distributor, the producer and the exhibitor. The result is that the exhibitor gets a really small amount, and for a cinema like the Liberty, it was just not enough. Consequently we had to not show films unless it was a good product. Now, multiplexes were given a five-year tax-holiday and they mushroomed, because they invested all the money in the five years that they had. Naturally it was at the cost of the single-screen cinemas. Those five years are over for most of the multiplexes, they are back in the mainstream and they are also paying forty-five per cent entertainment tax, but this has upset the exhibition of motion pictures completely. The result is if you look at any good product—and now it's mainly Hindi product, there's not much English anymore because the population has evolved over the years and it has become a Hindi-speaking population—if a picture is showing in Liberty, it's also showing in the other cinemas.

Even before the multiplexes came, television was also a competition.

Well, of course, this is a normal phenomenon worldwide, this is not specific to India. When television came, it had an effect on films. How can it not? When television improved from black-and-white to colour, it was another blow and it was bound to have an effect. But if you kept up with the times, the effect was less, in the sense that we had our surround sound, we had digital stereo. We kept up. We have the latest equipment, digitalized and the rest of it, so that did keep us going for some time.

With the exception that in India a lot of people go to the movies. Have you seen the audience decrease?

Movie-going in India is a passion. In the West, it would be a date, but here it's a family outing. This was very well-shown when we ran *Hum Aapke Hain Koun...!*, when the whole family—and the Indian family is normally a large one—would come with their food, because it was a three-hour picture.

Was it possible to eat in the theatre?

Well, we allowed it just to get into the festive spirit *(laughs)* and it was a riot. People were enjoying themselves. They were having a great time. It was more than a movie—it was an experience, really.

What do you think of Indian cinema today?

Today, the days of Indian cinema as a classic, as a form of storytelling, as an art form, are gone. Audiences want all the fighting, the *masala*. There are some lovely films being made, but the number of lovely films, from my point of view, has certainly reduced.

What is a lovely film?

You want a good storyline, a good production value, something that moves you. You don't want ridiculous fighting, stunts which are impossible; that's the mass-appeal.

But it was already the case in the 1970s with Amitabh Bachchan's films ...

Not to this extent.

You find movies more violent now?

Oh, definitely. The movies are more violent, the women are wearing less, it's a complete change. I am not saying it's better or worse, but it's what today's public wants. *Udaan* [Vikramaditya Motwane, 2010] and *Lootera* [Vikramaditya Motwane, 2013] are completely different products. I prefer the old products without the shadow of a doubt—V. Shantaram films, Raj Kapoor or *Awaara* [Raj Kapoor, 1951]. Two paintings of *Awaara* are hanging on the wall till today. They were different days, better days, as far as the themes of the pictures were concerned. I can't say technically, because technically, there's progress. What we have today cannot be compared to what we had in those days. There's no comparison. As far as the Liberty is concerned, this cinema hasn't changed at all, only the technical aspects, but as far as the architecture is concerned, it's exactly the same as it was. The street has changed of course. The traffic was much less, the people were better behaved. Now we've put a compound wall because you've got little shops on the pavement and we don't want them to get mixed up with people who are coming here.

In your opinion, what is the future of Indian cinema and Indian theatres?

There were about one thousand something theatres in Maharashtra. Now there are six hundred something. Indian cinema is going down as far as numbers are concerned. As far as multiplexes are concerned, it's a completely different class of audience now. People who come to the Liberty are not the people who go to multiplexes, and the people who go to multiplexes are no longer the people who go to single-screens. Where it goes, where it ends, I am afraid I can't hazard a guess.

Who comes to the Liberty?

The masses come here. My daughter would go to a multiplex. My driver's daughter would come here.

Because of the prices?

Of course, our prices are much lower than the multiplexes.

It is a paradox, because your cinema is so much classier ...

It is a complete paradox. I had numbers of photographers who have come here, including a French photographer who was totally enamoured by the Art Deco architecture of this cinema. But then, I have met so many people who have been to the Liberty so many times, and they've never seen the cinema. They don't realize how lovely this cinema is. They go inside the auditorium, see the film and go home. Now that we are changing directions, that we're having music shows and doing other things, people are suddenly beginning to realize how lovely this cinema is. That makes me very happy because that's the audience I am looking for. I am not looking for the ten-and-a-half anna guy anymore. I want an audience that appreciates this place.

Would an explanation to these reactions be that cinema in India is not considered as a form of art?

You have both. You have cinema that is for the educated people, which would be the direction I am hoping Liberty would take, with the weekdays devoted—one show a day—to good, intelligent cinema. Whether it is European, whether it is another country, or even Indian, it doesn't matter.

Can you fill one thousand seats with European movies in India?

I am not saying we are not filling them. We do on occasions when the movie is a blockbuster, on a weekend—but not on a weekday. As far as the theatre aspect is concerned, we only use the downstairs, which is seven hundred twenty-eight seats. For stand-up comedy, we fill it. And our turnover is better, because the price of a ticket for stand-up or a music show is much higher.

Recently, Australia wished to celebrate the hundred years of Hindi cinema, and discovered that one of our silent movies' actresses, Nadia, or Fearless Nadia, was Australian. So we showed one of her films, *Hunterwali* [Homi Wadia, 1935]. The Australians have helped in its restoration and we had nineteen people on the stage playing music. The combination was fabulous.

The changes you are making show a change also in the art scene of Bombay.

I feel in my bones that it's changing and I am delighted to show that it's changing. You'll have to come back after a period of time and see the change!

PART 2

THE 'BOLLYWOOD' SHOW

The guidelines of Indian cinema, and especially of commercial films, are most unfamiliar to Western audiences, to the point that the first word that comes to mind when one attempts to define it is the derogatory term 'kitsch'. One will see an excess of colours and sounds, a pompous self-expression and actors who flaunt their way through never-ending and unbelievable plots. However, who could really say, after watching their first Bollywood film, that they were not captured by its magic, that they did not indulge in the guilty pleasure of pure entertainment?

The interviewees in this chapter are decoding the elements of the famous Bollywood formula and its necessary ingredients—musical numbers (as far away from the story as possible), absurd comedy sequences, and a love story with unexpected developments, including all the romantic clichés. On top billing, one will find a superstar capable of the most spectacular stunts, including the ability to pass himself off as a teenager when he is actually fifty years old. The heroine will be the perfect plastic doll with tresses that blow in the wind without getting the least bit entangled. She will be respectful of traditions, but ready to do anything for love. Over the last few years, she will also have gone on a severe diet and begun to wear her dresses shorter.

These popular cinematic elements may seem ridiculous to an audience who will only approve of realistic or intellectual cinema. Others, who have been brought up with superhero films, westerns, musicals or epics from Hollywood, will acknowledge that there is sometimes a very thin line between a work of art and a commercial debauchery, even in the same film industry. Business-driven Bollywood, just like any other film industry in the world, can also produce wonderful films.

But one is not here to ignore some of the terrible flaws of the Indian industry out of sympathy for some marvellous films that have come out of the Bollywood studios. The disengaged, casual attitude of most producers towards talent promotion—one will have a difficult time finding really good actors amongst the youngsters on screen today—has led Bollywood to a point of no-return. The industry seems to think that there will always be an audience to save the most appalling movies of the time. Is it necessary though to look down upon this audience? Isn't it possible to give them better entertainment?

The old-fashioned Bollywood cinema was good as long as it kept up with the times. It is breaking down today, under heightened pressure from an audience that is less and less interested in these films—confirmed, in the case of most films, by the empty Mumbai theatres after just one week of the film's release—and young artists desperately hoping to find greener grass somewhere else. The interviewees of this chapter condemn the dullness of an outdated system, while still recognizing some of its positive aspects. The argument remains that the 'B' in Bollywood should not be lost along the way and Indian cinema should not ignore the specificity that makes it so rich. Still, the formula for a show that would be both art and entertainment, along with being essentially Indian and universal at the same time needs to be rediscovered.

ATUL MONGIA
Casting Director

Being a close witness to the making of Dibakar Banerjee's *Detective Byomkesh Bakshy!* I had the pleasure to meet Atul Mongia twice and observe the multi-faceted man both at work and in the comfort of his Versova home for the interview. Atul's journey is indeed all the more interesting to my research because his personality is so characteristic of the young generation of the Bombay film industry: eclectic and full of energy, yet conscious of the challenges of living in a city of all possibilities, dreams as much as nightmares.

First an actor, then a casting director, Atul is now hoping to tell his own stories by directing movies. While he waits for his script to find the necessary funding, he still conducts workshops for young actors and joins the crew for films that he believes in. On a workshop for *Detective Byomkesh Bakshy!*, the Indian equivalent to Sherlock Holmes, I watched in awe as he asked the two male leads of the film, Sushant Singh Rajput and Anand Tiwari, to improvise as the legendary godly partners Ram and Hanuman. One could easily tell from his precise though reserved direction that this is a man who has spent time and thoughts on understanding how to get what he wants from an actor.

To say that professionals like him are much needed in the Hindi Film Industry is almost an understatement. Even though truly talented actors, such as Nawazuddin Siddiqui or Radhika Apte, are getting more and more work, their struggle is a proof of how most producers would still prefer to bet on pretty and fair faces, family ties or fame from reality shows to create their new stars. Acting skills are their last concern. This sad situation is all the more striking in an industry where actors rule over anything else, from the crazy numbers a Salman Khan movie makes at the box-office—giving no chance to potential competitors—to a national holiday being declared in Tamil Nadu on the first day of a Rajnikanth release.

The Hindi film star-culture is a fascinating but endless subject. Luckily, with Atul's humour and down-to-earth personality, one is sure to get to the heart of the matter.

You started your career as an actor ...

In our country, there are very few avenues to understand cinema. So most people who begin working in cinema, or aspire to work in cinema, start by thinking of becoming actors. When you watch cinema, you don't see the people behind it, you only see the people acting in it. So it was a very natural movement. I was kind of artistic, I was a performance artist, I used to dance, I used to sing and I quite enjoyed it as well.

When did you begin singing and dancing?

That was just in school. You perform for your festival, you represent your school. But from there, it transformed into performing arts and studying theatre, as an actor and as a director.

How old were you when you began?

Nineteen.

So you began right after school? Most people first try to get some kind of a college degree.

For one year I did. *(laughs)*

To please your parents?

Yes, and to try to get a few jobs: three months in advertising, three months in marketing, because that was my background—marketing, business administration. But I knew this was not what I wanted to do. So by twenty-one, I was fully into theatre. I was assisting Barry John, I was teaching in his school. He's one of the reputed theatre directors and teachers in this country. I was working with him for two years and then I moved to Bombay.

Twenty-one is very young to be teaching. Was it a challenge?

Yes, it is quite young actually. Honestly, it came naturally to me. Also because I was going through various weird phases in my life, including a spiritual one. So I already had the calmness a teacher requires. I was going to different ashrams at the time, staying there for two weeks, practising silence. I was not behaving like a twenty-year-old. From nineteen to twenty-five was my very spiritual phase. *(laughs)* And then I came back to life.

Did you get bored of it?

No, I got disillusioned with it. I didn't find the answers.

Did you use to watch a lot of films back then?

I've loved films since the age of four or five. I was four years old when television was introduced in our country. Since the day it came into our house, I've been watching television. And we used to wait for Sunday movies, because Sunday was the only day when movies were shown. I've enjoyed theatre because it's given me all the learning, but I've always fantasized about films.

What kind of films?

Any kind! I even saw Tarkovski's *Mirror*, as a seven-year-old. And I saw it again when I was twenty-seven, because then I was exploring world cinema. I remembered watching this film when I was seven and how it haunted me for days together. Now when I see it, it reminds me of my childhood a lot. So I would watch anything, right from commercial Hindi cinema to some really odd films with or without subtitles.

Would you have been able to watch *Mirror* without subtitles?

I don't think I could have read them, as a seven-year-old. But I remember seeing it. Maybe it was on a videocassette, I don't know. But I think it was on Doordarshan. My dad was in the army, so we shifted base every year and I've lived in fifteen cities in India. At that time, the concept of going to a cinema hall wasn't as normal as it is now. The only avenue was VHS tapes, which were introduced in the late 1980s. We used to hire them for ten rupees, fast forward the boring portions and watch the good parts. We used to watch two-three films a week. In the vacation time, we would watch one film a day.

So your parents were into films too?

Yeah. We used to watch Hollywood also, because by that time Hollywood slowly started coming in. But only the action movies, only the very popular Hollywood films, would be shown in India through videotapes. My father liked watching Hollywood films more than Hindi films, because of the army background, which is very British.

So your family wasn't too much against the idea of you going into films?

They were very supportive. They never objected. They only said, 'think about it'. My father just wanted to be sure that I really wanted to do this. I just sat down and calmly said this is what I want to do, and he thought 'this guy is slightly mature for his age, so maybe he knows what he's doing'.

What exactly were you doing in Delhi, with Barry John?

I was acting with Barry John, directing student plays, not professional theatre. And I was teaching people who were training to be actors. Barry John's school followed a certain three-month course.

How did you learn to be an actor through this course?

Barry John is a very good teacher. He's not directly involved in teaching children now, but when I was working with him, he used to teach kids every day. And that's where my fundamental comes from, because now I train a lot of actors, especially in films. His philosophy is that acting has to come from the self and until you know who you are, you cannot be somebody else. So a lot of the focus was on exploring who you are. That was primarily the first month of the workshop, which is something I really liked.

How do you discover who you are? Through improvisation exercises?

Lots of exercises. Because theatre is a physical medium, you physically get down on the floor. While you're doing them, you learn how to be aware of what you're doing. Studying yourself is really something that we really put a lot of focus on. I still do that, with a lot of actors, when I work with them—even with film actors. Our culture in cinema is very different, very external. We do not go internal when we act in our cinema. The few good contemporary directors who are pushing actors to go internal are making all the difference now. What we miss in cinema as a country, largely is this: the psychological and emotional aspect of the part, because we just play the emotion physically. We don't really go into it, understand it and then play it. We force it on the screen and that's where it often looks fake.

Are we talking about a kind of an Actor's Studio method?

I've not yet worked with an actor who's got into the part so much that he needs to come out of it. *(laughs)* But because this is cinema, what you see is what you get—apart from prosthetics, because they can create wonders. You largely play your age, your personality type, your class. You're cast for who you are, ninety per cent of the times, unless you've proven yourself as an actor after ten years for instance, like Naseer [Naseeruddin Shah], who can play anything. I like to break this when I am casting. When we come to the character and the acting aspect of it, I think it's a two-way process. It's not always the actor who's trying to be the character. I also discuss with the director and the writers. You've written a part in your head, but suddenly you've found somebody who's not exactly that part. Even your character will need to work towards the actor. You'll probably change your script a little bit. Instead of forcing the actor to become this person and do it in a fake way, why not be flexible with your part and adjust it to the actor? Because at least then the performance will be more organic. The story of course is the most important thing; you can't do it at the cost of the story, of what the director's vision is.

Shouldn't an actor be able to play different kinds of characters though?

Yes, he should be. But unfortunately the system also has to provide that. In India, the system doesn't provide for it. There are a lot of good actors who say, 'I don't want to play myself, I only want to play parts'. They don't want to be typecast. Unfortunately, in Bollywood, we always try to capitalize on something: money dictates almost everything that we do. The truth of the system is that once you do something and you're successful at it, five more people want you for the same reason. If you're funny in that film, then five other people want to cast you because you're funny, not because you're a good actor. That's the sad part for actors. But I always tell them—because now I've been in this industry for some five years and I understand how it functions—'do it, be typecast'. Because when you will be in a position of power after doing ten films, you can dictate what you want to do. As painful as it is for them to be typecast, it's very important if they want a career which stands both in art cinema, parallel cinema as well as commercial cinema. Only the commercial cinema will give you the money and the fame as well as the possibility to choose what you want to do. If you keep doing alternate cinema, you won't get money, you won't get to do what you want to do. But now, there are so many contemporary directors and so many scripts coming up, that it is possible to not be typecast.

And still earn money?

Well, Nawaz[uddin Siddiqui] is making money, so.... *(laughs)* I don't know about the others!

Do you know any actors who have found fame and chosen not to be typecast?

Yes. One example could be Rajkummar [Rao]. He's in *Kai Po Che!* [Abhishek Kapoor, 2013]. He was in the second story of *LSD* [Dibakar Banerjee, 2010]—the guy who dupes the girl and makes the video. After doing *LSD*, he had to do three more parts of a guy who dupes or ditches girls. But he kept doing smaller parts. A lot of mistakes that actors make after doing lead roles is they say they'll only do lead roles. Which is stupid. I think Rajkummar has been very smart in how he's chosen his career path. He's done a small part in *Gangs of Wasseypur* because he got the lead in *Shahid* [Hansal Mehta, 2012]. He's brilliant in *Shahid* and in *Kai Po Che!* So now after four years of doing some seven-eight roles, he's getting where he can start choosing as an actor. That's one example that comes to my mind, but there are lots: Manoj Bajpayee played an angry guy for almost everything. It's the only way he can break it if he wants to.

There are no big Bollywood stars in the names you're giving. Does it mean that stars are happy to be typecast?

I think that there is an extreme pressure on Bollywood stars. Firstly, most of the Bollywood stars come from film families, so there is this whole school and philosophy that their parents inculcate in them. Then there's the peer pressure. Ranbir Kapoor started with a lot of experimental stuff, whether it's *Rocket Singh* [*Salesman of the Year*, Shimit Amin, 2009] or *Wake Up Sid* [Ayan Mukherjee, 2009], where he's not playing the hero, he's playing the confused kid. In *Rocket Singh*, he's playing a Sardar, a Sikh, which is unusual for a Bollywood star to do. Then there's the pressure of the one hundred crores. You're not a star till you've done your one-hundred-crore film. I think some of the stars are trying to break away, but some of them are also getting pressurized. I am sure after five years, Ranbir Kapoor will do another alternate film. Ranveer Singh wants to do both. But because he's just started, he'll probably want to do the other films after a few years. So there's a lot of pressure on these guys, more than we can understand. If we had been in their position, what would we have done? But then there are actors who choose to say, 'no, we'll only do this'.

When you moved to Bombay, had you already decided to be a casting director?

No, not at all. It happened by chance. I came here to be an actor. But I had very specific notions of acting in my head. When I say actors make mistakes, I was making the same mistakes. I didn't want to play the 'heehee, haha guy'. I used to go to a lot of advertising auditions in Bombay. Every audition was a disappointment, because the person auditioning didn't know what to ask for. They just said, 'Smile widely, or dance, or jump', just physicality. If there's a motive or some logic to the physicality, then as a true actor, you do it. But if there's no reason, you say, 'Why should I jump? Why should I smile?' I was that kind of an actor, I was too idealistic, very method-oriented, so I couldn't find any space for myself. I kept struggling for two-three years trying to understand where I fit as an actor. The boom that has happened in the last five years had not started then, ten years back. So even though Anurag Kashyap had seen me in a film, and he wanted to work with me, he was struggling himself to make films at that time. He was making a film in four years. Those opportunities were very few, to do roles that you want to do as true, idealistic actors. That kind of made me go away from acting. In parallel, I was somehow getting introduced to world cinema at that time.

Which kind?

Everything. It started with Bergman, Kieslowski, Kurosawa, Satyajit Ray, Tarkovsky. It started with the masters. But then it went to European, Iranian, Russian, Japanese, Chinese, Cantonese cinema, whatever I heard about, whatever my friends in film schools told me about—because in film school they watch world cinema every day. I used to get names from my friends and I started discovering them online, like the Criterion collection, which is one of the best. I think I've seen seventy to eighty per cent of their catalogue. It made me realize that what I thought was cinema was nothing compared to the world out there. And I started wanting to do this as well. Not just as an actor, but as a director. That's how my journey as an independent filmmaker began. I made three short films in a span of four years. I was not happy with any of those three films, because I was comparing myself to Bergman and Kieslowski and thought, 'What the fuck am I doing? These guys are so good, and I am a no-gooder.' Roughly around that time, when I was confused about being an actor or not, being a good filmmaker or not and thinking of returning to Delhi, I got a call from Dibakar [Banerjee]'s office. They were looking to make *LSD*. They wanted only newcomers, so they needed somebody to train them. In the eight years that I was in Bombay, the one thing that I had been doing consistently to make money was acting workshops. By that time, people were talking about me as a decent teacher in Bombay. So that's how they asked me if I would even cast for it, and not just train the actors. I had never cast before. But if you know acting, if you understand direction, then it's only about sourcing. And I did it, just like that.

Where did you source from?

I went everywhere. On the roads, to a lot of theatre groups, in the theatre fraternity, in colleges, in schools. I tried to spread the word as much as I could and then obviously when you begin something, luck also helps you. A lot of people happened by chance.

Were there any actors in *LSD* who had never thought of being actors before?

One of the leads of the film is a non-actor. She's called Neha. Dibakar found her in Sneha [Khanwalkar]'s wedding video. I got in touch with her and I started testing her. We did some three-four rounds and she didn't want to act. I said, 'Why don't you come and assist me in casting?' She learned acting with me and then she acted in the film.

More films came after *LSD*...

LSD will always be a very special film. It was the first.

You also acted in some of Dibakar's movies.

I didn't want to act, but he said, 'You fit the part'. I said, 'No, no, I'll get you a good actor' and he said, 'No, no, you'll do fine.'

So now you feel you're not a good actor? It seems like you got really disillusioned with movies.

Yes, I was. I was in my twenties, it was my dream, my passion and then obviously the system is very different from what you dream. I think if I go out now to act, I'll get better opportunities. But I am very focused on making my first film.

So casting is not something you enjoy?

No, I enjoy casting. Especially if it is for films that I really believe in. Obviously, there will be some films that I might do just for the money.... But I thoroughly enjoyed *Titli* [Kanu Behl, 2014]. It was also Dibakar's production and Kanu, a very dear friend, was the director. I was very happy to cast for that. With my associates, we did a lot of hard work to find the right people. They went all over the country.

Are you excited about a film just from the script?

I think script is everything at the end of the day, with the director's vision. Sometimes, the script might not be great. But the director's vision must be brilliant. I feel that in a film like *Lootera* [Vikramaditya Motwane, 2013], which I worked on, the director's treatment and vision is so good and the script is just above average. Sometimes really good scripts get fucked up, because you just went wrong with the treatment. And sometimes, above average scripts can also be good films. But that happens with very few directors. Only very few people can do that. Hence my decision-making is always based on scripts.

Can you tell me about a bad experience on a film?

It would be unfair to take their names, because they have their own school of thought and I have my own. I think whenever schools of thought clash, that's when problems arise. Because otherwise, one thing about us Indians in general and people who are working in indie cinema, is that we are extremely hard-working people. We work twenty hours a day to make our films. For no money. But we do it. All of us. It's not like commercial cinema people don't work hard.

It's just that schools of thought are different and when that clashes, you don't enjoy that process. You do it because it's your commitment and you can't leave somebody in the lurch at the last moment.

You worked on a lot of alternate cinema...

And hence I made no money.... *(laughs)*

What would you say is the vision of this new cinema when it comes to acting?

I think one would have to go a little back to try to understand the phenomenon that's happening in Bombay right now. In the 1970s also, we had a huge parallel cinema. Even in the 1980s, we had some really good films. A lot of actors were coming from film school. But in 1991, we opened our market. The economic liberalization happened. Our whole economy changed. Now it's a one-billion strong market. Everybody cannot be served a, b, c. Some people need x, y, z. So with time, people have realized that there's a niche market for cinema as well. If you work within a certain budget, you can make that certain kind of cinema, sell it, make money and also be critically acclaimed for it. A lot of filmmakers have understood that, a lot of producers too and it's only the multiplex boom that has allowed us to do that. Because earlier, there were halls which were only five-hundred seaters, so why would you call a fifty-people audience in a five-hundred-seater theatre? Now we have one-hundred seaters, two-hundred seater theatres and we have six theatres under one roof, so one of them will be catering to the niche, which also includes Hollywood cinema. That's the market aspect of it. The visualization aspect of it is that many filmmakers, like me, have started watching world cinema. A lot of places started renting out DVDs, giving us access to world cinema. Now the Internet gives us access to world cinema, you can just download it for free. And I do that. I know it's wrong, but I am not ashamed of it, because my education has come from piracy. So it's bad, but it's good for me. *(laughs)* A lot of that piracy has helped us understand the world, so we aspire to the best, to what we connect to. Acting is just one aspect of it. We understand that stories can be different. We understand that production design, camera work, treatment, acting and actors can be different. Which is why these filmmakers begin questioning the melodramatic school of thought typical to our country. When actors can do it without melodrama and be much more efficient, why do we need to indulge in melodrama and why is it the only way to do it? The other advantage of doing that, of taking actors is that, at the end of the day, the director becomes the star of the film. Even though our great filmmakers are talked about, like Manmohan Desai, and they're great in the commercial cinema that they did, they made films at a time when the big stars were happening and the audiences only knew the actors' names. They didn't know the names of the directors. Now the general audience know the names of directors. Anurag [Kashyap] is one of the biggest brand names that we have right now. People like Dibakar and Anurag have cast actors and not stars and made great films. They became the stars of their films. When you don't cast the star, then a lot of restrictions go out of the picture. A star is a brand. Brand means image. Image means they're going to function only within a certain precinct. They're not going to step out of it. So an actress will say, 'But I can't kiss that man, because that man has a wrong image, it goes against my branding. And if I kiss this man, then I have the right image.' All the actresses are now seeing how they can win four Filmfare awards by stepping out a little bit, because the Indian society is a little more open. Actors want crazy, edgy, different things. They don't worry about what people will think about them, because they're not a brand anymore. That's where the acting aspect of cinema has changed.

Do you think that these new filmmakers will be able to keep their freedom or will they have to give in to the system at some point?

I think the right way to do it is how Anurag and Dibakar are doing it. They made a certain number of films the way they wanted to make them, without stars, then people respected them. If you come up with your first film, go to a star and act like a star would, he will say, 'Fuck off'. Because he doesn't know you, he doesn't believe in you. But once people believe in you, they're ready to listen to you.

Now Anurag and Dibakar are really big brandings. If Anurag is working with Anushka [Sharma] and Ranbir [Kapoor], they will listen to him, because they also know they're working in a certain kind of a film now. It's not the typical Bollywood movie, it's slightly different. The reason to work with big stars for directors is not just to make money, not just for fame, it's just that for certain stories, you need more money. And for that money, you need a star. It's as simple as that. So for example, if tomorrow I am making a sci-fi film for twenty-five crores, nobody is going to give them to me unless I have a star.

What happens when a filmmaker is forced to work with a star that he doesn't want for his film?

That happens. You have to be very careful with who you are casting. The star needs to be open to this side of cinema or it doesn't work. It doesn't make sense also. Why would that star work in this film if he doesn't believe in it? And why should that director cast that star? If you see this kind of directors, they are casting big stars, but a lot of them are young stars also. Those new boys, Ranveer [Singh], Sushant [Singh Rajput] are more malleable, they haven't got as fixed as some of the older stars might have been. If I start my workshop with them, I'll be breaking them for one month, so they'll be open to me as well, not just to Dibakar or Anurag. I worked with Ranveer Singh in *Lootera*, and he was very open to whatever I had to offer, and he did everything without questioning, because he wanted to see where this process takes him.

Are acting schools a new thing in India?

FTII [Film and Television Institute of India in Pune] was one place which was training actors, and that's where the parallel movement happened. In the last ten years, a lot of acting schools have opened and learning acting has become almost a norm. People who can afford it go to America to Lee Strasberg and those who can't afford it go to Anupam Kher, Barry John and a hundred other acting schools that we have in Bombay, in Delhi, Chandigarh, Lucknow, all over the country. It's become a big business now.

A big trend in Indian cinema is that most stars come from film families. Is it changing now, is it easier now to become a star if you don't come from a film family?

No, it's not easy. It's very difficult. But possible.

More possible than before?

Yes. What happens is a star has a life cycle. Probably a life cycle of say twenty years.

Especially for women, right?

Women have a life cycle of six years, *(laughs)* at the most ten years, if you're Aishwarya Rai. I am talking about stars, not actors. Male stars have a life cycle of obviously forty-fifty years, because you can keep playing parts. But to play younger parts, you have a life cycle of twenty years. Even though Saif Ali Khan, Shah Rukh Khan, Aamir Khan and Salman Khan still play guys in their twenties, there has to be a time when they stop. And that time has come. That's when the space gets vacant. Now is the opportunity, where all these guys are jumping in, whether it's a Ranbir Kapoor, a Ranveer Singh. Because now the first line Shah Rukh says in his trailers is, '*main chalis saal ka hoon*', 'I am forty years old', which is a very big thing for a star to admit. He's admitting it, he's telling the audience: 'I am forty and I am playing a forty-year-old'. So that means this space for a twenty-seven-year-old is vacant right now. But eighty per cent of the newcomers will be from film families. For example, in *Student of the Year* [Karan Johar, 2012], all three guys are from film families: Varun [Dhawan], Alia [Bhatt], and Siddharth [Malhotra]. It's difficult for them as well, but it's much more difficult for people who are not from film families, who will really need to find space for themselves. After three years, newcomers will not be welcomed so much, because these guys, Ranbir [Kapoor], Ranveer [Singh], can play a twenty-year-old for the next ten years. Once we have enough stars—now we need ten stars instead of four stars, because the number of films is increasing—the industry will shut itself and we will have to wait another ten, twenty years. When Mithun [Chakraborty], Rajesh Khanna, Amitabh

[Bachchan], Vinod Khanna and Dharmendra stopped becoming stars in the early 1990s, that's when Shah Rukh Khan, Aamir [Khan], Salman [Khan] were all introduced. *Maine Pyaar Kiya* [Sooraj R. Barjatya, 1989] was late 1980s, *Baazigar* [Abbas-Mustan, 1993] was early 1990s. Akshay Kumar and Saif Ali Khan came a little after. Those holes were there to be filled in and they grabbed the opportunity. They didn't allow anybody else to take their place and ruled it. Akshay Kumar, Ajay Devgn, the Khans, and Hrithik Roshan, these were the people who came in the 1990s.

How come there are such few stars and so many films?

I don't know if Hollywood people used to do this, but at least in Bombay, at least till some time back—not anymore—one actor used to act in three films a day.

A day?!

That's why you had the same look in every film. You had a nine to twelve shift for one film, then a two to six shift on another film, and a eight to eleven shift for a third film. Every star was doing three films at a time and that's how they managed to do so many films. Now, filmmakers are not ready to shoot only three hours a day. They are saying, 'No, I need to finish my film, I need to do it in one schedule, I can't wait for two years to finish my film.' So most actors are doing one film at a time.

But there are still only ten filmstars, twenty if you count the women.

Yeah, the A and B-listers on whom ten crores will be put are about twenty.

Another trend in Hindi cinema is that of fair skin and light eyes. Is it also evolving?

We are a fair skin-obsessed nation, especially in the North, not so much in the South. I feel it's a globalization thing. It was there always, but now it's crazy. I think a lot of it has to do with how suddenly Miss India's started becoming Miss World and Miss Universe. The times when Miss World and Miss Universe happened were also the times when the economic liberalization happened in India. Beauty became very important. Beauty brands had to sell their products. For that, they needed icons and for icons they made Miss World and Miss Universe. It's all connected. Our fairness products which were only two or three in the 1980s became three hundred in 1990s. If you suddenly want people to buy three hundred instead of three, then you need to bring a change in the society. Cinema, beauty contests were a small way to do it. The market dictates who we are and holds the reins of what people's tastes should be. If somebody like Dhanush is cast in a film like *Ranjhanaa* [Anand L. Rai, 2013], everybody says, 'My sweeper is more good-looking than him.' They don't realize how stupid their comment is, saying that the sweeper cannot be good-looking and that the only criteria to be a hero is to be good-looking. That's the mindset we function in.

To go back to something you said before about acting, why would the Western way of doing things be better than the Indian way? Wouldn't copying the way Western cinema works mean losing the Indian soul?

I don't think it would be un-Indian to make a non-entertainment film. It will be different from how we've been making films. A lot of us make art cinema, just for the heck of art cinema. But a lot of us have something to say, which is very true to our culture. It's just that it might not be as entertaining. I thoroughly believe in entertaining cinema. What I am against is mindless entertaining cinema. I feel that in the name of entertainment cinema, we don't work enough. We need to work harder on our scripts, even in entertaining films. We need to work harder on everything. Still, entertainment is very important. I will give you the example of my wife. She doesn't work in films, she's a food blogger. When I say, 'Let's watch a film', and it's some arty film, she doesn't want to watch it because she has worked all day and she needs to relax. She loves watching serious films with me, but once in five times she'll say, 'Let's watch this chick film.' I know where she comes from and I know where the entire country comes from. All of us need to de-stress and cinema is de-stress for us, like food or cricket. The day we will make only serious cinema, everything will become very sad and morose. What's missing in our culture is we are not ready to look at problems. Whenever there's a problem, as long as we are not getting affected, we turn our face away. And I think somewhere that's why alternate cinema is also important, to ignite something in you. As a seventeen-year-old kid, you want to express something, you want to learn something, understand something, and our culture is not giving it to you. We need to have meaningful cinema.

How do you create groundbreaking cinema in India, while still keeping it Indian?

We don't have a market for niche films right now in India. So the model is to go abroad and sell your film. That's one model that has been coming—which Guneet Monga, one of the pioneers, follows brilliantly. But over all, you just have to be honest with your story and a lot of filmmakers make a very personal film in the beginning. I think you should have a personal connection with your first or your second film. Then you have to take your personal connection to a universal connection. If a guy who lived in Kanpur all his life has now been in Bombay for the last seven-eight years, it'll be nice if he talks about people in Kanpur and not people in Bombay or Delhi, because we want to know his experience. That's how you can make the film Indian: by telling your story and not borrowing a story that has already been told.

Can you talk about the film you're writing right now? Is it a personal film?

Yes, it is. It is personal, and I hope it is universal, not just personal. It's about people in their twenties, and how they don't know where to go and what to do in life.

Do they go to ashrams?

No! *(laughs)* You have to make it slightly more glamorous than that!

When do you start shooting?

When I get the money!

How do you plan to finance it?

Right now the scenario is that it's not difficult to make the film, it's difficult to release it. So even though I am getting money to make it, I'll have to be really careful of the distribution.

Why is the system like that?

It's because the studio system has become very strong in our country. It's almost mirroring Hollywood. Corporates have taken over. They dictate the production space, the cinema space, so unless your film is being released by them, there's no guarantee that it'll be released....

SNEHA KHANWALKAR
Music Composer

You can't help but immediately fall in love with Sneha Khanwalkar. In addition to her natural beauty—she can wear spectacles, bed-head hair, have her arm in a cast and still be the first person you notice in a coffee shop—she infuses you with the kind of passion that makes you want to be like her when you grow up. Even if you grew up a few years before she did.

Whether her fascinating life stories are completely true or slightly exaggerated for the sake of her captivated audience doesn't matter. She is so cinegenic that you want to believe every single word she says, much like the kid from *Princess Bride*, who becomes a fairy tale buff thanks to Peter Falk's fantastic storytelling. Tales of audacious trips, heartbreaks, family pressure, early successes and self-doubt: this is a Bollywood *masala* movie in its own right and you have been invited to, on a lovely afternoon, in the suburbs of Mumbai.

At thirty-six years old, Sneha could easily show off her impressive resume: the youngest female music director in the Hindi industry, she has composed music for some of the most well-known 'indie' films released in the last ten years: *Oye Lucky! Lucky Oye!* [2008], *Love Sex aur Dokha* [2010], *Detective Byomkesh Bakshy!* [2015], with her mentor Dibakar Banerjee, and Anurag Kashyap's *Gangs of Wasseypur* [2012]. In 2012, she also hosted MTV's popular TV-show,

Sound Trippin', for which she travelled to ten different Indian cities, in search of new sounds and local artists.

Call her music 'folk', and you're most likely to face a small disappointed look—she's too nice to frown at you—for putting forward such a simplistic comment. Like many artists in the Hindi film industry, she gets annoyed at how easily your most recent work ends up labelling you as 'so and so'. Ask her about being one of the only female composers in the history of the Hindi film industry, and she dismisses your question with the smile of someone who has heard it too often. Is it because genres hardly matter when you do what you love? Or simply because Sneha is compelling for everyone, man or woman? She would rather be known as a free spirit, who likes to go with the flow—even during interviews. She sometimes forgot my foreign origin when, passionately caught up in a story, she would spontaneously shout a word in Hindi.

And what about her music? For Sneha, it is less alive in words or long sentences than in a song quickly hummed or a beat drummed on a coffee table, next to the teapot. This fabulous woman is simply an experience.

Your family is very much into music.

My mum's family is into the Gwalior *gharana* of Indian classical music. So I have seen my relatives, my cousins, my family, doused in Indian classical music. You had to shake them out of it, because we didn't know of any other culture so we thought that this is quite normal. Later, I realized that we had a peculiar thing going on in the family. At four o'clock, our grandparents would wake up, one of them would tune the *tanpura*, sit down and sing. We would have our separate homes, we were not a joint family, but we would come together at various religious occasions or festivals and that's when we used to stay in this two-storey house, where at four o'clock in the morning sometimes, you had to get up because your grand-uncle was singing. His children, my cousins, uncles and aunts, would also get up and do their thing. And they were teaching in music colleges. They would talk about *ragas* and each one of us was assumed to be able to sing, play or know about a *raga* or about *taal*. I was really young and I used to listen to Ace of Base, because it played in my aerobics class. I used to like that also. At school, I sang the Lata Mangeshkar songs, in my free periods, and my friends would make fun of those songs. I never really understood why people didn't like other people's music, but really held their own as something important. I liked all of it! We used to gather for family functions, family friends' dinners and I was made to sing each time. It was terrible because there were these judgemental eyes and in Indore, where I grew up, you really had to be a good kid. It was indispensable. You had to show promise about the future that you're out to become something really big and a genius. *(laughs)* There was this pressure of performance. Being a girl, you otherwise never got to speak or emote too much. You had to be respectful and at the same time good at singing. There was one cousin who used to stay in America, she had come and she asked me once, 'What is this, a talent show?' That's the first time I saw it as, 'oh I need to stand up against it'. But it was too late, I had already done a lot of damage to myself. Now in retrospect, I feel it was the best thing because I thought a lot about music, there wasn't any controlled performance or learning, but a lot of listening and a lot of questioning.

So you never learned music.

The basics were naturally there because of my family, but I also learned a lot through hearing music. Some things you just effortlessly do, because you keep hearing them. Doing an *alap* with a *harkat* by hearing it was very normal. Understanding of it came much later.

Did your family want you to be a musician?

No. They should have put me to learn the piano, or something. I think at that time, because I sang well, they must have thought that if I work on it, they will encourage me to become a singer and find myself in that career. Which also got fueled by these reality shows that had just started coming out. All kids were expected to practise, do *riyaz* [practice] and then become Alka Yagnik and Lata Mangeshkar. In my family, there was other classical referencing, but it was still Lata Mangeshkar and Asha Bhosle; we are a Marathi family and they are Marathis....

So they were okay with Bollywood, even though they had a classical background?

They were okay with some songs of Bollywood. I was not allowed to sing all kinds of songs. In fact my dad was picky, but he picked the right songs—for example, *Roop Suhana Lagta Hai* by [A. R.] Rahman. He picked Rahman instantly when he came in. Other uncles and aunties were not taking to Rahman that easily, because it was a different sound. But my dad liked the *Bombay* [Mani Ratnam, 1995] soundtrack, *Roja* [Mani Ratnam, 1992] and he would make me sing that also sometimes. I mostly sang from the album of *Lekin…* [Gulzar, 1991]. The music was by Hridayanath Mangeshkar, Lata Mangeshkar's brother and there were some amazing songs in there.

So you were not watching movies at home?

I watched a lot of movies but whichever everybody was watching. There was no, 'I want to watch that movie'. There was no opinion on films, there was an opinion on film music.

Not even world cinema or Hollywood?

No. Films weren't brought inside the house too much, there were no posters in our rooms, no Bollywood chat, it wasn't encouraged. Our cousins used to come and then we would watch *Honey I Shrunk the Kids*. I also used to watch a lot of animation, I grew up on *The Aristocats* by Disney, *The Jungle Book, Terminator, Titanic*. I also saw a semi-porn film, which was Japanese—when I was in eleventh grade, with a friend. It was our first porn movie. I found it was very artistic and I was like, 'Why isn't it making me horny? Why is it making me [feel] something else?' The music was one of a kind, very *In the Mood for Love*. Even the foreplay was very artistic. *(laughs)* So I was like, 'Ok, this must be porn.'

You started working in animation. What led you there?

My parents shifted from Indore to Bombay. They just wanted a better town for us. I felt great, supremely liberated. I didn't want to come to Bombay at first, because the last time I had come to Bombay, I was in the seventh standard and I had got lost looking at a B-grade movie poster—a poster with a lot of gore and nudity. *(laughs)* I was really young. My mum and my aunt started to walk around the market. I just stood there for one and a half hour and lost them. They came back crying for me. I was right there. My mum slapped me, and I was like, 'But I didn't move, I was right here!'

You didn't move for an hour and a half!

I think, because she yelled at me, 'I've been looking for you for one hour.' That's how I remember it was one hour—definitely around forty minutes. There was a lot to stare at; it was huge, painted, dirty fluorescent. So, I had very shitty memories of Bombay. Also it was too crowded, you could never feel important. But by this time, when I came here, I think not being given attention was the best thing for me. Indore is not that good for girls—you couldn't step out alone, you couldn't take a rickshaw by yourself, you couldn't wear things, people always stared at you just because you're a girl. Bombay made me feel a little less sexual. So I was quite happily shocked: I was suddenly coming to a new college, interacting with peers who were different from me. I used to doodle a lot and animation was the thing at that time, so I decided to do it.

Where did you study animation?

I studied at C-DAC. It was from Pune University, but there was a branch here in Bombay. I didn't study further because I didn't want to sit at a computer and it turned out you have to sit at a computer for too long. At that time, I thought if I go to Los Angeles, I'll spend too much money, sit at a computer and not be happy. Ironically that's what I am doing now, sitting at a computer! *(laughs)* Then I started doing an art direction internship at Omung Kumar Productions. At this point, I had just done my twelfth grade. Omung Kumar is an art director who directed that *Mary Kom* film [2014]. I literally snatched the job from him because I stalked him for a long time. He finally took me on and that's when I realized that films is the best place to be. I knew nothing about films, I had no passion for films—there was no good film/bad film for me, no awareness, no sensitivity towards films. But what I saw on the sets—working shifts, going early in the morning, how even the smallest department was so important on the set, and how everything had to come into harmony without knowing how it will come out in the end—I found the job quite brave, quite patient, basically very exciting.

Did you start watching films then?

No. Ah, I remember watching *American Pie*, in the first week that I came to Bombay. I watched it with a bunch of friends who thought I was from a village, so it would be cool to hang out with me and show me *American Pie*! *(laughs)* I also saw the first Hrithik Roshan film, *Kaho Naa... Pyaar Hai* [Rakesh Roshan, 2000]. Those were the films that were there, there was no Anurag in the picture, no Dibakar in the picture, they weren't born! *Jaane Bhi Do Yaaro* [Kundan Shah, 1983] was my dad's and mum's favourite film, I used to like the music. My mum and dad may not have had a lot of knowledge about films, but they spoke very respectfully of certain films. Their analysis was not shallow, like, '*Arre*, what a picture, I love it, I can see it hundred times.' They were very subtle. So if they liked something, they would say: 'The acting is superb, the story is beautiful.'

So after nine months of art direction, you switched to composing. Why?

My dad was really worried because I had just skipped animation, started doing art direction and I hadn't decided what my career will be.

How old were you?

I was about to enter my first year of graduation, so seventeen, eighteen years old....

You were seventeen and your dad was worried?

I think he told me in the eighth standard that I should do IAS, Indian Administrative Services—and I said, 'Okay, I'll do IAS.' The next day, I was found in the library reading about IAS. My teacher led me to the comics section. I think all middle-class families at that time, and in smaller towns, were too career-minded. I saw that each time somebody got a report card or a degree or a job, it was celebrated. So my dad was pissed off and I was really genuinely confused. I knew I wouldn't spend my time in art direction, I was a doodler but it wasn't clicking for me. Then I decided to compose.

You were eighteen.

Around eighteen. Or less. Not more. I started writing down and composing songs on a walkman, putting down some dummy lyrics and at the end, in the last two lines, I would write what singer I wanted. So I would write Hariharan, and Kavita Krishnamurthy for this song, as if it was going to happen. I would give one star for good songs, two stars for better ones and three stars for a super hit song! *(laughs)* All this without even stepping inside a studio. This was my dream job. At that time, my insomnia sort of had begun—and by insomnia, I mean you just don't want to sleep, you want to sneak out, have a cigarette in the middle of the night.... Sometimes, I would wake my dad and my mum up at three o'clock in the morning, go to their bedroom. Because they liked music, because they had made me sing so much, I would subconsciously get back at them, say, 'Listen to this new composition' and I would start singing. I knew that they had always shown me respect for my singing, so they had to sit down.

I started looking for work once I had fifty, sixty tunes. Now, when I look at them, there was one line from there, one line from here.... If people liked songs about *chunri*, I'd make a *chunri* song. It was still an exercise. The intention was correct, but I hadn't gone deep and got the punch yet.

What did your parents think of these songs at three in the morning when you woke them up?

At that time, they used to like them, but I never got a clear answer from them.

You're a composer, so at one point you might have wanted to make them proud.

I think people don't understand composition or music direction so much in India. They only understand singing. My relatives must think I know how to play the *tabla* or the harmonium very well. But I don't. That's why we don't have many female music directors. I don't think any parent tells their child to become a music director.

Do you play an instrument?

My voice is my instrument. I can play the keyboard by ear, but I don't play an instrument to perform. I get people to record but because I am not a real musician, my party of musicians is very diverse. It comprises of really good musicians and unlearned, but passionate village players also, who don't do music for their bread and butter, but just get drunk at night and play. I don't only pick singers who have done ten years of learning or sound super correct. I am receptive to others, probably also because I am not from the institution.

How do you compose your music without knowing the theory?

I understand Indian classical music. I know how to write the Indian notations. But it's not that I'll put down the entire chord structure. I'll sit with somebody to see if it works for me. I am also interested in odd sounds. Sometimes they have an impact on me, a little more than designing a harmonized piece. So if I have to put down a song, it could start with anything, like with a bang....

We'll come back to this later. Let's go back to you being eighteen with your fifty songs.

Ignorance was bliss. I thought the industry was dying to meet me. *(laughs)* I thought I just had to go there and everything would sort itself out, that because I liked Rahman's music, whatever played in my head would automatically come out. I realized it was not enough to be a listener when I started meeting people and tried to get my songs on a CD. I realized that I have to look for a film, so that I could excite myself. You can do anything in a film song. You can weep, you can yell, you can be angry, you can be passionate about something. That's what really excited me. There was no urge for independent music. I don't think I had woken up to any concept like that. Also music wasn't spiritual for me. It was just a career—do your job, you know a bit of music, do a song if you feel like. I actually didn't start like, 'Oh man, I want to express through music.' *(laughs)*

I called Tigmanshu Dhulia and told him I want to meet him, but that I hadn't seen his film, *Haasil* [2003]. He seemed like an approachable guy and he had worked with Mani Ratnam, so there was all this talk of 'Mani Ratnam, great filmmaker'. I met Tigmanshu and did two songs with him. The film hasn't released yet. With him, I met Piyush Mishra. I would go home, sit with Piyush's lyrics, start composing like that *(starts humming)* and come back with the song. Then Tigmanshu said, 'Okay, let's record, how much money do you want?' I said, that much, he said, 'Okay.' I was like, 'Really?' I came back and I thought this was my best decision to compose. I obviously was a slow, dumb eighteen-year-old—I was quite ignorant to all these big things they spoke about. Camera work and all that, I couldn't relate to it.

Around the same time I also met Anurag [Kashyap] through Piyush *bhai*. Anurag sent me to Ram Gopal Varma, which was quite big, because Ram Gopal Varma had just made *Rangeela* [1995]. After that, he was on a downfall—but still his music was great till *Satya* [Ram Gopal Varma, 1998]. I used to listen to this album a lot. Ram Gopal Varma asked me to do all the songs for a film which again canned. I had just done two songs. Those two songs went into another film called *Go* [Ram Gopal Varma, 2007], which my friends still tease me about.

Why? Because it's a bad film? I haven't seen it....

Yeah, it's a bad film. Why would you see it? Don't see it! *(laughs)* I don't think I had grown that much at this time. I was trying to learn software... I was also studying, I was twenty, twenty-one. I graduated and I had not done work as I had expected. I decided to stay quiet for a couple of months and think. I went back to my mum's and dad's house to stay with them because my money ran out. Then I called Dibakar, because a friend got the number somehow. I said, 'Look, I haven't seen your film *Khosla Ka Ghosla* [Dibakar Banerjee, 2006], but somebody told me you're very good with music and you give it a lot of importance, and I like the music of *Khosla Ka Ghosla*.' He said, 'It's okay, many people haven't seen the film.' *(laughs)* Then he took this long interview over the phone only about my musical background. I realized that, for the first time, somebody was listening carefully about where I've been. I couldn't tell him nonsense. Even now, sometimes when I think I am starting to bullshit, I go straight to his office and keep up the momentum so he crashes it down. I survived on bullshit a lot while growing up. I sort of made my way through bullshit.

You're not bullshiting me right?

No, no... I might... no, no....*(laughs)* Dibakar met me, much later, and I told him I wanted to do a film song, not ads. He said, 'Come for an ad recording, see if you can do this.' I went to the studio, I sat through the entire recording and in the end, before going, I said, 'But I want to do a film song, I don't want to work on ads, give me a film song.' My ego was hurt.

At twenty-one, such an ego!

I only survived on ego at that time. Dibakar said, 'Fine, here are some lyrics, you think of a song.' He gave me some lyrics, and then I disappeared for a month or two. Around the same time, I was also going through an emotional setback. A break-up. *(laughs)* I cracked the song I think, I showed it to him and he liked it. That song is not released yet, because that film never happened.

Again?

I know! But it's happening now. *Calcutta* is that film [*Detective Byomkesh Bakshy!* 2015]. He had started work on it long ago. So we did a scratch, he showed it to the producers, we recorded the scratch, it all went fine. Within a week, it was decided that he's doing *Oye Lucky*

[Dibakar Banerjee, 2008]. And he said, 'Would you like to do a song for it? Because there's only one song.' I agreed. Because the film was set in Delhi and Punjab and I didn't know that area, I was asked to travel. I picked a friend, promised him beer and he came around for one-and-a-half, two months. I slummed it out basically. I travelled in like dirty old jeans, backpack.... Also did all the weeping, the crying, all the drama, while on the travel. But it was very liberating because there was nobody, nothing. At that time, I had lost hope, so I would listen to any singer and feel real goosebumps. I was on a very emotional high and on top of it, Punjabi music is super emotional. Their notes and everything are very nostalgia-inclined, also because of their history.

I hadn't seen or travelled in India like this before. I had always travelled with parents, hotels, cars, train stations, airports, but I hadn't been in a village unguarded. And that was quite a change. I started drinking and I started to be sensitive towards every sound that'd hit my hear. This is my own personal journey. This had nothing to do with how the songs would sound eventually. I don't want to connect the two yet. So *Oye Lucky* happened and instead of one song, we did five songs, with amazing singers.

Why did you do five songs? Because Dibakar was really happy with your work?

We just had found great singers. And there were already two songs for sure—it must have been the producers.... It wasn't like, 'Oh you're a good person, I'll give you three more songs.' It wasn't that literal. *(laughs)*

Where did you find those singers?

In villages in Punjab and Haryana. None of them were playback singers, so they hadn't faced the studio or the mic.... Should I tell you a bit about that?

Yes, of course!

There was one singer who was around seventy, seventy-five years old, he didn't know his age. A villager. I wanted him to sing *Jugni*.

I played his voice for Dibakar, who decided, 'Okay, this works for this song, you can try this.' I went back after a few months to find that guy again to record him. Now I had a song, a composition and lyrics. I rehearsed with this old man, Mr Des Raj Lakhani, for two days. Then I took him to Chandigarh, put him in a lodge, stayed in the same lodge. The other singer came from Jalandhar, his name was Dilbahar, he was a twenty-four-year-old married guy, extremely shy on the face, but very naughty. I put him also up in the same lodge. I was staying on the third floor, they were on the second floor and there was one room for rehearsals. Dilbahar wasn't literate, so he couldn't read and write and his condition was that he did not want to let anybody know that he can't read and write. So I had to sit with him and make him learn the entire song, except the rap section that he didn't sing. In the other room, Mr Lakhani was rehearsing. Now, Mr Lakhani would sing beautifully, learn the tune... and forget it in an hour. Again, he would learn it and forget it. Dibakar was to come only for a day, morning to evening and in the evening fly back with me again to Bombay. We had only one day and this bugger wouldn't learn, that bugger couldn't read. *(laughs)* It was my first film, so I couldn't show my director that I was inefficient. When Mr Lakhani's turn came, he said, 'I want to take a nap for two hours.' And none of us could say anything because he had just had lunch and as per his rituals, he had to sleep for two hours after lunch in the afternoon. So he was sleeping on the couch, I was standing and Dibakar was like, 'What?' *(laughs)* Then, he sang, Dilbahar sang and it all went quite fine.

There were other singers. There was one kid whom we recorded in Haryana and brought to Delhi eventually. He was eleven years old. His voicebox was about to change. So he had a slight crack in his voice. There's this song, *Tu Raja Ki Raj Dulari*. Dibakar said, 'Let him sing high.' In their belt, singing high pitch was directly connected to their manhood. They have competitions based on high pitch. Whoever would take the highest pitch would win, whether he would be able to sing ever again or not. There are singers in Haryana who lose their voices forever, after twenty-eight, because they've sung enough and sung at such a high pitch. But they are okay with it. These are the kind of singers we interacted with.

Haryana, at the border with Delhi, is extremely high on testosterone. It's the rape capital in a way. Travelling alone in that region was scary, but I didn't know it. I didn't realize. Again, ignorance is fucking bliss! *(laughs)* I was roaming around, talking to everybody—they would ask my age, my caste, whether I was married to the friend I was travelling with or not.

Was it in Haryana where you went to a music festival where you were the only woman?

Yeah. You wanna hear about that? So we stayed with one singer, in a village called Kalka, extremely interior. That guy had some seven kids, and he kept saying, 'My wife is not beautiful.' And she was beautiful! They were heading for a competition where I was supposed to go with them. We got ready and these guys started loading guns. I even picked the gun. Slowly it occurred to us that we were not going to a great place. We got in a Scorpio, full of eight men who were drinking and smoking ganja. We would also smoke ganja at that time, but not like this and we wouldn't dare to ask them to pass the joint, you know? *(laughs)* The travel from the village to Bahadurgarh, close to Delhi, was around three and a half hours and in the middle of it, my friend whispered to me, 'If they try to rape you, I cannot do anything, because they have guns. So, do you think we should just get off of this car?' I looked around outside the car and there was just bare land. And I said, 'There's no point.' We reached the place, we saw some uncles, aunties, kids and we were happy. It was 9.30-10 pm. We were like, '*chalo, family hai*' [let's go, there are families]. They started eating dinner and slowly, there were no women anymore. And then no kids. Only men, who by then were drunk. So much that even the master of ceremony on the mic was saying, '*Yah kaun hai?*' [who are they?], pointing at us, '*Bombay se*' [they are from Bombay]. It was very interactive. Then I called Dibakar's office and I said, 'I think I need a car now.' One car came from Delhi. The driver was a Sardar. Now, you're sitting in a competition full of Haryanvi *jats*, and there's a Sardar in trousers and shirts, who says, 'We have to go.' And I am like, 'No, no, sit, the music is amazing!' So he's sitting in the middle of it and I am going around with the recorder, because by then the music is so brilliant.... I was also high on it, so I stayed as much as I could. Slowly there were some growls and some abusing happening. Then we just sort of moved out. I had taken enough videos and enough music.

Did you use the music you found in that festival for your composition?

I composed a *ragini*, for which I used the *madkas*. It's a traditional form of rhythm where they beat the clay pot with a tyre rubber. They also cover the mouth of the clay pot, with some sort of a rubber. It's all made by hand because all these guys are farmers.... It's not their job, they're not musicians. So recording them was another party because.... Haven't you seen the making of *Oye Lucky* on Youtube?

No, I haven't.

Please watch it. You'll get the images for your understanding. So that kind of recording happened there. I also went to Himachal to see the snow, I had never seen snow. I didn't tell the office. Anyway, I was not telling them anything. I was slumming it, I had no money, they didn't give me much money to travel. I thought I had nicely hidden it from the production department, but later on in the videos they saw me abusing in the snow.... *(laughs)*

Oye Lucky happened and it was released...

Yeah, it was released *(laughs)*, but two days after the bomb blasts [of 2008 in Bombay]. We all were in Goa. There was a film festival where the film premiered. It got a great response, but because the blasts had happened, nobody wanted to talk about a film. I felt really bad for Dibakar, because you couldn't even go to a public theatre.

That was bad luck for your first film...

It was worse for Dibakar, because the music had released a month before and it had done its job I think. People were listening to it, people liked it. It was being heard.

You continued working with Dibakar.

I worked with Dibakar on *LSD* [*Love, Sex aur Dhokha*, Dibakar Banerjee, 2010]. In between, I was getting only work on films which had Punjabi songs, because *Oye Lucky* had Punjabi sort of songs. I wouldn't take any work. I was also a little bratty—I thought I could hibernate like this and only do good work. *(laughs)* Which was a good idea, because *LSD* happened. I kept learning during this time. I was wondering: what exactly is working for the people? You can never find that out—that I realized much later. You make a song and you're not thinking about the people at that time. When your CD is ready, you don't want to listen to that music for at least two-three months. At least, I would run away. And then, slowly, you would see me alone, listening to my own songs. *(laughs)* After *LSD* happened, I got this folk tag on me. I don't know why. I am not a folk musician. I am not working towards the development of folk. I only felt that because classical music comes from folk music and classical music had been intimidating me forever, I wanted to go to its mother and complain to it. I like the simplicity of folk music, its ignorance. I like that musicians don't care about performance and that the voices come out of the jobs they had, the hardships, or the weather, or the food they ate. Their music is what their life is.

How do you work on a movie? Do you read the script or do you write your songs first?

I read the script of *Oye Lucky*, but more like an exercise. I never went to Dibakar and discussed the script. I didn't have it in me to have an opinion at that time. My director had an idea about the intensity and he knew whether or not I could apply that intensity. So half the job was done by Dibakar picking me, at the right time, for this film. For the song *Jugni*, Dibakar said, 'Just take out your anger! You have anger, right?' I picked just these instructions and I learnt to express my anger. More than me, there are a lot of people who have a very good reason to be angry. That's why I must have related to the script and the voice of that man. It all just fell into some sort of understanding: the history of Punjab and how their notes are....

Did the same thing happen with *LSD*?

No, for *LSD*, I didn't read the script. There were a lot of people chasing Dibakar for the music of *LSD*. With Dibakar, it's not like,

'I've done one of your films, so now you have to give me priority.'... He's very reasonable, he's not sentimental, which is great. I also had to do a scratch for *LSD*, to show him whether I can crack it or not. I did that without knowing anything; I just knew the title was *Love, Sex and Dhokha*, over which I had a two-hour long conversation with my dad who explained why the word 'sex' shouldn't be in the title. Dibakar said, 'My parents are also saying the same.' *(laughs)* I was playing the scratch loudly while working on it, in my parents' house: 'Love, Sex aur Dhokha'! By then, my parents were used to it. I had done a scratch, a song in gibberish, which Dibakar really liked and he wrote Rajasthani lyrics to it. Then we made two other songs for the film.

So you got the job.

I got the job after having done the job. *(laughs)*

What happened next?

I did *Gangs of Wasseypur*. I had done music for two films and they had both done well, musically also, but both of them were with Dibakar. I felt that coming-of-age feeling of stepping out and doing something on my own. *(laughs)* The other reason I wanted to do *Gangs of Wasseypur* was that I got this folk tag I was telling you about. People were saying that I got the right pulse and I didn't think I got it entirely. Could I repeat that, could I go deeper? Somebody like Anurag, again, you can't bullshit and he doesn't know music. He told me the first day only, 'I'll hear it, and I'll say if it works or it doesn't. It may be great, but whether it works for me, that's all I can tell you. I cannot explain why and all that.' So I said, 'Yeah, cool.' There was this Anurag cloud, you know? *Dev-D* [Anurag Kashyap, 2009] had happened and the music was great. Anurag had arrived.

So I took it up, and the travel started in Bihar .... Because there is this Maharashtra/Bihar clash, and I am a Maharashtrian, my kick was to go to Bihar and say, 'Hi, I am Sneha Khanwal*kar.*' *Kars* are mostly Marathis, and I've seen amazing faces! I would play with it. *(laughs)* I went to Patna, above Ganga and under Ganga and then to Ranchi also, close to where Wasseypur is. Now, I had also heard about chutney music in college, because of the song *Lotela*. I felt it was Indian, but it was not. It was a little African also, but I didn't understand it at that time. I saw a documentary about Trinidad, about chutney music and I realized that Biharis had gone to Trinidad, migrated as indentured labour, in the mid-1850s and have stayed there ever since. There's a Bihari community in Trinidad and of course in Fiji and Mauritius also. But Trinidad seemed more romantic and also it was closer to Jamaica.... I told Anurag, 'I'll do this film, but you'll have to let me go to Trinidad.' With him not knowing Trinidad, he said, 'Yeah, sure!' There, I saw the same women, same faces, same bodies, but here in a saree, there in a frock that showed cleavage, dancing and listening to chutney music. The instrument is the *dholak*; in Bihar, it will play at a tempo of let's say one hundred and twenty max. There, at one hundred and forty, one hundred and fifty—and all you could move was your bum! *(imitates the movement of the percussion on the table).* In Trinidad, they also have this weird instrument, a percussion shaped like a triangle, which is extinct in Bihar now.

I stayed in Trinidad for two months, alone. It was my first trip out of India. I recorded a lot of singers, kept composing, got lyrics on line, speaking to Anurag over the phone, getting things approved, tune and lyrics. There are a couple of songs in the films which have the influence.

There's also a song called Womaniya for which you recorded women...

For *Womaniya*, I was in Allahabad listening to some *nautanki* singers when Anurag called. These guys had planned the shoot for *Womaniya* within a week. I wasn't ready, but they said, 'Just come to Benares and do the recording.' I called a singer from Patna and a singer from Benares. Both these women never really did a recording. The Benares woman was a *paan*-eater, *jagran* singer, who was more outgoing; the woman from Patna was a housewife, she would only sing in choruses. These two women were brought into a room, we all sat together—it was a one-take recording. It was done in an old format, where the micing was dressed in one place—they were not sitting in booths. These women never talked to each other, they were put in front of each other and they were teasing each other. That whole recording was something else! In the end, in the chorus, they were like, '*Yehe, womaniya, yehe, womaniya*' and they were pointing at me, because I was tiring them out of their wits, by recording and rehearsing.

Did you feel that you had more freedom with Anurag because he didn't know about music?

I had more freedom, but I felt I could have taken the wrong decisions.

You're working with people who are mainly non-mainstream. Do you want to do mainstream cinema?

It would be exciting. Now, I wouldn't want to do something which is inclined towards the interiors or folk. After a film releases, you get similar kind of work. I've also been dodging that, because people think of a UP [Uttar Pradesh, state of India] film or a Bihari film so they call Sneha, or ask me for Marathi songs because I am Maharashtrian. *(laughs)*

What are your next projects? What would you like to work on now?

There is Dibakar's film which will happen after August or September [*Detective Byomkesh Bakshy!* released in 2015].

So on that one, you're working for sure?

I've done that one song. And there's another song which he liked the tune of, some months back. Oh, you want to know how I sang that tune?

Yes!

We were going towards Juhu and I wanted Dibakar's driver to drop me in his car. He was going for a meeting—I think he was meeting his writer in Juhu. Dibakar didn't want to talk and the atmosphere was depressed, dark. He said, 'I don't want to speak about anything, I just want to go quietly, finish off this meeting and go home.' So I said,

'Okay, I'll also stay quiet.' Then I said, 'Can I sing a song? Should I sing a song? I'll sing a song, it's a new tune!' He said, 'No, maybe later, because *abhi* [now], I won't be able to react well.' So I said, 'No, don't react, I'll just sing.' I sang some tune that I had in mind. He dropped me, he went and then called me from the meeting, 'I like it, just keep it!' *(laughs)*

Would meeting A.R. Rahman, who was such a special person in your learning of film music, be important to you?

No. My fascination doesn't involve meeting the person. I'm learning from his music, that's pretty much enough. There's so much learning that's happened from Rahman's music. The keyboards came in and he used them in his soundtracks—and the bass. When I play the bass in my family, they'll not hear it. They'll be like, 'This guitar doesn't play? Can't hear it!' You can't hear the bass as such. But he played it loud and clear in pop songs and I think he's made soulful music.

You're only the fourth female music composer in India, how does it feel?

I've never found the right answer for this. The last time I was having a little tiff with my mum, I used this. 'Have you ever asked me what it is like to be a woman and live alone in Bombay?' *(laughs)* It's there, it's an undercurrent thing, but I don't think you can sit with it for too long. On the films I've worked on, the crews have been quite equal. The directors never treated me like I was just a girl. Anurag sometimes even talks to you as if you're a boy, '*Kya kar raha he tu?*' ['What are you doing?' in a familiar way with masculine forms of address] He treats you like a comrade. Dibakar on the other hand never shows his leadership. Sometimes he says, 'I am confused about this.' However, in recordings, you feel you are a woman all the time. Sometimes, your musicians are not listening. Earlier, some musicians didn't look me in the eyes—they would look at the sound engineer. For instance, I am telling the *sarangi* player: 'Play *ni sa sa* and then *re*' and he's playing '*ni sa sa* and then *re*', not looking at me! Later, I realized it was fine. Also, after travelling in the interiors, all these things hardly matter. Because that's where you get the extreme action: you're a female, you're from a town and you're bossing them around. I think that made me tougher also.

[The interview is almost over, but Sneha and I get to talking about Dibakar and I mention the fact that I've interviewed a few people for my book that have worked with him, especially women. Sneha insists on adding something about him]

You can't bullshit Dibakar, and Dibakar mostly doesn't bullshit you. Initially, when I was starting out, I was denying all the learning that I got by default from my family. I was denying it because I was being rebellious. And I think that's why I was not finding ground. But somebody like Dibakar made me look into that learning again. He told me whatever you've learnt, whatever life you've had, it's individualistic, it's in your bones. You can't deny that, because it's your wealth. That sense, I got from Dibakar, although my parents have been saying that all the time. Also there was something he said about some song tune I was writing. He said, 'This is sentimental, it's not emotional.' And I was like, 'What the fuck is sentimental, what the fuck is emotional?' *(laughs)* He's just got good parenting skills. He just says these right things which make you think. And Anurag lets you be so you can continue thinking. *(laughs)*

MANOSHI NATH AND RUSHI SHARMA
Costume Designers

As the saying goes, 'clothes make the man'… and the Bollywood star. There is no other film industry in the world where clothes play such an important part that they have become fashion in itself. Ample evidence of this is the influence of the Hindi film industry on the wedding trends or the multiple 'Bollywood' clothes stores that have opened all over the world—to the extent that in the West, audiences might not always like the *masala* film they just went to watch, but most of them will comment on how pretty the costumes were, and funnily enough, expect all Indians to be dressed accordingly. Only Hindi films can make poor villagers in Rajasthan look like they have just stepped out of the Ambanis' residence.

How do you make your way from self-proclaimed realistic urban films like *Oye Lucky! Lucky Oye!* [Dibakar Banerjee, 2008] or *Once Upon in Time in Mumbai* [Milan Luthria, 2010] to a more traditional romantic comedy such as *Sanam Teri Kasam* [Radhika Rao, Vinay Sapru, 2016]? Simply enough, answer costume designers Manoshi Nath and Rushi Sharma, you enjoy both as long as you stay true to the spirit of the film. They might not want to go back to actresses dancing in the snow in their tiny sarees, but they appreciate the creative freedom in a country with such a diversity of styles that you can draw your inspiration from thousands of sources.

I met Manoshi and Rushi in an Andheri West café after going back and forth with the date and the time of the interview. These two young women are very in demand and go effortlessly, almost magically, from prepping the clothes they design for a Bollywood star in the morning to a work meeting on their next film. Though they did not have time to sit with me for long, it was with a spirit of love that they answered my questions.

To put it simply, Manoshi and Rushi have 'found each other'. They work as a dream team and a well-oiled machine, and it was easy to see even from my very informal interview, that they seem to complete each other. When one started a sentence, the other finished it. The passion that they have for their work has made them first and foremost specialists of independent cinema, but also of more conventional Bollywood films. No matter what type of film they are working on, they always follow two rules: fierce professionalism and passion.

Working as a duo in the film industry is quite original ...

Manoshi Nath [MN]: We started off as two people, though we are both from Delhi. Rushi used to do a lot of international films, and I used to work with a particular director who made commercials. Work increased, and Rushi met our production house, so we worked together on a couple of commercials. Then I stopped working with the director and I worked with her on an international film. That was our first feature film together. Then we travelled for a while, and by that time we had figured we both want to work with each other. Basically, work with the best, and you have no competition! *(laughs)*

Rushi Sharma [RS]: That's when we opened our own company, Fools' Paradise, because we believe we are two fools who are living in our own paradise, and films as you know are as far away from reality ...

MN: A make-believe world.

What are the pros and cons of working as a duo?

RS: Our background, as far as our studies and education, how we started off, is quite different. Manoshi started storyboarding in a production house. She comes from an ad background. I studied design at school. Our own strengths and weaknesses are quite different. Sometimes we give absolute opposite ideas to one character, which really works wonderfully when blended together. Also we try to do our research separately and we discover that we have found the same kind of picture or the same kinds of things. Nobody can make out the differences in our sketches. Our principles are exactly the same. I have no doubt in what she is going to say if there is a call that I have to take. She is going to say exactly what I am going to say. It is fantastic to have support like that. It's a marriage of a sort.

MN: It is a complete marriage!
RS: And a good one at that! A marriage without the complexity of sex. *(laughs)*

So there are no negatives in this arrangement?

MN: No, two creative people working together do have creative differences. One person would get stuck on the red, the other one on the blue ...
RS: Or the same blue she calls green and I call blue! *(laughs)*
MN: Now we've come to terms with it and we say, let's put a pin in this and somehow some solution comes out.
RS: What's fantastic is we have never compromised with our work. We may have fought with each other because of something that is troubling the two of us, because we are working so closely.
MN: We are also very good friends.
RS: Yeah, she's my closest friend. I don't know about you though...
MN: Sort of. *(laughs)*
RS: We do fight. I spend the maximum time with her, not with my family. We are working so much.

You have always agreed on the films that you want to work on?

MN: We don't work separately, we are partners. Our creative decisions, brainstorming, is always done together. The film finally on set can be executed by one of us, but the design of the film is always together—whether it's a commercial, whether it's a music video, whether it's theatre, whether it's a feature film.

You are also working on ads?

MN: Very little. Mostly because we have a love for feature films, for crazy hard work *(laughs)* that drives us mad, because we love characterization—going into a character, living his life.

RS: Making our own backstory for him.

MN: That's why we love working with Dibakar [Banerjee], because when Dibakar tells us, 'This is the actor which is playing this character', it doesn't end there. It is a character that has a backstory that is never going to be seen on the big screen. Dibakar explains to us where he comes from, which family, which clothes he used to wear when he was a kid. We also start living with the character.

RS: In *Shanghai* [Dibakar Banerjee, 2012], Emraan [Hashmi]'s character in the film is a Rajasthani from a small town in Rajasthan. His character belongs to the *chote bhai* clan, people who were royalty at some point. But in royalty, all over the world, the younger son always ends up with nothing. When the royalty goes away, the younger brother who didn't get the property, no royal rights, still wants to show off that he is royalty. This *chota bhai* is a phenomenon in itself. When such a character is given to you, you have to understand him. There's a portion in the film where Emraan takes his watch off, showing his wrist, and says: 'I am actually fair' [because that portion doesn't get tanned], 'I am royalty.' The best part about this character was that the actor was the complete opposite. This actor is known as a serial killer ... kisser! *(laughs)* Because all he does in his films is kiss women. He is this romantic, lover boy kind of a guy. We had to convert him into a small town man who is a porn filmmaker on the side. In a small one-room apartment, on a dirty bed, he makes dirty porn films. It was quite a task, because Emraan is very nice, fair, a sweet looking boy with pink lips. Dibakar told us, 'Let's paint his lips black!' So that's what we did and we stained his teeth. He was a guy you would not shake your hands with. That's what we turned him into. *(laughs)*

MN: We were quite proud to turn that kind of an actor into that kind of a character. One day, as we were shooting in a strange town in Maharashtra, Latur, Emraan was sitting in character, in costume, in makeup, next to Dibakar. Dibakar was ready for shot and said, 'Let's call Emraan from the vanity.' Emraan was sitting right there! He didn't recognize him because he had blended into the geography of that place, of the people who lived there. That was a big compliment for us. *(laughs)*

So you do more than just work on costumes...

MN: Yes, it's the entire look, from head to toe.

RS: Actually, I think one of the biggest things that has happened in India is the change in these boundaries, that the production and the costume designer have to work together. For *Talaash* [Reema Kagti, 2012], every character had a colour attached to him. We didn't decide on the colour between ourselves, but between the director, the cinematographer, the production designer and the costume designer. It's a new way of looking at cinema, where a character is built from a colour, to his character, to finally becoming a costume, which is in sync with the set. We have succeeded in working with a lot of directors like that.

MN: In fact, one of our films is a completely character-driven film [*Queen*, Vikas Behl, 2013]. There is this lady actor called Kangana [Ranaut]...

RS: Sorry for interrupting, it's not only character-driven, it's a woman-centric film, there is no male lead. In itself, it's a big phenomenon.

Like *Kahaani* [Sujoy Ghosh, 2012]?

MN: *Queen* has a female lead as well. But this is much softer. We feel that surely every Indian woman has gone through what Kangana in this film is going through and will relate to it.

RS: Getting your heart broken is universal! *(laughs)* The best part about this character was her journey: what she is, and what she becomes throughout this experience. That has come out pretty well, we have taken Kangana out of Kangana the star.

MN: She is one of the most well-dressed, trendiest, sexiest looking actors right now. You can put her in any clothes and she looks fantastic. She knows how to style herself very well. We have taken her out of that world.

RS: We made her a small town girl who lives in a very orthodox family. It's her journey of getting over herself, getting over her inhibitions. How we've spoken those sentiments to the costumes has been quite interesting.

MN: It's not like she was burqaclad and got into a bikini. It is a journey of her own sensibility. When you take people out of their comfort zone and you put them in another world, in another life experience, they change drastically. The girl travels out of her own home and goes out of the country. In fifteen days, she has a different perspective of the world. Not only does she go through that, she also goes through a very emotional change in her life. And how that transforms her as a person in the way she does her hair or she wears her clothes, that's fantastic.

RS: Towards the end of the film her body language has changed. This is why the costume has worked beautifully there as well.

You're saying Bollywood has changed, that technicians work now in harmony. How are films made usually? Have you ever worked on films where there was no harmony?

MN: We are very careful with what we choose. Except once in our lives, we have always read our scripts before taking a film. We don't talk money or who the actor is: none of these criteria are important to us. Only the script. If it challenges us enough, it doesn't have to be of a particular kind. It can be a mainstream Bollywood *Hungama* kind of a film. We have done *Dhoom:3* which is one of the big blockbusters. That's the only film we have said yes to without reading the script because the actor called us. We also style two actors now: Aamir Khan and Ayushmann Khurrana. Aamir Khan is a veteran, among the top two in India right now and Ayushmann Khurrana is a new actor whose debut got every award (best actor, best debut actor).

Those are opposite worlds for us—working with somebody who has no experience, and somebody who knows himself, his body, his character. These are the two kinds of actors that we also style personally.

Why would you choose to style people personally?

RS: Actors, whenever they are in public, are always in character. What they are at home is a completely different thing. They always have to look presentable in public, even more so in Bollywood. Aamir asked us to style him personally, for events and commercials. We wanted to take up Ayushmann because we thought it was a challenge, since he comes from a television background. Now that he is into movies, it's a different kind of styling that he needs.

How is it interesting for you to style an actor as opposed to a character?

RS: We have two aspects of our life. One is completely style, design, fashion, trend-oriented, where we want to go to Milan, pick up stuff and style our actor. Then there's the other one, which is characterization, where a Dibakar comes in. Real cinema is something that has come to India pretty late, ten years ago, with Dibakar's first films. Both sides of our life interest us. We don't just style, rummage through the shelves. We are designing—for instance, everything that Kangana is wearing [in *Queen*] has been designed and made by us. But in a period film like *Once Upon a Time in Mumbaai* [Milan Luthria, 2010], costumes have to be absolutely in sync with the fashion of that time. We love cinema; but at the same time, we love fashion, which is why it is fantastic to be able to do all kinds of films.

MN: Plus, being an actor here, you have to be at par with whatever the trends are in Milan, Paris, New York, London. You see Daniel Craig wearing a Dolce and Gabbana black tuxedo, and Aamir is wearing a similar tux. It is our job to get that kind of quality, that kind of a look in our Indian actors, because that's what we are all aspiring towards.

Why not use Indian traditional clothes which are so beautiful?

RS: In fact, Aamir had been nominated as one of the Hundred Most Influential Men in the World by Time Magazine. He had to go and attend the Time Gala. What he wore was an absolutely Indian outfit—an asymmetrical *pankawalla* with breeches called *jodhpurs*. That is an important part of portraying to the world what India is about. However, at certain times, the actor wants to be not the one who stands out, but the one who blends in.

What are your influences in fashion?

RS: We ended up in Milan because of *Dhoom:3*, which is a very glamourous, big Bollywood blockbuster kind of a film. We have actually used lots of our Indian fabrics and made a very modern silhouette out of them. But we also wanted these to be at par with the Milan fashion.

MN: A film like *Dhoom:3* is aspirational. Fortunately or unfortunately, Indian silhouettes are not aspirational for Indians because we have seen them for centuries. However, our fabrics are being used and exported everywhere: cottons, silks, knits.

If I understand you correctly, Bollywood films like *Dhoom:3* are not about the characters...

RS: It is still about the character, but it can be aspirational. It demands a different category of an actor. It depends on where it is located also. The minute you have an Indian staying in another country, he would be a part of it. He can't be sitting in Singapore and be dressed in a *kurta pyjama*, like an Indian. He'll be dressed in whatever clothes he's buying off the malls there. Even blockbusters like *Dhoom:3* can still be about characters. But the flight of fantasy is a little more.

MN: Also now directors know the kind of work we do, that we do a lot of character-driven roles. Even if it's a big film like *Dhoom:3*, you know that there will be a lot of realistic elements given to the character.

RS: When they called us for *Dhoom:3*, we were so excited. We said we'll do an out-and-out glamourous, sci-fi film. We got the brief and thought, 'This is very real!' *(laughs)*

MN: This *Dhoom:3* is slightly different.

RS: Back to reality! That's what we do! *(laughs)*

MN: Having said that, it is still a fantasy.

RS: This film, this character has been a challenge to us, because we had to break out of our mould of being so gritty and so real and still getting into the latest trends, fabrics, and colours. Because every season has its right colour, a different silhouette, so we are trying to sync that with our character.

MN: For us, to get into this song-and-dance routine...

RS: Wow!

MN: The famous song-and-dance Indian film is larger than life, like firecrackers. That was something that we had never done. Out-and-out three-four songs which are complete performances. It was an amazing experience.

RS: A song breaks out and then the character does something else. *(laughs)* We had to listen to the songs, to the music, follow the words, the lyrics, where is he emoting, where is he walking, how is he dancing. That was quite a challenge for us, to make a costume for dance.

And in a song, you have fifty more dancers...

MN: We were not doing the rest of the film. The films that Rushi and I normally do are films that we take up completely. So from the main actor, the hero and the heroine, to the last guy who's riding the tricycle behind, we will be styling everybody. We'll be dividing the look and having a backstory for everybody. There's another film that we were doing called *PK* [Rajkumar Hirani, 2014], where everything has a characterization, even the last guy that you see in the background. However, for films like *Dhoom:3*, each actor has a separate stylist or costume designers. The background and the secondary artists have a stylist. A lot of times, what it does is that all the costumes don't marry each other and they don't look like part of the same world.

On *Dhoom:3*, have you tried to work with the other costume designers?

MN: In a few places, yes, because this film has a lot of stage performances happening. So there, we have spoken to the production designer, to the secondary costume designer, to the main lead costume designer, just so that we can all match up colours and fabrics a little. In fact we fought for it.

RS: They shouldn't look like they are performing to two different songs.

MN: In two different worlds. But they said we were all given the brief. Brief doesn't help. One has to consult the other designers.

As a costume designer, isn't it more interesting to work on a period film?

MN: For us, it's the reverse. It's a challenge, actually, to work on something that you're wearing every day.

RS: If you see how India is, every social strata, every caste, every town, every village—so many languages, so many different cultures—every person looks different. In Bombay, which is a cosmopolitan city, you can go on the road and say, 'Ah this guy is from the film industry, that is a person who is from Maharashtra and is probably working in a bank.'

MN: We have to do so much of research on characters, on actors...

RS: To travel on a local train, in a bus, to sit in a train station, to go to a mall and see how different these people look, is a fantastic experience in itself. To get that nuance right, without actually making it out-and-out, traditional clothing of Bangladesh, of Bengal, traditional clothing of Punjab, you look at the person and you sort of make your own story. It's like Sherlock Holmes: he looks and tells you exactly what your profession is, what you are doing right now, 'You do a lot of writing because this bit of your jacket is shining while the rest of it is not.' We are the little Sherlock Holmes who are getting into the character. For us, it is a lot of fun to do beautiful dresses, period cinema, like *Detective Byomkesh Bakshy!* [Dibakar Banerjee, 2015], but it doesn't happen so much. I would really like to work on a Baz Luhrmann film as well. Costume design is about the filmmaking process. There is a story to tell, even in costumes.

MN: Our research differs a lot. Once you're doing a character development, you can do any research from books or the Net, then you get down to the roads. If it is a small town, then you travel to a small town, you take pictures, you take interviews, you go into people's houses. For *Shanghai* [Dibakar Banerjee, 2012], we had a team running around in Maharashtra, in Gujarat, small places. A few girls went up north, to meet people on the streets, to take their pictures, to go into their houses, to tell them, 'Can we go and see your wardrobe?' So people have opened their wardrobe and said, 'These are the shirts we wear'—such strange shirts, we hadn't seen those shirts in our entire life. We had to construct and fabricate them, and age them.

RS: New clothes into old! *(laughs)*

MN: And they were completely inspired from those people in the streets.

RS: Since we are not living this reality, it's difficult to know it.

MN: It's difficult to go there and think what these people are thinking. They put their outfit together in an entirely different way.

RS: For *PK*, we were shooting in Rajasthan and we went to the markets in small towns. There are probably eight to ten shops. In those shops, we had to buy things and then we made friends with those people, who got bundles of clothing from their own homes. We said, 'We don't want new clothes.' So they sold their old clothes to us.

MN: I think half the village was following us, saying, 'Take my clothes, take my clothes.' *(laughs)* It was not about money.

RS: Finally we asked them, 'Why are you following us around?' They said, 'You're lying, you're not here to buy clothes, you both are actresses and you've just come here to meet us.' *(laughs)*

MN: That was quite an experience, to buy clothes off people's backs. There was this guy saying, 'I'll give you this shirt, but how do I go home, do you want me to go home naked?' So we arranged for a jacket for him and he gave us the shirt. We got those clothes cleaned and our Aamir Khan is wearing them.

Do you know why Aamir chose you as his personal designers?

RS: I would like to quote his interview in *Filmfare* for *PK*. He basically said that we bring life to a character, through our own vision, which not many people can do.

MN: An actor like Aamir is completely character-driven. As long as we are cracking the character and we are true to the character, he's fine. Secondly, he's an actor who needs to look good. I think what Aamir got from us is someone who figures out what are the weaknesses and the strengths of his body, so he can look correct on screen. Anushka [Sharma] told us she never looked like that in any film. She's wearing regular clothes. It's not that she's wearing eccentric things, or things which look ugly. She's wearing very nice things. But she said no actress would dare to dress like this, because everyone wants to look spectacular.

RS: Especially in the film industry, women are meant to be glamourous with their hair flying in the air. *(laughs)* We've not done any of that!

MN: There are films where there is rock climbing and the girl is wearing a mini-dress.

RS: *(laughs)*

MN: There's been a film where this girl has been kidnapped and she's supposed to run in the forest. When you're planning this film, why the hell did you give her heels in the beginning of the film? She's supposed to wear the same pair of shoes through the film! Give her sensible shoes. People don't dare to do that, because eventually they'll want their actresses to look like a virgin diamond. *(laughs)*

What would you do if a filmmaker asked you to do a scene in the mountains of Switzerland where the actress is wearing a saree or a mini-skirt?

MN: It's beautiful to watch! But we would put up a fight. We would say that this is not what we want. But if the director and the producer say the film is going to bomb because the audience doesn't want to see this A-list actress looking different, we will give in.

RS: Once you take up a film, you know what everybody is going for. If this is the script, and this is how glossy the film needs to be, we go glossy. The biggest challenge coming from doing all those realistic films for us is to do glossy. We keep asking so many questions. A lot of commercials are like that, none of it is reality. We also love doing that, it's a full fashion show!

MN: What we have targeted for ourselves is that in a year, we should be able to do at least one film that we can go back home and sleep peacefully about. That's all we want.

What does wearing a saree mean to an actress? Or wearing a mini-skirt?

RS: Traditionally speaking, a saree would mean this is a more homely, a more manageable, a more decent, less vampy girl. Wearing western would not necessarily mean the opposite. It would mean she's got education, she's travelled the world, she's aspirational. However, there have been actresses who have really transformed. Mandira Bedi for instance. She wears the sexiest sarees differently. She has just brought the vamp to the real world. She was a cricket host. When she started coming on television, she would wear the sexiest of blouses, teamed with a pair of jeans, or a pair of shorts, or a skirt, what we call Western clothing. Nobody has judged her saying she's not a decent girl. For the Indian audience, saree is the most sensual, even now. Even though you may have Western clothing on an actress, there will be this one scene in the film where she will be in a saree. And the sexiest scene will be in the rain, with a wet saree.

MN: Our men in Indian cinema have also become women now. They have become sexier, more body conscious, more beautiful, more fit. They are ready to expose more. And people are ready to watch them!

RS: Even I want to watch them!

Who's the best-dressed actress in Indian cinema?

MN: Sonam [Kapoor] and Kangana. Kangana is fabulous. She's so intelligent and smart, picking up the right things for her own body. She has a very Audrey Hepburn kind of an aura.

RS: Sonam is fantastic. Such a sense of fashion and style, the opposite to most actresses. Vidya Balan and Rani Mukherji, in their own zones of wearing saees, are dressing really well too.

MN: They don't have to give into this fashion of little dresses, they're reviving the indigenous art and craft. They're combining and they're experimenting.

Why do those actresses choose to wear a saree? Is it because of their own personality or because of their audience?

MN: Personality.

RS: I think it's also because of the audience. The audience is more accepting of Vidya [Balan] in a saree because of her body type. Her films have done better when she has worn sarees.

MN: It is also about her personality that she refuses to be anorexic. She has the typical south Indian body, and she accepts that, without going into diets to look like a particular kind of person. In fact you name four actresses who've done women-centred films—Vidya Balan, Rani Mukherjee, Preity Zinta and Priyanka Chopra—two of them regularly wear sarees.

MN: I think at some level, once you're representing your own country in Cannes, in New York, it's a very good idea to go wearing sarees.

What do you think of Indian fashion right now?

RS: I think Indian fashion internationally has been coming into its own, it is distinct, it is not a copy of the West.

MN: Some designers have realized that our fabrics are so rich. And using our own strength to portray our own fashion on an international scenario, like Manish Arora.

Why did you come into fashion?

RS: I've been interested in fashion since early childhood. I used to dress dolls and Barbies when I was a kid.

MN: She always wanted to be in fashion.

RS: And I am completely obsessed with films. I am this person who watches a film and forgets about my own life and world. I become a part of that film. When I was at fashion school, I realized that when you design a costume for the screen, it's worn only once, which fascinated me.

MN: I always wanted to be an artist. Theatre for me was a very big thing. Films have come into my life at a very late stage. There is no other expression that takes all art forms and brings them together like films do.

ANJUM RAJABALI
Scriptwriter

Boy meets girl and falls in love. But before both can aspire to a happy ending, boy and girl have to prove themselves worthy by dancing and singing their way into each other's hearts and overcome religion, horoscopes, caste, misunderstandings, family expectations, evil stepmother, sickness, sometimes death and lots of tears/rain. If this storyline rings a thousand bells, you're probably familiar with the Bollywood romantic-comedy formula, which has been responsible for the success of the Hindi Film industry for decades.

The endless debate between film-buffs on the importance of the script to determine the quality of the overall film, intensified by the popularity of contemporary TV shows, has somehow been avoided by Bollywood in the most radical manner. Until very recently, scripts would be so underrated that they wouldn't be ready at the beginning of the shoot; and film stars could decide to change it on a daily basis, according to their own wishes. Even today, most actors choose a film on the basis of a narration, and rarely read the script itself.

I met Anjum Rajabali at the office of Mumbai Mantra, in Worli (South Mumbai). He has been a scriptwriter since the movie *Droh Kaal* [Govind Nihalani, 1994] and has acquired fame for his collaboration with the filmmaker Prakash Jha (notably with the political film *Rajneeti*). He writes scripts in many different genres, such as historical dramas and thrillers. Moreover, Anjum has pushed his involvement in this profession by teaching aspiring filmmakers at FTII Pune and Whistling Woods International in Mumbai.

Over the years, he has become a strong advocate for Indian scriptwriters, whose profession is poorly recognized by the industry. Not only does he try to understand the flaws of the system, he also works to find solutions. Mumbai Mantra sees him as one of its most active members and aids his efforts. They set up scriptwriting workshops and provide support to other scriptwriters, in order to bring about a real change in the industry. In this interview, Anjum explains articulately (and in parts, passionately, to the point of outrage) the obstacles one would have to overcome to make this change happen.

During an interview I did in Paris in 2004, Yash Chopra told me that one of the problems of Indian cinema was the lack of good scripts. As a scriptwriter, do you agree with this statement?

As a conclusion, I agree with that, actually. But the important parts are the reasons why we don't have good scripts. Is it that we don't have any storytelling talent in this country? Impossible, because this is the longest storytelling civilization in the world. It's a cliché, but we have great stories in our heritage. So what is going wrong here? The scriptwriting function, the particular process and its place in the filmmaking programme were not really well-defined for a very long time. The scriptwriter was, and to a certain extent still is, considered merely to be the pen of the director. The director has a certain kind of vision. This is what he'd like to make the film into, that's the kind of drama he would like, these are the issues that he wants involved. So the scriptwriter is supposed to execute that vision. Unfortunately, that seems to be the best position that he has been able to reach.

The other thing is that, because it is not regarded as an independent skill, the kind of respect, or the kind of space, or the kind of reward which is remuneration that is put on it, is in fact pretty low. You feel like the main thing is the director and the performers.

When you see the other professions involved in the directing process—the cinematographer, sound technician or art director—you feel there's a need for a very specialized skill, because it's technical. In the technical field, we'll feel that if you don't know the job, you can't interfere. Whereas everybody knows stories. So if you have a story, everybody has a comment on the story. This is where I think we have fallen short: to carve this out as a specialized function, to recognize that it is a very specialized craft, that it is written with a certain degree of understanding and precision. You take a couple of things off, the whole thing is likely to wobble.

Unfortunately, a large proportion of the writers' community seems to believe that when we receive an assignment from the director or the producer, we are employees. Very rarely do they allow their own vision of what the script should be, do they stand confident on that. The script does not have to be designed to somebody else's view. If there's a story that you've undertaken, the story has a life of its own, a particular vision, structure, rhythm. Your loyalty is not to the employer, it's to the story. It's like a doctor dealing with an operation, you can't have everybody in the family telling the doctor what to do. Even though it is your child, it's his job. He is supposed to do it. You can't say, 'You can't cut here.'

That kind of specialization is not even acknowledged by the writers themselves. Why? One reason I feel is of course the fact that the film industry has been organized in a way that the collective attitude towards the script is that it's not a terribly important function in most cases. India makes one thousand two hundred fifty films a year. Rarely do you see that the script has been worked out in an independent way. If the film's rule already says that the writer can't sit here, he has to sit there, then he'll say, 'Okay, if that's the rule.' Instead of questioning, 'Oh, wait a minute, I am a writer and the writer has to occupy a certain position. The craft has to occupy a certain status.'

Number two is that we are a country full of very good ideas, good with stories. But we are not very good when it comes to the craft of scriptwriting. There is a certain kind of framework within which it has to be put. This specialization has to be learned, be practised, be perfected. It takes time, it takes a lot of effort and attention. Not too many young writers look at it this way. The degree of preparation which they may need to reach that stage of specialization, of a certain degree of expertise and confidence in the craft, is not practised. There are some artistic people and naturally gifted people in every field. But most people who join a profession have to learn. You do find Hussain and Da Vinci becoming great painters because they had a skill in them. But most people go to art school to understand what you mean by frame, colour palette, how to express certain figures, in order to discover your own individual artistry in that framework. You need that framework. A lot of scriptwriters don't subject themselves to that. I am not saying that only formal training is necessary. I am saying that a learning and an understanding is important. It's a job like any other job. You have to learn that specialization, you have to practise it.

Only very recently have we noticed that young writers, new writers, are writing independent scripts on their own, without a contract. That's what we've been trying to encourage. When you step out in the market, don't just say, 'I want to write.' Show that you can write. Bring a script that says, 'This is the script.' But even in that, merely because it has some good ideas, it doesn't necessarily make it a competently written script. I read about sixty-seventy scripts a year. Less than two per cent measure up to some merit, where you feel, 'Yes, this can be recommended.' Which means those people with all their good ideas and great intentions, why are they not actually learning how to write better? You have to do a lot of rewriting, a lot of practice has to go in to it. Many scripts will be thrown away, even after you've written them, because everything that you think, that you write, doesn't necessarily become gold. In Mumbai Mantra, we receive hundreds of scripts. The number is very reassuring, very heartening. But for most of them, you feel even the story hasn't been constructed well. You want to be a storyteller, you should understand what the story is. So there is a certain demand for good scripts, yes. But there is a gap between the supplier and the demand.

Let's try to go deeper into the root of the problem. Is it because of India's strong oral tradition that people don't feel the need for better scripts or is it simply because cinema is first and foremost a visual medium?

What I find problematic in the submissions that we get is that they are not thinking visually, they are not thinking in terms of screenplay. When they write a story, they don't have the objective in mind that it is going to become a script. There is a certain rhythm that a screenplay has, which is different from a short story, or a literary piece of work. We, on the one hand, are at a great advantage because we have a long tradition of storytelling in this country. But that same thing can turn into a disadvantage because the form is different. Oral tradition? Yes, most of the films that were made before the last twenty years were not written! They were discussed. There is a certain kind of accountability which comes when you actually put down a design. There is a precision—this scene will start here, this is what will be said, this will be the action, this is where the scene will end. It's an industrial document. Because crores of rupees, millions of dollars are going to be put on that. It is important therefore to be responsible, that it fulfils its task, which is not being done here. Because, once again, training is important. It forces you to think along certain lines—this is the objective, so be careful about your structure, be careful of the rhythm in which the plot is unfolding, of the consistency of your dramaturgy, of the premise. Do those scenes which are unfolding have anything to do with the premise? Is there a thematic consistency? Is it the same story at the beginning and at the end? People lose it along the way, so in the climax you're going somewhere else. A lot of the comedy is occupying huge chunks where it was not necessary. There is a lot of guesswork through which films are made. Intuition is good. Impulse is not.

There was a lot of impulsive filmmaking taking place with a lot of interference coming from others. People working on the script behave like six blind men and the elephant—if you remember that poem—where each one says, 'No, no, but my audience wants this!' And the other one, 'But this film ran well, so therefore we should make it like that.' Someone says, 'We should have a marriage song!' Where is the consistency? Where is the homogeneity? Who is controlling this? We have inherited this bloody tradition.

I know in every industry you have studio executives also interfering with that, it's not like Hollywood is away from that. And yet, even studio executives and others, which might be giving notes, respect the fact that when the script finally turns out as it is, it will be fixed. Then, everything else moves around that. We still don't have that kind of primacy here. We had an industry that never behaved like an industry, with good business practices. There was a rank plagiarism which took place. Because you like something, you take it—that used to be the norm. And to hell with whose copyright this is. Now people are getting a little particular—and yet, I am saying the directorial function tends to overshadow the scriptwriting function. It is dangerous and it is encouraged by filmmakers and producers.

Where should the scriptwriter ideally stand?

His function is the only function where what he does is a complete work, in the larger filmmaking process which is regarded as work-in-progress. Which means it has to be handed over to somebody else, who has to execute it. If the document which is handed over is competently done, if it has been accepted that this is the film that we are trying to make, then the director's job becomes to execute the vision of the script. The vision in the script may have also come from inputs of the director, because the last few drafts are debated and discussed with the director. Fine, I have no problem with that, because the director is also a storyteller. He's using the medium of celluloid, taking somebody else's story but he's directing it. So in that sense, he becomes a narrator. You tell me a story: if I go and narrate it to my child, I become the narrator of that. You have no control over what I will tell my child. The director is the one who is actually reaching the audience. The consonance between the director and the script has to be a very strong one, because this is the most important relationship in the entire filmmaking process for me.

Filmmaking has also been a very approximate process in this country. With some people who practised while being approximate, it worked. A Guru Dutt, a Mehboob Khan who was completely illiterate—they had no problems at all. They were not trained. Today however, they all recognize that the writing credit is a very precious credit. They all try to muzzle it, so the writers feel disheartened. Most of the time, directors want a co-writing credit without writing. What do they do? They discuss it. That is the function of the director! To discuss the script. How the hell does that make them a writer?

So it is true that there seems to be almost a conspiracy of factors which is undermining the growth of the scriptwriting function in this country. We should consider it seriously. People do say that films make money because of merchandizing, music, satellite. But the fact is that if the audience is rejecting your cinema, eighty per cent of the time, there's something to be questioned there. It's very well to have four thousand screens and create so much hype and so much excitement that even if they don't like the film, people will go and see it, out of curiosity. But this is not the way to sustain an industry. It's a storytelling industry. Stories are the repository of today's culture. They have to be treated with a certain degree of understanding, sensitivity, respect, engagement. If this doesn't begin to happen, the economy of the mad rush for opening weekend will come under question. In Hollywood, the largest films mostly manage to make their money because of the whole technique of marketing across the world. In Mumbai, even that is failing. Therefore, it is important to recognize where the attraction for a film is coming from: people are watching a film to experience a story told in an interesting way, using cinematic elements. It continues to elude the structure of the film industry. It's like when you're working in the building industry, you know that the architect's blueprint is very important, and you stick to the blueprint. Don't change the pillars of the building or it will collapse! Likewise, the entire film is available in the script. So make sure that it is done well.

The other thing that I didn't mention is that not many people here know how to read scripts. They are beginning to pay attention, yes. And yet I am surprised at the kind of notes that scripts receive. They are looking at a very different film altogether. They have not understood what the structure is. They're merely going by certain marketing considerations that they have been told by studio heads—this film that we do should have those elements, because that's what is used for marketing. This is not the way to judge a script. Even now, with so much money being available, rarely do our films get confirmed on the basis of the script. And I feel our films should get confirmed only on the basis of the script.

Films mostly confirm on actors...

Actors, budget, props, that's what seems to make it happen.

Most of the stars don't read scripts, they need a narration.

That's the degree of investment that the stars are giving to a project on which they are going to earn four to five million dollars. It's huge money in India, it's enormous! Your investment is that you want a narration and you won't even read the script. This is something very odd. Scripts seem to make everyone very nervous. *(laughs)* Which is why scriptwriters most of the time are not welcome on the set, which is why the director keeps going on telling people, 'I wrote the script', 'my script', 'I've been thinking about it for so many years', 'written and directed by' and 'film by'. How can it be a 'film by'? It's a collaborative process, there's teamwork involved, there's a collective vision which is going into the execution of that. Without the cinematographer using his skills, your film won't look good, without the costumes....

It tends to reduce the level at which you're treating the script. You give scriptwriters eighty per cent of what they actually deserve, they will give you sixty per cent. You give them one hundred per cent of what they deserve, they will give you one hundred and twenty per cent. There is massive disheartenment. Which brings me to the union. The scriptwriters' union that we have, it is like banging your head against the wall. We're bleeding from the head, trying to push some basic reforms through.

Which ones?

Like credit should be guaranteed. It is a very simple thing. Contracts often say that the credits will be decided on the discretion of the producer. We're also talking about no arbitrary termination—if I have handed over the script to you and you accepted it, you cannot fire me midway and hire somebody else. Number three is minimum wages should be there. Writers are desperate, they are paid peanuts and they accept. Even the writers don't have the confidence to say, 'No, I won't do it.' There is a law of copyright being amended. All we are saying is that keep the contracts consonant with the copyright act, with the law of the country. Producers are afraid to do that, because it involves royalties. So constantly, if you are looking out to exploit writers, then you have no business to complain that you don't get good scripts. Because you don't want to pay for good scripts. You don't know what a good script is.

Could the situation of scriptwriters in the industry be a result of the Bollywood formulaic writing, where ninety per cent of Hindi films tell the same story over and over again?

There was a certain template which did get formed, which is what we call formula, with certain fixed elements—for a story to not become too grim, you need to have a lively phase in it, which is the initial phase of thirty minutes. There should be comedy, a certain kind of exuberance, there should be music, so that people enjoy it. Then you get into the drama of whatever the story is. If you look at early Indian theatre, it had a certain framework. Bharata Muni (the Aristotle of the East), with his *Natya Shastra*, pointed out that stories work very well because they contain certain feelings, what we call the *navarasa* theory. Therefore, there is a certain completeness of the experience. You come out with a certain wholesome entertainment. We did not have genres and it's a good tradition. But instead of us allowing ourselves to seek those emotions out in that, what happened is the industry tended to make a formula out of it. I want comedy also, I want a little bit of sex also, I want dancing. Why? Because that seems to be the thing which works. This is not how stories are written.

Have you heard of Christopher Vogler? He was a studio executive for Disney, he used to read scripts. Then he discovered Joseph Campbell, the author of *The Hero with a Thousand Faces*. Vogler said, 'Ah, this is a great formula.' He picked that out, rearranged the elements and asked scripts to be written like this. For twenty years, people from different generations started writing scripts like that. Everybody loves the formula, because it makes your job easier. It takes away the creativity, which is the difficult part and it gives you a certain format into which you can put it. If you look at those old films, like *Veer-Zaara* [Yash Chopra, 2004], there is a conflict taking place which turns out in a scene of confrontation and an outburst. They wanted melodrama. They also wanted a certain underlined morality: a film should actually stand for certain values. If there's a criminal, he should reform. All these things got embedded into the scriptwriting expectations. There was a time when music was really big in India because film music was being purchased before. Then the electronic and digital business began and now people are downloading. But earlier, it was a big commercial prop. Even I used to be told, 'Write your own script but there will be six songs in the film. Four before interval, two after interval. This is fixed, we will not negotiate. If you don't put it in, we will.'

Why four before and two after the interval?

Because after interval, they thought the story becomes dramatic and serious. There is not enough space for that. But there is a rhythm that we are talking about! There is a certain narrative culture within the story. You can't just insert a song in there! This character doesn't sing! *(laughs)* Very few people who made films in India were actual filmmakers. They were producers. They could produce phones as well if that worked well. What they were attracted to was the glamour. It's that kind of people who began determining it. There was this phase where there was a lot of black money. Filmmaking was not taken seriously. It was a completely unorganized sector. These things became a norm. We are trying now to make sure that these things become more professional, more accountable. But the attitudes of the past still carry forward. The producers still believe that the scriptwriter is an employee. If you look at the contract, they are so one-sided. All the rights are mine, all the responsibilities are yours. All the assets are mine, all the liabilities are yours. All the safety is mine, all the risks are yours. This is not professional. You are asking somebody to give you some work, something that is of value to you—you need to be able to learn how to value it. This has been led by greed. But at the same time, when the stars demand the sun, the moon and the earth, you're happy to do it. The power balance is disproportionate. A lot of writers are becoming directors. For two reasons—one is that they don't like their work to be interfered with and the second thing is that they don't get the respect and the money that they think they deserve. A director gets it, directors get paid humongous amounts and the writers are paid shit. If you look at Hollywood, the maximum difference between a writer and a director would be twice. If the scriptwriter is getting one million dollars, the director is getting two. Here, it's a difference of ten times, twenty times. In one sense, if you really look at it, the most creative function in the entire process of filmmaking is writing. Because it is original, it is creating something out of nothing. The others are responding to that. They already have that document in front of them. The actors don't have to invent it; the writer has to invent it. It's the most difficult function.

PART 3

A NEW GENERATION IN MUMBAI

To say that the Indian film industry can be equated to only Bollywood implies a simplistic view that needs to be examined. Admittedly, it is difficult for people in the West to understand Indian cinema's diversity without matching it to known patterns. For example, French cinema could be summarized through a dichotomy of independent films/arthouse films against commercial/popular films, though numerous films tend to break those barriers. The same could be argued about Hollywood. However, in India, this view falls short. First, one has to take into account the dozens of different industries, each one corresponding to a language (Tamil, Telugu, Malayalam, Bengali, Hindi, Bhojpuri, etc.) and each having its specificities. Second, in a country where cinema is primarily considered to be a business, arthouse films stand absolutely no chance against commercial films.

To simplify, arthouse and independent cinema in India (a so-called realistic cinema, without songs and dances, or any other structure characteristic of commercial Bollywood film) always existed, but in a small proportion. Above all, it is still despised by distributors. Almost invisible in India, this genre must seek refuge abroad at international festivals, preventing most Indian viewers from partaking. One would also find fundamental differences between Bhojpuri cinema, which is made with very little money to feed the masses of Mumbai slums and Bhojpuri-speaking audiences in the North, and the expensive Hindi blockbuster which comes from the studios to win national and international success (meaning the Indian diaspora).

In Mumbai over the last few years, as a result of several factors (economic liberalization of India, construction of multiplexes, arrival of satellite TV), another element has been added; one which is still commercial cinema, but rejects the domination of the Bollywood romance, to answer the demand of a growing middle-class who was fed on European and American films. Political thrillers, social dramas, period films, themes such as the life of the middle-classes in the urban centres, sexual abuse, corruption, drug-trafficking, organized gangs; what defines this cinema is that it speaks of a contemporary India that has been completely ignored by Europe, to whom a whole subcontinent only means either Maharajahs or Mother Teresa. A dozen filmmakers, producers and actors—Anurag Kashyap, Dibakar Banerjee, Sudhir Mishra, Vikramaditya Motwane, Vishal Bhardwaj to name a few—initiated a movement, that many would call 'new wave', though the filmmakers themselves dismissed this as simply inapt. Emerging as a type of rebellion against Bollywood, the movement has no theoretical approach, though it encouraged a lot of others to follow its path. Anurag Kashyap, who mentored a few of his assistants into becoming filmmakers, is the best example. Will this movement succeed in standing up on its own against the studio machine or will it eventually merge into it? Will it be able to make sure people abroad know that Indian cinema is not a *Slumdog Millionaire* but more of a *Gangs of Wasseypur*? Will it be able to find a place in Indian culture to sustain itself so it does not become a carbon copy of the average American film, but on the contrary rejuvenate a culture lost in the homogenization of globalization?

We will see that the very articulate interviewees of this chapter cite the same reasons to be optimistic rather than pessimistic on the subject. Filmmaker Dibakar Banerjee and film critic Mayank Shekhar both came from this movement, and know its pitfalls as well as its hopes. Much like India itself, torn between its image of a potential economic giant and its poverty-stricken masses, Indian cinema might be at a cross-roads, but it is impossible to predict which direction it will take.

DIBAKAR BANERJEE
Director and Producer

Often associated with Anurag Kashyap and the 'anti-system' directors, even though their cinematic universes are radically different, Dibakar Banerjee, forty-nine years old, is today one of the only Indian filmmakers capable of making non-Bollywood films which will be distributed in theatres and appreciated both by the critics and by the middle class. If one was to mention his name to any film-buff, one would always invoke a reaction of admiration coloured with deep respect. Dibakar is famous for his knowledge and intellectual conception of cinema, but also for some of his political views: in November 2015, he returned the National Award he received for his first film, *Khosla Ka Ghosla,* to protest the 'growing intolerance' in the country. In October 2016, he publicly voiced his support for Pakistani artists when extreme-right wing movements claimed they should be banned from working in India.

Hardly an activist though, Dibakar would probably be best understood by his desire to confound expectations. One could have easily labelled him as a filmmaker with a message: both his first films, the comedy *Khosla Ka Ghosla* and the thriller *Oye Lucky! Lucky Oye!* were a take on the Delhi middle-class; *Shanghai* was an Indian adaptation of the French novel *'Z'* (which also inspired French filmmaker Costa-Gavras in 1969) and *Love, Sex aur Dokha* denounced TV voyeurism. But in April 2015, Dibakar released, in his own words, a 'pure entertainment' flick, a detective movie set in 1940s Calcutta with an emerging film star, Sushant Singh Rajput, and co-produced by the biggest Bollywood studio, Yash Raj (*Detective Byomkesh Bakshy!*).

True to his reputation, Dibakar is a journalist's dream. He had so much to say that I barely felt the need to revive the conversation with questions. I came back almost frustrated after recording only a one-and-a-half-hour long interview with him, but completely convinced by this Bengali intellectual, a French cinema lover, so self-assured, even while laughing at himself. He welcomed me into the office of his production company, Dibakar Banerjee Productions, in Parel—he is one of the only industry members who live in South Mumbai. While I introduced myself, explaining how it remains difficult for an Indian film specialist to make French audiences understand the distinction between Indian cinema and Bollywood, he started the interview without any formality ...

[Dibakar Banerjee begins]

I know many French people who don't drink alcohol. But still, when you think of the French, you think of French wine. So when you think of Indian films, you have to admit that ninety per cent is Bollywood kitsch. It's changing, it keeps changing, but it is that. And one has to accept it for what it is.

But then, you are talking only about Bombay cinema, because Tamil cinema wouldn't be Bollywood kitsch.

It's another kind of kitsch.

We don't even know that there is Tamil cinema abroad.

Absolutely, that's a different issue. India is not Bollywood. That's a very pertinent issue because that's something filmmakers like Anurag [Kashyap] and I have been fighting. Fortunately, we have been to enough festivals to get a move on in terms of spreading the idea that we are Indian filmmakers, just like an Iranian filmmaker or a Peruvian filmmaker or a Sri Lankan filmmaker. And yes, we live in Bombay and make Indian films, but as a genre, we are not Bollywood.

Do people talk to you as a Bollywood filmmaker?

We can't fight it. At least I try to fight it as much as possible. It's a strange schizophrenia because when I am in India, I am seen as a part of Bollywood. In fact, after the four films I have made, I have no idea why I am still counted as a kind of established figure of Bollywood. Somehow, I have been accepted as a part of this commercial industry. It's the greatest surprise to me. When I am in India, I am part of the establishment. I am interviewed by the same journalists who are interested in big Bollywood stars. Of course, they know that I make different kind of films. And that's the inclusiveness of Bollywood that I am quite interested in. It's very inclusive. It's the typical Indian ethos, which is to accept anything and make it a part of you, so that it slowly loses its force of change.

So you think it could be dangerous?

Of course it is. You have to keep fighting it. After I made my first film, which became a cult hit [*Khosla Ka Ghosla*, 2006], everybody was expecting me to make a sequel. And everybody had already stereotyped me into a kind of middle-class comedy kind of a filmmaker, which I was extremely uncomfortable with. So my second film, *Oye Lucky! Lucky Oye!* [2008] was a direct accusation at the middle-class, when you see middle-class for all its hypocrisy from the point of view of a common thief. The film is based on real life and it's very dark. So a lot of people that were expecting a *Khosla Ka Ghosla – Part 2* were completely shocked. Today, somehow it's included with *Khosla Ka Ghosla* as my 'Delhi series of films'. But at that time, I remember my own family was shocked. They said it's a very dark film, though very funny. It was seen as a thief adventure. In fact, one of the producers at the studio had said, 'Why don't we end the film with that guy gone to Jamaica? On the beach with lots of women.' He actually meant it. Then I was being talked about as the Delhi guy who had brought Delhi into the scene. There were articles written about me, analysis, surveys. There's a book somewhere which features my film on the cover—how Delhi has come on to the screen because of my films. I started to go away from it and that's how *Love Sex aur Dhokha* [2010] was made. Nothing of that sort had been seen on an Indian screen before. So it completely threw everything out of gear. I was a favourite of all the National Awards but the graphic nature and the absolutely confrontational images of *Love Sex aur Dhokha* stopped me from being a favourite with the establishment. When a film is picked up for the National Awards, you become part of the Indian panorama that goes all over the world. It was said that they couldn't choose *Love Sex aur Dhokha* to represent India abroad because somebody is being beheaded in the first film, there's somebody having sex in front of a camera in the second film and in the third film, you have somebody sort of setting up a trap in front of a spy camera. It's a very negative image of India. It was good that I became the *bête noire* again. When you are being included, you're slowly seduced into being part of the establishment, so that you lose your dissent. The trick is to be inside, to be subversive and not give in to the seduction of inclusion. *Shanghai* [2012] again sealed my fate because it was a totally out-and-out political film. In Europe, you have seen hundreds of films like that, but it's very difficult to explain to a European filmmaker that though we live in politics all the time, there's a tendency to ignore the elephant in the room. Now, people are a lot more wary of what I do. At least they know that I wouldn't be able to be seduced that easily, that they need to give me more money. *(laughs)*

If they give you a lot of money, would you do a typical Bollywood romance?

Not really, but not because of any other reason than that there are many other people who know that genre, who know that kind of story by heart. I won't be contributing anything to it. I would rather make a film about rape and its aftermaths. Or about the memory of love, because I think you fall in love for about two years, five years maximum. From the third or the fourth year, I think it becomes a memory of the first two years. All of the happiness is a memory. You don't realize it at first. You later define it as the happiness. So I'd rather make a film about love being a memory of the love that you once had. Those are the kind of things I am interested in, but one will have to sneak them in and do it in the way that people don't expect it until it's on screen. That's what I did in *Shanghai*. I had to take [Emraan] Hashmi, I had to take Abhay [Deol], for this thriller, because

I knew that it would provoke a lot of people. Now it's out there, no one can take it away. That's what I'll have to do with my other films.

So you want to provoke?

No, the need to provoke doesn't come first. I think the first thing that happens is the need to say something. And what do you want when you say something? You want people to agree with you. Everything that you've said in your life is informed with the hope that it will find resonance. I make a film to see if I am not alone. It's essentially a way of finding other people who think like you. Instead of saying it, I will make a film about it. It's a rather expensive way, especially with other people's money. *(laughs)*

Did you find people who agreed with you then?

I guess so. A lot of them agree with me because it seems to them that something that I am saying is sort of powerful. A smaller segment agrees with me because they understand what I am trying to say. And a large segment just go there because they see my name and they hope to see something, so it's a mix of everything. After a film is made, you can't really control it anyways.

Who is your audience? Who do you think you are talking to?

Roughly there are two kinds of films: one filmmaker, Spielberg for instance, will make a very good film after having thought what his audience would like to hear. Nine people out of his audience go to see that film. One guy will make a very good film about just what he wants to say. And he knows that out of these ten, three people will watch it. Both are right in their own way. So I say what I have to say and take my chances. Then you need to make your film cheap. My core audience is the Indian urban elite unfortunately. It's the most ineffectual and the weakest, because they control everything, they control the media, they control the banks, they control the money, but they have no desire to change anything. I know my films are made in an idiom which is not really obscure. I think any Indian can understand it. But perhaps because I come from an urban background and because my films are produced by studios—which are populated by this section of the Indian elite—the way they are projected, and marketed and seen, they become an exercise exclusive to the elite. Sometimes my face is seen in newspapers which are mostly English, mostly elite—it really preaches to the converted. It's a bit of a grey zone to be in, but that's what India is. To understand cinema that's coming out of India, you have to have an understanding of India which is not informed by the mythological trash that has been sort of doing the circles of the bridge between West and East. You have to see India for what it is.

And what is it?

I think it's an ex-colony. I don't think the West has understood the full impact of colonization yet. The last word on colonization and colonialism hasn't been written yet. We are still on the colonialist period because the shadow of colonialism will stay with us another hundred years. Everything that happened since cannot be separated from our colonial past. Only then you can judge and understand it. I don't think you can understand France if you don't understand Enlightenment, Revolution or Counter-revolution. I don't think you can understand Britain if you don't understand the Industrial Revolution. You can't understand America if you don't understand the puritanical migration from England to America in the seventeenth century. The biggest curse of an ex-colony is that it tries to wipe away its past and invents itself from the moment it got its political independence. But there are so many ways that you are colonized. Your heart, your brain, your liver, your kidney, everything is colonized, and it takes a lot of time to get out of it. You have to understand that *plus ça change, plus c'est la même chose* [the more it changes, the more it stays the same].

How is Indian cinema still under the influence of colonization?

One thing about colonization is that it is the elite exploiting the poor for taxes and for money. You support that exploitation by convincing the poor that they need the elite. One thing that all colonialist powers do is that they bring back feudalism. When the British came to Africa, a lot of African societies used to live as republics, as tribal egalitarian societies. The British came and said, 'They can't have this, because they will decide some things for themselves and it's just not good for us.' They created a system of feudal chieftainship called 'warrant chiefs' who would be on top of these tribal societies, collect tribute and pass it on to the British. It's just an example of how colonialism promotes feudalism because it's easy to collect taxes. What the British did in India is that they completely magnified and re-invented the Mughal system of tax collection. Out of that comes the social system. So colonialism actually brings back feudalism, elitism and completely breaks the backbone of a large part of the thinking masses. In a way, we are there to think for you, give you values—education is good, family is good, preserving the traditions beyond all relevance is good, royalty is good. All those feudal and colonial aspects can be seen everywhere in India. We expect our politicians to have children who are politicians, because we don't want to think, and we want them to think for us. Similarly in films, that person comes from that rich family, that's the guy we should put out there.

The films, more or less since the 1940s, have been made either by the feudal elite, or the urban elite. What the feudal elite do is that they show more or less rich people who are good at heart, who rescue people and have very dislocated story about family and love. Rich people start becoming nice people. All the actors, the stars, with all their rich glamourous cars, they're always nice. What happens is that the director starts talking down to the masses. That is at the core of all Bollywood. It's about the rich trying to tell a huge poverty-stricken country that we are rich and we are good and you should believe us. Because we love and we are beautiful, fair skinned—colonialism is extremely racist—we wear expensive clothes, we cry like babies when we are in love. And we have a heart. And of course we have a BMW and this is the way to be.

The urban elite derives from colonialism. All political and artistic ideas of India come from the colonial period, including neorealism of mid-1940s and early 1950s. So if there had not been any De Sica or no Renoir, then Ray would have probably developed in a different way. Ray was essentially a foreign man, because in addition to him being formed by the neorealism of the 1940s, he was inspired by the late nineteenth century Bengal revolution which was a direct brainchild of Europe's influences. So he had two influences in fact and there are many directors in India who haven't travelled as much as Ray. Bimal Roy's films are extremely leftist neorealistic films. That's the urban elite—and I am a part of that—who has no knowledge of how the poverty-stricken parts of India work. But their understanding of poverty is a derivative way of looking at the poor, where they define how they should uplift the poor. Of course they are thoroughly on the poor people's side, but they have a nice flat to go back to.

Should one go live in a slum to understand them?

It can't happen. There was a very interesting phase, in the 1970s and the 1980s, where some directors, usually rich and coming from a nice feudal background, caught on to the absolute unrest of the common people, when the myth about India being that peaceful New Age country broke and we saw that we were as violent as any other ex-colonies. With certain things working in our favour, which is why we didn't become a banana republic. But there was a seething mass of violence and discontent. These guys tackled that and that's why, in the 1970s, you had heroes who were labourers, tonga drivers, taxi drivers, criminals, or loony cops who would use violence and beat dumb, rich, politically-connected people or criminals. In the 1980s, the things changed even more because the financing of most Bollywood films came from the underworld. So you have a series of films which completely idealize the underworld Don by going into his childhood. 'I did this because my mama didn't give me milk.' Their obsession is about the underworld man being the wronged here and the politicians become the poisoners who have made him like this. All these films are a projection of who's making them.

I think we should do a survey, on the path-breaking films of our industry, take the director and the producer, research from which family background they come from. A huge part of the early film industry, which forms the bedrock of the industry now, was made up of refugees from Pakistan. They brought their refugee culture—coming to India with nothing and making everything. They lost their house, their land, their family, their brothers. As a result, most of the blockbusters are about a family, brothers, getting separated at a village fair and meeting twenty years later. And the family comes back again. Our obsession with family is deeply related with the partition of 1947.

What about the 1940s?

1940s are a completely bizarre interesting phenomenon where you can really see cutting-edges social protest. Bourgeois protest nevertheless. *Neecha Nagar* [*The Lowly City*, Chetan Anand], made in 1946, is a complete allegory—and another film called *Roti* [*Bread*, Mebhoob Khan, 1942]. This is a combination of a whole series of extremely socially-motivated cinema. But the fact is that it always was a social movement, never a personal agenda. Therefore only a few directors took that auteur road because you always belong to a family, or a tribe, or a clique, or a club.

What do you belong to?

I am an outsider. So it's very easy for me, to be a lone ranger. The advantage that I have, which other people who are entrenched in the industry don't have, is that I am a proverbial outsider, so I have automatically a way of standing out. It's an unfair advantage that I have, but I am making the most of it. I've been in a kind of lonely journey. In fact, *Bombay Talkies* is the first time I am part of a club of big directors, known directors. To be in the same film as Karan Johar, Zoya Akhtar and Anurag Kashyap is a big thing.

You're still part of a group, who works with the same people.

You can follow your own vision. But at the same time, you need the raw material. That raw material is often shared. Anurag used my Greek director of photography, who did his first film in India with me, and then went on to do *Shanghai*. Richa Chadha, who was introduced in *Oye Lucky!* was in *Gangs of Wasseypur* [Anurag Kashyap, 2012]. There is this incestuous kind of situation. Anurag and I are seen as these two guys who are pushing this new wave.

Like Truffaut and Godard. Which one would you like to be?

Neither. Both are perfectly nice filmmakers and they should be allowed to do their own films. And when I finish thirty or forty films, that will be the day to figure out. It's too early now. Anurag and

I have lots of commonalities in terms of other people that we work with, we are working on subjects which are slightly confrontational and by chance, we have broken through with some films. But otherwise, you can't imagine two filmmakers so different. Godard is three filmmakers in one filmmaker's body. That's one thing I would like to do and I am a little kicked by the fact that if you see *Khosla Ka Ghosla*, my first film, and if you see *Shanghai*, you can't imagine they are by the same person.

Is there a new wave in India today?

When you're inside, you always protest. When you see from outside, you always belong. If I was you, of course I would solidly put Anurag, me, Sudhir Mishra, Vikram[aditya] Motwane in the same bag. But it all depends on the point of view. When you look at the earth, it's the earth. But ultimately you have to differentiate between India and France. An alien wouldn't see much difference between you and me. The more you zoom in, the more differences start creeping in. So, if from the French perspective you are looking at India, yes, Anurag, me, and all the other filmmakers belong to that group. The good thing is that we are trying to tell the same stories in very different ways. It's not as if we're evolving non-stories and try to tell them, and say, 'Look what we have done.' It happens sometimes when form becomes alienated from content. We try to engage with a new kind of audience. That's the commonality. If you want to zoom in further, then I could tell you the differences.

Are you also influenced by the West? Are you a colonialist?

Of course, anybody who lives in India and says that he is not a product of an ex-colony, would be wrong, except the original aborigines living in the villages, in the jungle. That is not possible. The thing is there are almost three or four waves of the cinema protest. I talked about the 1930s cinema where the mainstream was dissent because there was a strong theme of reconstruction that was going on in the 1930s and the 1940s. In the 1950s, a bit of it carried on. But I think from then onwards, the big families captured the market with their feudalism—rich people and their love affairs, rich people and their family affairs, rich people and their families getting separated. That's what kept happening. And how a poor person was actually a rich guy but he didn't know. It's the oldest mythology of how a king was found as a pauper on the road and actually was the son of the Sun God or something like that. It's the Jesus myth.

[Satyajit] Ray carried the dissent cinema on his shoulders alone because he was such a subtle man, such a European man who hated any kind of stridency. All his anger, all his dissent was subtly permuted through it. *Pather Panchali* is really a film about what poverty does to you. But it was told with such a degree of beauty in it that you see the humanism first and the poverty later. Indians were very sharp and a very famous Indian film actress [Nargis] actually said at the Indian Parliament, 'How can a film talk about Indian poverty?' So Ray was dissenting throughout, Ray was angry and he reinvented himself in the 1960s and the early 1970s with his Calcutta collection. He looks and sounds like a young French filmmaker who is twenty-eight years old.

Shyam Benegal films are anti-feudalism, even if he came from a very different point of view. I don't know what his background is, but all his films are about breaking down the feudal structure which is hugely exploitative. So that was the second level of dissent.

The last level of dissent that we are populating is a kind of urban dissent, which is really dissent and protest against banality, mundanity. Because with India being liberalized in the 1990s, a certain amount of popcorn and lemon-popsicle romance continued in the 1990s, which is what we protest against at its core. We are trying to say that things are not so rosy, not always so sweet. There are beautiful things which can be dark, which can talk about protest and what is wrong about our urban society. But this generation of filmmakers is even more cut off from rural India, poor India than the earlier generation, because consumerism and liberalization of the economy has divided India even more into two Indias, where you have no connection with what is happening in our villages. Earlier, there was some kind of a connection. It's a paradox, that connect was feudalism. Feudal families would send their children to study in colleges in Bombay or Delhi. But they'd go back for their vacation and see the real, poor feudal India where they would be the lords. If you see

Benegal's films, they have that element about it. Today, our themes are centred around urban politics, urban unrest, riots, deep brutalization because of consumerism, which is a complete brutalization of the society.

[A pause in the conversation, followed by a conversation around 'good' commercial films, during which I turn off my recording device. Without warning, the interview starts again].

I have no idea what good or bad cinema is. I can barely tell the difference between a well-made film and badly-made films. So many Bollywood films are made so badly that I think it's a crime to talk about the deeper elements of Bollywood when so many are made at a nursery level of filmmaking. You really can't talk about that genre of Bollywood. But then you only have a few filmmakers like Sanjay Leela Bhansali, whose films at least have a visual level and a theme. You can discuss his fantasy. But most Bollywood films which we call fantasy, celebration of love, are so shoddily made. You are trying to make too much of something that is not there. Where is the fantasy? Let's get a good cut first! Let's do something that has one part, and not many parts. That's another discussion all together—why Bollywood films are what they are.

Karan Johar represents this kind of movies. How did you work with him on *Bombay Talkies*?

They are all extremely intelligent people, extremely frank, extremely clear. Their films are made to supply a myth to a largely feudal country where a lot of people watch films to project themselves into that story. Their films succeeded then, not now. Because the story of urban young India was a story of abject sexual repression. Therefore, when you tell them about a romance, the average young guy and woman would live their love life through that. It's almost at the level of *Tristan and Iseult*: talking to the Indian man of the 1980s and 1990s is the same as talking to a young French man from the seventeenth century, who will listen to the romance of Romeo and Juliet and think about courtly love. It's an answer to repression, that's what we supply. It's about an Indian man or woman's life. You study, you prepare for education, you get a job and then you're just waiting to get married to have sex for the first time. And all your fantasies, and all your stories are about when you fall in love and marry. You can't think beyond that. That's what all Indian stories are about—the Indian marriage or the end together. It's really about not fucking enough. Karan [Johar] is a very different guy from me. The film he has made for *Bombay Talkies* is truffauesque. The premise reminds you of *The Soft Skin*. The nature of the story is at that level. A real, true triangle. Sexual ambiguity. Karan is trying to push his language further. He's taken *Bombay Talkies* as a way of breaking free. In terms of technique and language, you can see he's struggling, because he doesn't know how to tell a story of that level yet. But in the middle of his career, he's trying to completely change, to give an alternative view of the sexual politics throughout our lives. People who work in Bollywood are all intelligent people, perceptive people, successful people who succeeded out of their own vision. But the reality is it's essentially a feudalistic, patriarchal and repressive society to which they are catering a myth and a road to escape. When you're selling a myth, the person you are selling it to is entrapped, and so are you. When you come to the execution is when the schizophrenia comes through and that's where the film starts confusing you; what are you trying to do? You start with something, you go somewhere else, etc. Bollywood doesn't trust its audience and is trying to control it. People are stupid, they want to be manipulated. I've not seen more stupidity than in a group of people. A group of people coming together has the chance of becoming extremely stupid and being susceptible to manipulation. They want it—'Come, give me that shit.' I've seen it everywhere in the world. Somebody will be there to give you that shit. Luckily, myths can break; that's why we are here. If our films didn't exist, this urgency for freedom might not have happened.

So is the fact that Bollywood is changing partly because of you?

There is this myth of success around us and it's been a good publicity campaign. Also, the elite media, the elite English-speaking media didn't have much of a role before we came in, because they would just tell a story in the critics section. They wouldn't be able to show how much they can appreciate cinema. Our baby steps and small efforts have given the Indian media something to be proud about, to write about. They were at the same time going through a revolution because there was more money in media. So there were more newspapers, more supplements, more TV channels, more critics, who were all from the urban elite which had seen world cinema. That created an image of success. The way the media put us on a pedestal was almost as if we could do no wrong. That image of success—when it's being repeated by the elite media which is being read by all of Bollywood—made the Bollywood industry think, 'Are we missing on something? These guys are being praised for what they are doing and we are being seen as dinosaurs, so let's try and see if we can reinvent ourselves.' Every studio has a small wing which tries to invest in new independent films, like Fox Searchlight, five years ago. With people interested in talent and in films. UTV had Spotboy.

There's a flip side to it. My Greek cinematographer told me, 'Dont you guys ever make bad films?' *(laughs)* He said everybody is praising every film! Everything is superb, *c'est magnifique*, everything is fantastic, is mind-blowing. It's a mutual back-scratching that happens. Anurag is at the forefront of it, he praises everyone and everything. And then again, everybody is praising him.

As if India couldn't make those kinds of movies.

Exactly. It's the colonialistic need to be acknowledged by the ex-colony which is being supplied by the paternalistic uplifting extended arm of the West, 'Come my child, sit here, now we will tell you how to go further from here.'

You are getting some kind of recognition from the West.

You need to know it for what it is. And I think—this is my personal ideas, nobody but I am responsible for it—all ex-colonies in Asia have this need to be acknowledged by the West which is kind of obsolete. Because when I look at the West, there is such deep lack of confidence for the last fifteen-twenty years, that it's almost bizarre for us to be accepted by you when you're in a complete crisis. But that's how history functions. For some reason, the West is looking for champions to promote. What happens is when political power and economic power goes away, what remains is political power. Hence the cultural paternalistic behaviour, 'Who is my next champion? Africa? Turkey? India? Can I now uplift India? Now that I have uplifted Korea and they don't talk to me anymore, can I find the new child from the jungle?' As a result, what happens is, a lot of us start ignoring the quality of the films. Just because you made a darkly-lit film about a boy who has been kidnapped and fucked in the ass five times, your film becomes the new Indian urban, whereas it's probably an average and shoddily-made film. I still haven't figured out why we are not being able to make a series of films which have this common denominator of quality, like a Korea, like a Thailand, like Turkey in the 1980s and 1990s, like Iran. I think unless the feudalism of India is completely broken down, any meaningful cinema that stands the test of time will be difficult to come by. Cannes will celebrate one or two films and somebody will become the flavour of the month, but to have a genuine standard of quality cinema which stands for our own way of telling a story, like Chinese cinema—I've not seen that out of India. And the reason for that is we essentially have no time for aesthetics. Our colonial history is gone in a way that aesthetics have become the last priority. Social position, money, material success are more important to us than the joy that comes out of aesthetic quality. You can see it in our roads, in our buildings, in the way we dress, in our graphic design, in our gardens. It's the tragedy of India: from being a country where aesthetics ruled everything, including politics, we have come to a stage where aesthetics have become the last priority.

So India is in a very difficult position, of trying to reinvent itself aesthetically, to be counted in the world. When you go to China and you see a Chinese garden, it's a complete aesthetic statement. When you go to Iran—and I am not saying Tehran, because it's just like India—when you see a jug from where they're pouring out the water, you see modern aesthetics. When you go to Korea, you see that their aesthetic is based on sitting and eating on the floor and everything follows from there. And when you see the graphic design, the photography that comes out of there, or the book designs, or architecture, you can see that their films can go forward from there. We never had that, for a long time. And now that the colonial experience is slowly going away, we don't even have the copy of European aesthetics. All we have is Hollywood trash to connect with.

If you watch South Indian films made in the 1970s and the 1980s, you'll see what true Indian aesthetics can be. How dark skin can look magnificent along the long expanse of a white wall, which is the essence of Indian architecture. When you go to an Indian village, you will see that beauty lies in dark skin against a white background, lit by a harsh sun, yet having the darker effect of the tree that is planted in the centre of the courtyard. If we don't emerge from there, if we don't come from there, where will we draw from? I know I am sounding very philosophical but we need our own aesthetic foundation. And we are lost. Which is why we borrow. When you see Coen Brothers, you can see that their aesthetic is drawn from Midwest America, from the open expanses. When you see Truffaut or Godard, their aesthetic is Parisian. One hundred years of modernization, one hundred years of industrialization, the cars, the scooters, the taverns, the cafés, the coffee shops, the colour of the jackets, the posters of films—all of these gave a Truffaut, a Godard, a Gaspar Noé a bank of aesthetics to fall back on. Look at Ray—because he was so localized, so Bengali, all his films are deeply aesthetic. They are so rooted in the Bengal renaissance of the nineteenth century. His music is based on Bengali folk music which is what Tagore was heavily into. He took that and merged it with European music. That was the core of its synthesis. Where do we draw from?

India is so rich!

We have to look for that. For my film in *Bombay Talkies*, we went and shot in a chawl. I can't tell you how electrified we were in that building. It's an early twentieth century structure, it was made so lots of families can live together but those families were not related. So you had to create privacy for them because the Indian system was always about a joint family living around a courtyard *(he begins to draw a typical Indian house)*. This is the true Indian aesthetic from three hundred years ago. In the late nineteenth century, they had urban labour and they had to find public housing for them. They created this beautiful structure which had rooms and balconies, which would look out onto the main road, a central courtyard and this courtyard would be the place where they would all meet, talk and there would be a playground for kids. They would have common toilet facilities and common washing facilities. We could modernize the plumbing and the sewage and this could become such an alive space, because everybody is connected to everybody. None of the Indian modern architecture has been taken from there. We have cut off our aesthetics fountainhead. And that we need to find, otherwise we'll be copying forever. Copying is fine, as long as you're original. As long as you have something to say, then you can copy from anywhere. But if you don't have anything yourself and you start copying first, then it's dangerous. And it's there in all our films.

But you would actually think that Indian cinema is very different. Bollywood doesn't look like anything that we know!

In Bollywood cinema, there is something that you have to take out. And from there you have to go forward.

Is this why there are songs in *Shanghai*?

The producer wanted to add songs in *Shanghai* because it's an Emraan Hashmi film. Emraan Hashmi is like the Will Smith of India. Will Smith is the only consistently profitable star in America. Emraan Hashmi, with his romantic stories, makes huge amounts of money. People come to see his films because he personifies the lonely sexually-repressed Indian young man who falls in love with this mysterious girl who is above his status. With *The Dirty Picture* and *Shanghai*, he has become an object of art. There are no songs in the international version of *Shanghai* that was screened at Toronto. The presence of songs is me talking down to the Indian audience, 'Take your song.'

You said you have to take something out of Bollywood to create Indian aesthetics, what is it?

I would say that the thing that separates us from Europe is that we are psychologically at a stage where Europe was in the Middle Ages, where raw emotion and sentimentality played a big role. I would say that you have to take that and go somewhere from that. If we take European *ennui* and the cold loneliness of the average European, we won't reach anywhere. Because in India, no one is lonely. It's happening in certain urban centres, but you have no time to be lonely and also you are rarely separated from your class. An average European is an island. An average Indian is a representative of his class, his group. So we have to come from the fact that we have no personal lives, we only have social lives.

If you see my film in *Bombay Talkies*, you'll see that I've made the first step towards that. I have no idea how it works out, but it's extremely emotional and it's social. The personal parts of the film are emotional. Whatever our weaknesses are, we have to make them our strengths. If you see Iran's films, they are immensely social films, like Jafar Pahani's—except *This is Not a Film*. The way the characters talk to each other, you know without that social bond, there cannot be that film.

The last thing we can do also is forget this obsession about the West. One unhealthy trend that has come with us, filmmakers like me and Anurag, is that everybody wants to be at Cannes and Berlin. And I've said it many times—at least for five to six years, forget about festivals. We should forget about being uplifted by the West. Make movies about what you want, but that aim of being screened at the festivals tires your anger. And it lets people patronize you even more. If we forget the festivals for five years, I think we will be there in all the festivals afterwards.

India has no Ministry of Culture. It has a Ministry of Information and Broadcasting which controls arts and culture. That's a colonial thing, the name itself. The Ministry had a memo called, 'How can we increase the presence of our films in the world's top ten festivals?' This is not a good aim. A good aim would be to have a script-writing software which lets an Indian write in an Indian language rather than in English which he doesn't know to find Indian stories told by Indian people. When *Shanghai* was considered for Cannes, my producers were petrified because they knew that if it was selected in Cannes, people in India would see it as an art film and won't go to watch it. There are so many paradoxes working in the system. Let us first make films which are as good as a bunch of Korean films, of Thai films and let's not worry about the West.

Is there something else that needs to be improved other than the aesthetics?

Technique.

Why?

Too many films are being made, technicians are being underpaid, things are being made in too much of a hurry. I think as a society we are not really planned. We have to understand that films are essentially art and technique together. India doesn't have a comfortable relationship with technology. We can write a very good book, but we can't print it very well. The ethos of doing something technically perfect is not there, the way it is there in China. And our film industry is chaotic. When critics come to me and start talking about the philosophy behind my films, I am trying to tell them that filmmaking is like carpentry—get your joinery right, get to turn the wood fast, get to polish the wood, things will follow. By technique, I don't mean special effects or expensive technology. I mean the right sound and the right cut at the right time.

Another thing that happens is that Indian storytelling is a cyclical storytelling. Indian aesthetics come from the oral. The European cinematic tradition comes from psychoanalysis, the novel, the short story. The oral tradition is totally gone. When art started failing in the 1930s and the 1940s, artists realized that cinema was the next big thing to grab on to. So Europe has this tradition of pretending that their cinema is art. The filmmakers are the new artists because art somehow lost its course after the Second World War. You have transferred that elitism to cinema. But here, what happens is that storytelling would be done in front of a huge amount of illiterate people. One storyteller would go to a village and tell a story in a cyclical way, with re-embellishment, over seven days, so he could get seven-days pay. Repetition and re-emphasis are a form of our art. If you read Mahabharata and Ramayana, you realize somebody sang it in the original telling, that's why it reads like that. At one point, people used to remember it by heart and listen to it. So Indian storytelling essentially follows that circle. The songs emphasize the emotions to the people sitting ten rows behind you. In case you didn't get it, here's the song to tell you the pattern. When we repeat again and again, we forget why we are repeating. That's why now we are becoming shoddy.

Another reason is we are complacent because there's no other art form in India. Theatre is dead, dance is dead. An average American or European on a weekend can go to a coffee house, to a rock show, to a club gig, to a Broadway play, an installation, a museum, ski weekend, camping weekend. We can only go to the cinema, where you can kiss your girlfriend. And also it's so hot that the cinema theatre is the only place where you have air conditioning. Married couples go there to hold hands. When an art form, or anything else, gets such a monopoly, you necessarily have shoddy products....

MAYANK SHEKHAR
Film Critic

Had I never come to India, I might not have understood so well the French concept of *exception culturelle* (cultural exception), stating that art has to be treated differently than other commercial products. I might have never known that only the French language would commonly define cinema as the 'seventh art'. Fighting over a movie with my colleagues or my friends as if my life depended on it, as if we were engaged in a political debate, had become completely natural. Being part of a profession that people loved to hate—the infamous film critic, who supposedly disagrees with the audience's choices on purpose—made me proud. Because cinema is such a highly respected art in France, and because of famous names associated with the title, film criticism could easily be chosen as a career for any film-buff.

In India, cinema is the only source of entertainment for the majority of the population, but searching for a serious magazine on cinema would be in vain, even in Mumbai. For a long time, the profession of a film critic was limited to a few names, whose only requirement was to rate films out of five stars and have those stars displayed on the film's poster or DVD cover like a badge of honour. Hosting a talk-show to interview film stars (mostly actors) was considered enough to call yourself a critic. But in the last few years, the sudden boom in websites and social media, has resulted in many more voices—from the less to the most serious ones—being able to finally express themselves, and start building the profession from scratch.

Mayank Shekhar, who is thirty-eight years old, started his career sixteen years ago at the newspaper *Mid-Day*, followed by *Mumbai Mirror*, and the prestigious *Hindustan Times*. He succeeded in establishing himself as one of the most respected and talked about journalists, using his humour and unique style. He was presented with the Ramnath Goenka Award for Excellence in Journalism in 2007. He is also known to have an open mind about Bollywood, capable of appreciating an arthouse film as well as a commercial one. What would be his dream, one may ask? To write a book on the worst films ever made in India! Or, more seriously, create a website for film reviewing. Meanwhile, in 2016 he published the bestseller, *Name Place Animal Things*, which gives a large place to cinema as a part of the Indian popular culture. While I was writing my very first article on Indian cinema, in 2005, he introduced me to what we used to call 'independent cinema' then, for lack of a better word. We met ten years later, in a Bandra restaurant, for an assessment of the evolution of Indian cinema and film reviewing.

In a country like India where film reviews are not very respected, why would one become a film critic?

Why did I want to? I don't know. It just happened. I used to cover various bits in my first job at a newspaper, at *Mid-Day*. Of course, I was always interested in films, but then who's not? So you don't see yourself particularly as a film-buff in India, because you're surrounded by them. I used to watch many films in college, but then so did a lot of my friends. I would also watch a lot of films on video when I was a kid. We didn't have a video player, so we would rent one for three days and for those three days without sleeping, all night, we'd just watch films. So that's about eighteen films over three days. But then I wasn't the only one. My brother was watching it too. In hindsight, perhaps I am a film-buff, but it has never occurred to me to think of myself that way, because it's not such a niche thing to be in, it's not a hobby that most people don't have. If I was interested in a certain kind of plant, or certain aspects of making glass, that would set me apart. But I think being a film-buff, you don't realize it if you are one.

Then I got a chance to review a film during my first job—a mainstream big release on the weekend. It's a funny story actually. The movie was called *Boom* [Kaizad Gustad, 2003]. I got to see it in a preview theatre at about six or seven o'clock in the evening. I was supposed to fill my review for the next day so I had about two hours after the film to write my review. As it happened, the preview theatre caught fire. I didn't know what to do; my review was slotted for the next day. By this time, I had seen about thirty minutes of that film, which was beyond bizarre, to a point that there was no way in hell I was not going to talk about it. It was a very well-publicized film. It was Katrina Kaif's first film, with Amitabh Bachchan, Padma Lakshmi, a pretty top-grade movie in that sense. I wanted to see more of it, how bad it could get from here on! So I called my office and said, 'listen, there was a fire in the preview theatre. I obviously can't quite watch this film right now, but I really want to. There's a show late in the night in another part of town which starts roughly at around ten o'clock, which also means that it will finish around twelve. The deadline was supposed to be eleven thirty, so if you give me half an hour, I'll try and do it.' As it turned out, the film just wasn't starting. I was in touch with the copy desk, where they kept asking me, 'So has it started, when are you filling?', and I said, 'Listen, the movie hasn't started so I can't help it.' It reached a point where for that review to be in the paper the next day, they would have to hold the page. I said, 'Trust me on this, hold that page. It's so bad it will reach the annals of bad cinema. It's history in the making.' My editor trusted me, and they kept the page open. But they could only keep it like that for so long. The movie got over at twelve thirty, I filled my review by one o'clock. The only page that could be kept opened—and only because my editor trusted me on this one—was the front page, so they ran the review on the front page of *Mid-Day*, which I think a lot of people found hilarious. That's how it really started. I had reviewed movies before that, but they were really the movies that nobody had wanted to watch, and usually Hollywood stuff because that has no market for readers here—the Hollywood audience already has the reviews well before the movie is out in the theatres here. The anticipation for the Friday release is really for Indian films.

How would you define your profession as a film critic? You say everyone is a film-buff. To me, a film-buff is someone who, for instance, would want to watch all the films directed by his favourite director in order to get a full grasp on his universe.

That makes you French. You are the guys who invented the idea of auteur cinema, which, personally, I am not a big believer in. It would be auteur cinema if the director also edited the film, acted in it, wrote it, shot it. There are so many factors that go into making a film for it to be seen as auteur's work. It does apply to certain filmmakers, but it's been used to make a lot of filmmakers believe that they are the creators. I noticed it gives them a lot of arrogance, which I think is completely uncalled for. If the same filmmaker has done the worst films but also some good films, isn't he the author of both those films? A lot of other things might have gone wrong—the associates weren't right, the writers left them, the actors stopped working with them.

There are very few filmmakers, and fewer still in India, who can be considered authors of their work. I mean this also because it's largely a commercial industry, so the only way a film gets made is by the contribution of the paying public as against a film foundation in Europe, or various other trusts and bodies, who would sort of support a film financially. The only reason a film is being made here is because someone pumped in some money, expecting a certain rate of return on the investment. So it's likely that the director does not have full control or command over the work. But the way a lot of them plant their name as a 'so-and-so film'—even the first-time directors do it—is the negative effect of the auteurist theory. Back in the day, there were studio films. It mattered to very few people who the directors were. Even in world cinema right now and commercial world cinema, you can count the numbers of auteurs on your fingers. There will be an Almodóvar, a Christopher Nolan, a David Fincher, a David Lynch, etc. But the number of people who claim to be the auteurs of work just because they're directors is a bit appalling. So it's not that I completely dismiss the auteur theory but I think it applies to very few filmmakers and it should be something that we sort of give as an award, instead of calling every director an auteur.

What makes you want to go watch a movie?

Watching every film should be my work because in some way or the other, I could use them in the column I write, in a review or in some other conversation. But I don't think I watch movies because it's my work and therefore from six to nine every day, I'll watch a film. I do watch a film every day, but I do it because that work is really my pleasure. Of course, knowing who the director is important. But if enough people told me that is a shit movie and I've read enough reviews already, I will not go watch the film just because that director filmed it.

How does it work in India for a film critic? When do you see the films?

You have special previews. When I started, there used to be about four or five people—or for a really big film, maybe ten people in the preview theatre. But now, with the proliferation of media in general, blogs, websites, newspapers, television channels, these preview theatres have turned into massive halls, auditoriums, in regular multiplexes which are usually packed with people. I sometimes wonder if all of them actually review those movies, but they certainly land up at the show. The movie screening depends on the producer. My theory is, the earlier you show a film, the more convinced the filmmaker is of it being a good film. So some of them actually show it to you on a Wednesday, some on a Tuesday and already you walk into a theatre with a certain air of positivity. Because in my head, I am thinking at least these guys think they made a good film. There is a certain amount of confidence that they have in their work. A lot of the people who come to the screenings may not necessarily wait for a Friday to write their review. And so it's already out on Twitter, on Facebook, on blogs. And there are some filmmakers who don't show you the film at all. I love them the most. The biggest production house in India, Yash Raj, does not. Yash Raj would not have a press show before Friday. Of course, you get much less time to think about the film before you put the review out. But sometimes I like it, because you really don't owe the filmmaker anything. There is a subconscious freedom—it's always subconscious, I don't otherwise feel I owe them anything.

But watching it in a regular screening cinema hall with a paying public also has its own charms. That's why we started loving films, with the theatre first. But it would be a nightmare if all producers decided to have the screenings on a Friday.

Did film reviewing change in the last few years? Did it follow the evolution of Indian cinema?

There's a lot of public that loves to read about cricket, the other Indian national passion, but not in the same way that they love to read about cinema. Earlier, you would typically go to four or five mainstream publications and read reviews there. Now you get it all over the place. The buzz is also created through social media and each person is a film critic in that sense. All they want to know is—is it good or bad? Earlier at least, I would hear far more from people about what x, y, z film critic has said about this film. Now, and I am talking about general public of course—sometimes even film-buffs—they put together all critics as a monolithic entity and say, 'Oh the reviews have been good.' It's never an individual review, it has become an aggregate, which is dangerous. Every filmmaker can always find ten people who loved his film. When you see posters now, you see four stars on every film, regardless of the quality, or even if they were meant for reviews in the first place. So whilst democratized, the whole aspect of film reviewing is now open to all kinds of influences. Because when there are fewer publications, there are fewer reviews and these reviewers are taking themselves seriously, then each time, their credibility is at stake. But if it's a reviewer who's taken it as a hobby, he can always say, 'It's the best thing ever made', it can be plastered on the posters and that's good enough. Critical acclaim becomes easy to get, which is never good for cinema. And serious reviewing is something that filmmakers must aspire to. That's the only way, as only the French will know best, cinema really comes alive in its truest form.

So you're saying that there are more film reviewers nowadays and film reviewing has become less serious?

Infinitely more and infinitely less serious. There would be certain film-buffs who follow certain film critics and I am not denying that.

But largely, the discourse around film criticism is around whether they should exist in the first place. It's the first question that you get asked more often than not. And the second is, why should your review matter more than someone else's? And technically, it shouldn't. In that scenario, it has become an aggregate which does not distinguish one person's opinion from the other's, which is obviously problematic, because if critics have thought it's a good movie, it means nothing. It's as good as saying the public has loved it. I am different from you as a person, I didn't love it, but somebody is saying that the public loved it, therefore we should all go and watch it. Or somebody is saying all the critics have loved it, so we should all go and watch it. Clubbing opinion as representative of a larger voice, either the public's or critics', is dangerous.

Do you also think that critics are useless, that anybody could do their job?

Could I ever think so?

Then how are film critics important?

Considering film criticism or film critics to be useless would be as good as saying travel writing is useless, reviewing restaurants is useless, or writing non-fiction of any kind is useless, because all writings are from a personal experience. If reading about someone's experience is useless, then certainly film criticism is useless.

Can anybody be a film critic?

Anybody who loves films and cares about the writing world can be a film critic. If you love films, you will inevitably gravitate towards books on cinema. You will, whether you like it or not, engage with a lot of conversations around films. Many film critics are film reporters, that's not a coincidence. It just so happens that they are fascinated by the medium, and that's where they always like to be. It gives them a chance to converse about films, with people who know films like the back of their hands. I am not saying only a film reporter can be a film critic, but anyone with genuine love for films and care for the writing world could be a film critic. Which also means that they would be responsible because they love films. They will not suddenly say, 'This is a great movie', because someone asked them to, they genuinely love films, they respond to it in a certain way. They get agitated by movies a lot more than others who are indifferent. Only people who love films will hate bad films more than others. I get a lot of it sometimes—how I go overboard when I hate a film. But I genuinely don't do it consciously; it's just me pouring my heart out. If anything, it's a cry of despair instead of anger. Especially when you've seen good films; before every film you hope that it's going to be a good one, it's a cry more than anything else.

What changes has the Internet brought about for film criticism in India?

It has given everyone the position of a film reviewer, regardless of which website you write for, or which publication it gets published in, which blog you own. It's early days, I am sure a lot of good will come out of it, because a lot of film-buffs who may otherwise be engineers during the day, or working in advertising, or be jobless, know a lot about films and can apply some of that to writing reviews. You don't need to make a job application anymore to do that. And I think the ones that stick around for longer will survive as a distinctive voice. Commitment to that field is also very important. You can't call yourself a film reviewer if you've written thirty film reviews in your life. You'll have to put in the hours to gain the confidence of the reader, if nothing else. Right now, it's just pure noise across the board. Noise also driven by certain people whose job is to evaluate cinema in terms of how well it will do for the public, in terms of box-office alone. The box-office is also a film review of a sort—it tells you how many people went to watch it—so the viewer is thinking, 'Okay, maybe it's a good film.' Those people who only look at it in those ridiculous terms—of second-guessing what the audience will like—they've become hugely prominent. They were always big, but they are seen as critics now, which is odd, because they were always, if nothing else, trade-smiths. Film trade analysts, or astrologers, or psychologists, who are telling you, 'You will like this film, when I don't even know who you are.'

Is there an audience for a really serious magazine on cinema in India?

I think so. I think there is scope for a serious magazine—serious doesn't mean boring, don't get me wrong—it's very important to separate being serious and being a self-absorbed bore. One of the main reasons why mainstream publications haven't existed in the past is that there are only two kinds of mainstream publications in India. It's either box-office reporting or fanzine, celeb-gazing. There isn't even one proper cinema magazine. I don't even mean *Cahiers du cinéma*, I am not even talking about *Sight and Sound*. Something like *Empire* doesn't even exist. The Internet opens you up to a wider audience, because there aren't many readers in India and there are lovers of Indian films across the world. Even Indians living abroad, they might be able to access it. The genuine reading public, the ones who really love to read and the ones who really love to watch films, aren't that many people. But they are enough to support a few really good film magazines that would have, for instance, very detailed reporting from a film set, very detailed conversations with a cinematographer on how a film gets made, how a person shoots his film. That's not 'serious', I think it's damn entertaining. It's only serious compared to gossip. There hasn't been one magazine like this. I've been trying to work on a website for a while, but funding hasn't been easy. Wish me luck!

So your website would be ...

A starting point. Because to get money for my website, I would have to start something that looks like one, and then I go and look for funding, and use that to take it to the next level.

Where do you get funding for that kind of website in India?

You're asking me? If I knew, it would be up and running! The case that would have to be made would have to be a very business-oriented case, because you're looking for funding after all. It would have to be made from a very business point of view to show what it can lead to, what revenue models it can generate. It'll take me a while to even work that shit out, but there's no doubt in my head that there's scope for it.

Do you agree that cinema is being taken more seriously in India today?

I do agree with you. But it was taken seriously. There were pockets of film-buffs, who would go watch arthouse films, which were often state-funded, but there were producers also in the 1980s who would fund films which were for lack of a better word, more artistic, less of a circus, more of a storyline. But that audience wasn't big enough to sustain that cinema. The distribution system was the same. You had single-screen cinemas. If I am the owner of the theatre, I can either play a blockbuster which is nonsensical, or I can play this artistic film. I get ten people for this artistic film and one thousand for the blockbuster. So there was no way to watch these films to begin with. With multiplexes, because you have about six or seven screens of varying sizes, you can play all kinds of films. Even if there are only one hundred people who are interested, you only need one hundred people for that theatre anyway. And because at the end of the day the person who pays a ticket for a multiplex would pay about three hundred bucks, whereas the price of a ticket in small town India is still fifteen rupees, one person equals twenty people. This gave educated middle-class India a stake in its own popular culture for the first time, and that was about post 2003–2004. Thankfully, it coincided with the time that I began to be a film critic. Because I wonder sometimes: how do you review the movies of the 1980s which were shit movies? And what was the point of reviewing the arthouse films when there was no way to project them? So that was the best thing that happened to my job. The changing cinema made guys like me relevant because guys like me were talking to other guys like me and telling them whether this movie is worth it or not. Those guys were not watching movies in theatres to begin with, not Indian movies anyway.

So it's not only because of the multiplexes. People like you wanted to watch different kinds of movies, like European, American cinema.

People like me were watching these movies anyway. We were just using the alternate route to watch it. I would watch a Truffaut when I was growing up.

So those movies were easy to find?

For me personally, it was not too difficult because I lived in Delhi and there were places which would keep certain videos. It was a small circuit, but that circuit existed anyway.

It seems to me that they have blossomed.

It's a lot easier. Especially those who are growing up now are exposed to all kinds of films. Now you can download movies, DVDs are available. But the previous generation, which would be me, wasn't into Hindi films anyway. Now they are. And that is what changed. Therefore you can make films that sort of also appeal to them.

They are into Hindi films because Hindi films changed?

Yes. And Hindi films changed because of them. Because they existed with three hundred rupees in their pocket, which made them equal to twenty people watching a Salman Khan film.

Does it coincide with the fact that the West started to watch Indian films too?

No. That was a revolution of another kind, which was the Indian diaspora watching Bollywood movies, which were no different from the Bollywood movies before them, to some extent. It was just that they were set abroad. Because that audience had eight dollars to pay, which made them equal to forty people in India watching in a small town, those movies began to be set amongst the Indians abroad and they could spend more money on making those films. But that was a phase from the mid-1990s till 2003–2004. Not to say that one phase excludes the other. Those aren't the only films; you still have the Salman Khan front venture, hardcore, *masala* films. You have also some very artistic films, which don't have a song, or a dance. Likewise, you have films that intersect the two, which will be as entertaining as a Bollywood movie but as artistic, or as inspired by European cinema, or auteurist cinema, or Hollywood, etc. What it did was expand the choices. As the audience expanded, the kind of people who would watch a movie expanded, and so did the choices.

How come the rest of the world, not only the Indian diaspora, suddenly became interested in Indian cinema?

I think the rest of the world primarily—you're an exception—has taken Bollywood as a part of popular culture, as an exotica which is very relevant to the East right now, as against film alone. It's about the clothes they wear, the dances, the songs, not so much about filmmaking as filmmaking is understood to be. It's about a lot of other things that explain India as the exotic culture that it is. It's not wrong. The West was getting it wrong with the whole snake charmer, elephant and all that rubbish. *(laughs)*

Why should one be interested in Indian cinema?

When you think about it, India is home to one-sixth of the world's population—that many languages, that many cultures. To visually represent that culture, in some form or the other, through films for instance, through stories, alone makes it interesting. If I was not Indian, if I was French for instance, I would be very interested, if not for anything else then for their sheer numbers! Not being interested in Indian films would mean not being curious about one-sixth of the human race. And if you are a film-buff, to start with, if you love the visual medium, then you would want to see the stories that emanate from here. The reason why I like Indian films is because I like to see my own stories. It reflects the world I live in. In the same way that I love to see Almodóvar movies for the image of Spain I get. I go into a country I would not be able to understand otherwise, unless it was told to me through a beautiful story. It's such a human medium. All discourses on countries are political. But people aren't political. People do the same things. They eat, they make love, they drink, they make a living. But everyone does it differently, and newspapers can't explain that to you. Literature can to a large extent, but cinema is more accessible.

I've always thought that movies should be made to be seen by anybody.

It should. In fact everything that is culturally specific eventually can be universal. Because certain things are universal to humans. So the culture-specificity really comes from, 'Where is this place? Who are these people? How do they eat? How do they talk? How do they interact with each other?' But within this cultural specificity comes a very universal story, about love, about hate, about war, about losing a loved one, about finding a loved one, etc. One of the things about art that I most enjoy is its culture-specificity. I will not enjoy it if it's only talking to itself, because I will not be able to penetrate that culture. But all good films are universal by nature. Of course there are some bad films too. We don't love films for the sake of films, we love the good films.

There are a lot of Indian filmmakers who say that they only want to address the Indian audience, that they don't care about international recognition.

They are saying that because they haven't got it yet. The only Indian filmmaker who can be considered—or who's still considered—a master, is Satyajit Ray. He primarily made films not for Indian audiences, but Bengali audiences. He only made films in Bengali for Bengal. And they were all commercial successes first. Because at the end of the day, somebody is putting in money, right? And he's going to be putting money keeping in mind that it's going to be watched by people who will pay for it. So I think what those directors mean is that they're not going to tailor it to suit someone else because you can't, but will they be ecstatic if they pick up the Palme d'Or? Man, they will lose it. Everyone. Without an exception. Are they aspiring for it? Does it show consciously? No. Because you can't predict what people in France will like. But you can predict what you will like. And because you share a space with so many people like you, you can predict that hopefully they will like it too.

Are there Indian filmmakers who doubt the artistic quality of their films?

No. I think it's also a fully commercial industry, which is run largely by businessmen, based on return on investment, so they can't afford to think that. Whether they have a *Dancer in the Dark* in their head and they haven't made it, I wouldn't know. But they'll find it very hard to make that film. I think they could, but initially it's going to be very hard.

One doesn't need that much money to make that kind of film.

You know the kind of fame and adulation—because you've been here, you know—that filmmakers get here. Even film directors are now seen as genuine stars or celebrities and they're caught up in this world. They would be happy to live their life in this world, and there's nothing wrong with that. I do believe that the West has missed on a lot of good films that get made here because they also see it with certain presumptions. They say, 'Oh, it's a Bollywood movie?' If you don't see it as a Bollywood movie and see it as any other movie, you will be able to see its merits, for the film that it is. It's both ways. It's not like people in the West have actually seen, or appreciated some of the good stuff that comes out of here. Bollywood has become a pejorative. While it has done very good for the sales of various products—like saree brands, and bindis and shit like that—it hasn't done well for cinema, purely as filmmaking because it puts off a lot of people that will not enter knowing it has three songs in it. What they won't be able to appreciate is how well the songs are put. 'Oh, it's a Bollywood movie, let's not enter.' If they did, mainstream audiences in the West—I mean, they'll never be mainstream audiences in the West—but the film-buff audiences will be addicted to some of the stuff that's coming out right now. Because I do watch all these films, right? And I genuinely can tell the difference.

Would you consider the movies being made in India, by directors like Dibakar Banerjee or Anurag Kashyap, part of a 'new wave'?

I don't think it would be right to call it new wave, because of how abused that word is. But it's learning a lot from mainstream Bollywood and adapting a lot from world cinema. Some of the two are intersecting, which is sort of turning it into mainstream cinema, as against the new wave that happened in the 1980s in India, which was parallel. It means the parallel and the mainstream don't meet. Here, the parallel intersects with the mainstream. And that's one of the reasons why I would never use the word new wave, or even arthouse, or even parallel, because I am a mainstream film critic, and I know a lot of people get put off by those terms, they think, 'Oh, it's a boring movie.' So I'd rather not use these words and just concentrate on the fact that the films are as entertaining as what they regularly consume. These filmmakers also take themselves less seriously than the 1980s new wave—some of them were out there to tell the intelligentsia, or the upper middle-class or the elite how poor our country is, and how we must do something about it, try and live the life of a rickshaw puller, try living in a slum, try being the victim of atrocities in a village. It is all good, but if it doesn't entertain you, the point is lost. Then, it's a pamphlet. None of these new guys are into pamphlets. And they do have a message, but it's not so obvious and so grilled, and you can watch it for its own worth. There aren't that many films of that sort being made to be called a movement, but I have a feeling that we are getting there, if it sustains itself over the next few years. A lot of films that would have been impossible to imagine are coming out from the mainstream bucket. Of all the studios now in India, you have a Viacom18 that would make, say, a *Gangs of Wasseypur*. You would have a PVR making a *Dhobi Ghat* [Kiran Rao, 2010], a UTV that would make a *Paan Singh Tomar* [Tigmanshu Dhulia, 2010]. Those are studio-funded artistic films. Obviously, they are being made because there's an audience for them, and it's not the audience that's going to go watch a film at Angelica in New York. This is the same audience that watches it in a multiplex. If anything, we are at a better stage than American cinema is right now. American cinema has somehow co-opted what was an independent movement into a one-sided company. And they are making those movies for Oscars. *Silver Linings Playbook* is a formula film in its own way: dysfunctional American family, which predictably gets its shots at the Oscars. So in that sense, I find our cinema more real; it's truly funded by the public, and survives because the public will sort of endorse it in the long run.

What kind of people endorse it?

India has a pretty large middle class, about two hundred and fifty million. These numbers keep changing depending on which survey you use, but two hundred and fifty million is a good portion of the world. So if there are enough film-buffs within that public, it's good enough to sustain a cinema movement. At this point, there are about four or five really good directors, some of them turned into producers, mentoring the next lot, but it's all within a pretty well-oiled system. It's not that one movie being made and nothing else comes for a few weeks. It did well, so now they're working on something similar. Or they will at least be listening to scripts that are different. And that is a huge chance. I am only being optimistic, I am not saying it's all changed, but it's a lot better than it has ever been.

Could it not sustain itself?

If you put up say, two crores, into a film, and you make three and a half crores, it's all good because it's a one hundred and seventy-five per cent profit after all. But one huge Salman Khan or Akshay Kumar movie comes, and wipes off the board with its one hundred and twenty crores. So why put two and make three when you can make seventeen in one go? That's how investors think. You really hope that people don't get carried away. No investors are going to do it out of love for films. No one in the world has, sadly enough. So you really hope that people continue to hedge those bets; that the big exists with the small, and the medium. Which is what we are seeing everywhere, even in our literature. Our literature in English was always high-brow literature which spoke to a certain number of people and that's it. Suddenly you have this explosion of all kind[s] of writing, which has become mainstream and has increased the number of people who read books. It may not be great stuff, but any mature industry would have various levels to cater to all kinds of audiences. So I see literature maturing in India, and in the reverse way, I would hope that films would mature too.

So they haven't really matured yet?

It's tough to say it's already there, but it's certainly better than it has ever been. It's the best time.

In India, there are very different kinds of audiences. When you go to the Bombay suburbs, you see those posters...

Of Bhojpuri movies.

Yes. They are made for those from lower classes who will never see the movies we are talking about.

People love movies for different reasons. Those Bhojpuri films will exist and they always have. The problem before was, for people like me, that there was nothing that existed to cater to my taste. Can I have a stake in my own mass culture? And now we do, to a large extent, which is the heartening part. But yes, there are movies made in at least twenty languages. Within those movies, there are movies made for at least two different classes, which are the middle class and the lower class. The lower class would be the rural, and the urban—I mean semi-rural because villages still don't have theatres. That same audience, when it comes to Bombay, will have its own theatres, will go and watch those Bhojpuri films and it's fascinating. If there are that many cultures, there ought to be that many cinemas cultures and it's only natural. In fact, that part interests me as much—watching films, really bizarre films, with people responding to it—as the storytelling part does. They're going in for what we call *tamasha*. *Tamasha* is a style of theatre where Indian cinema came from to a large extent, where there will be an emotional scene, followed by a romantic scene, followed by a dramatic scene, followed by an action scene, followed by a song. This is where the word Bollywood comes from, which is B-grade Hollywood. But those are not the movies that you talk about in the West. In the West, they get put off by any film that has songs, 'Oh god, it's a *masala* Bollywood movie', but even if they have songs, it doesn't make them a Bollywood *masala* movie in the way that you've known them to be.

But then what is a *masala* Bollywood movie?

Those Bhojpuri movies. Some Salman Khan movies are *masala*. It has a construction.

Can the *masala* Bollywood movies disappear?

Oh, no chance. Everybody who has three hours to spare and couldn't be bothered with what they saw on the screen will continue watching them. They probably don't even discuss it when it's over, they'll probably say it was shit and move on with their lives. A lot of the film-going audience in India is not a film-buff audience. My mum watches a lot of films to see how beautifully shot Spain was and she may want to take a trip to Spain. Which is why a lot of tourism boards attract Bollywood filmmakers. Because immediately when the movie becomes successful, if it's set in Switzerland, tourism goes up. A lot of people I know watch films for the clothes—and you start seeing women with the similar kinds of saree at weddings. A lot of people watch it for the hero, because they just like the hero and the fact that he's such a virginal creature who's never set an eye on a girl except for the one that he's with and that he'll live with for seven generations. What he does doesn't matter. It's a world of fantasy that you can't deny. It's so dreamlike and a lot of people are fascinated by that world which they'll never see. Likewise, a lot of people are fascinated by a world where the hero is taking on the system and beats the shit out of the cops and the politicians. This fellow is doing things that they could never imagine doing. Only a fraction of them will be questioning, 'But hey, what was the story again? Haven't I seen that story before?'

Bollywood movies are still changing, in their scripts, in their structure, and I am guessing that they're trying to seduce the audience who is escaping from them.

And who, at the same time, wants a bit of that.

Is it really successful in the attempt?

I think that phase is on a decline. It was at its peak in the early 2000s. The starting point was *Dil Chahta Hai* [Farhan Akhtar, 2001]. That showed a few things: one, that it can be a pure Bollywood film, but it doesn't mean that people have to scream and over-emote, or that there should be a typical hero. But at the same time, it will be about impossibly rich people, really fast cars, lovely homes and at some level, not reflecting the concerns of people. It's escapist in its own way. That started the trend with movies like *Kabhi Alvida Naa Kehna* [Karan Johar, 2006], or *Salaam Namaste* [Siddharth Anand, 2005] in terms of the idiom, in the way people are behaving. Those films had the audience that had the money. They still liked Bollywood movies and they were tired of the melodrama in it. But I see much less of that being made because this audience now wants to take it to the next level and will reject a film that is so much like the last one that they watched.

So you mean Bollywood is taking a step back, that it's being more traditional?

Even when you talk about Bollywood, you have to bear in mind that there isn't one Bollywood. There are various Bollywoods. The kind of films that, say, a Shah Rukh Khan represents is Bollywood, so is Salman Khan, so is Aamir Khan. And the three represent completely different kinds of movies, even in the commercial zone, because it is a star-driven industry like Hollywood. An Aamir Khan movie would be necessarily different from the last one and that's what the audience expects from him. His films are as big hits, if not bigger, than Salman's or Shah Rukh's. Salman Khan movies, at least in the past few years, have been purely repetitive and have represented the same milieu, and roughly the same storyline. But they have been loved by people who usually don't give a shit about Salman and are just curious, 'Who is this guy? How do his movies make twenty crores?'

Films like *Dabangg* [Abhinav Kashyap, 2010].

Correct. They've started to get their city audiences, while still being in Bollywood. And Shah Rukh Khan would think of a film where he would pump in a one-hundred-and-sixty crores, like *Ra.One* [Anubhav Sinha, 2011], where he's tried to create a hardcore sci-fi fantasy/superhero film, within the same Bollywood construct.

Every time we talk about Bollywood, we're talking about stars; every time we talk about a different kind of cinema we're talking about...

Directors. But that would be true for mainstream versus off-stream independents even in Hollywood, to a large extent. There are about three hardcore mainstream industries if I am not mistaken: there would be Hollywood, Bollywood and probably Hong Kong. It's the movie stars who lead them and where the money is coming from. For the audiences, it's easier to connect with a movie star than with a director. Only film-buffs connect with directors. Everywhere. In France, it may be more the director sometimes. Was Gérard Depardieu as big as François Truffaut at his peak?

He was probably bigger. We also have this kind of star-driven cinema. We call it commercial cinema, popular cinema.

And we call it Bollywood. Except there's commerce in everything. It comes together, which is why Indian cinema is now at a very interesting phase.

When I first met you, I asked you where Indian cinema will be in five years from now...

What did I say?

You were really positive about it, really optimistic. I was hoping that it will be as celebrated as Chinese or Korean cinema abroad, and you said you didn't know, but you were really positive. It has not reached that point, but is it on the right path?

For Indian audiences' sake, and when I say Indian, it's one-sixth of the human race, I would like it if there were films that would lift the current crowd to another level, rather than simply hoping for a foreign award; because that never did much for cinema anyway. It's not like India never had certain wings at international film festivals, but the impact on the audience hasn't been as great. So this whole merging of the commercial and the off-stream is what really interests me. If we reach a point where the five nominated films at Filmfare for instance would be vaguely close to the five nominated films at the Oscars, that would be good enough. Unfortunately, that is not the case right now. Our award system is screwed up and what we don't realize is it's not about who has won that evening. It also means that appreciation and respect is easily bought. That will only kill the aspirations that a young filmmaker has, who will continue to worship some blockbuster filmmaker. And then you'll have repetitive films....

PART 4

WOMEN IN THE HINDI FILM INDUSTRY

Living on this planet means having heard of at least one of the many problems that Indian women face: female infanticide, a result of increasing pressure on a girl's parents to pay dowry for her wedding; *sati,* the practice of burning a woman alive on her deceased husband's funeral pyre (prohibited for more than a century but still practised in Rajasthan in 1987) or child marriage. The debate is coming back with the media addressing cases of sexual violence against women, such as the gang-rape of a young student who succumbed to her wounds in Delhi in December 2012, or of a journalist in Mumbai in August 2013. Every week, rape cases are making the headlines of Indian newspapers—a stark contrast in a country which tended to ignore them previously. In fact, India, especially in the North, is still a very patriarchal society, where the men dominate and women are infantilized—something that all the women I interviewed strongly agreed on.

The history of women in Indian cinema starts with unusual anecdotes. When Dadasaheb Phalke was making the first Indian feature film, in 1913, *Raja Harishchandra*, he could not find any women—not even prostitutes—to play the women's roles. He had to turn to male actors who were effeminate enough to wear a saree and almost look the part. It would be a while before women from so-called 'good' families would agree to demean themselves on the big screen. In the 1920s and the 1930s, it was mostly foreigners, such as the Australian Fearless Nadia, who were being chosen as heroines. The first Indian star to get first billing, before male actors, was the actress Nargis in the 1950s.

Even today, the career of Indian actresses is shorter than their male counterparts and their salary way lower. Once they are in their thirties and married, as in the case of contemporary actresses such as Kajol, Preity Zinta or Madhuri Dixit, they disappear from screens, except for some rare come-backs. In a few years, they will probably play parts of mothers, as Jaya Bachchan or Hema Malini would do. This ironical situation found depiction in *The Dirty Picture* (Milan Luthria, 2011), where an ageing actor plays the son of an actress who was his lover in a film made ten years before.

Still, actresses are essential to the film. One would imagine that the space behind the camera would then only be occupied by men, and that is where the cliché is smashed to pieces. Admittedly, one can count the number of female directors on the fingers of one hand, and amidst them only a few have succeeded in reaching a celebrity status as Aparna Sen has in Calcutta or Zoya Akhtar and Farah Khan have in Mumbai. But is it not the current situation everywhere else in the world, in Hollywood as much as in European cinema? Is this really a question of Indian misogyny? In fact, in all other technical aspects, women have succeeded in asserting themselves as equal to men, as I found when interviewing the women featured in this book. The phenomenon is definitely not new, but has seen an exponential growth since the beginning of the 2000s with India opening up to the world, and above all, the transformation of the young urban youth who is much more open to women's independence.

The four women interviewed in this chapter, two technicians and two actresses, all have in common their young age—not more than thirty-eight years old—and have been acknowledged in the industry very early on in their lives. With candour, they describe their work environments; they ensure that no man can outwit them and they raise their voices when necessary. A new generation is born.

THE FEMALE TECHNICIANS OF HINDI CINEMA

NAMRATA RAO
Editor

Interestingly enough, film editing turned out to be one of the most female-oriented professions in the film industry all over the world. India is no exception: well-established and prolific talents such as Aarti Bajaj, Shweta Venkat and Namrata Rao are now working continuously for both the commercial industry and indie films. Is it because most filmmakers are men and the special bond between a director and his editor works better across genders? Is it because the job doesn't require you to impose your views on a male-dominated set? Or is it simply a coincidence, after all? As women—I figured from my many interviews with female technicians that I was no exception to it—we always feel the need to justify something which should start to be seen as perfectly normal. Aren't we too obsessed with feminism nowadays that we try to find answers where we shouldn't even be asking questions?

At thirty-eight, Namrata Rao is one of the most sought-after editors in contemporary Indian cinema. She began her career with Dibakar Banerjee's second film, *Oye Lucky! Lucky Oye!*, in 2008. Since then, she chose to be more faithful to filmmakers (she edited all Dibakar Banerjee and Maneesh Sharma's films) than to a special genre of cinema. Being a YRF talent, she easily switches from out-and-out formula films such as *Befikre* [Aditya Chopra, 2016], to a more challenging *Titli* [Kanu Behl, 2015]. Lauded with awards, this unstoppable workaholic has edited seventeen feature films in eight years.

Namrata Rao's interview was the first conversation I had planned for this book, and I couldn't help but feel slightly nervous as to how the whole project would pan out. But it faded away as soon as I started chatting with this naturally friendly and warm professional. She welcomed me into her Versova apartment, in the north-western part of Mumbai, on a Sunday, and immediately apologized for the delivery boys coming and going. It was the only holiday she had in a long time and she was using it to get back to her daily life. With an interesting mix of passion and casualness, she started telling me about her career.

You said in an interview that you were always fascinated with films. What kind of films did you watch as a kid?

I was not really a film-buff as such, because my parents used to watch very few films, mostly religious films, like *Jai Santoshi Maa* [Vijay Sharma, 1975]. But I used to read a lot of comics. I was totally taken by them. I had this thing with storytelling. And that's probably how films eventually happened.

When did you start watching films?

On television. I used to have huge crushes on actors like Mithun [Chakraborty]. I was so crazy about him. I wanted to marry him. I don't know why. Now, I can't relate to him at all. *(laughs)* I used to watch films, but never in theatres. I had not seen any world cinema. I hadn't even seen Hollywood. The only Hindi films I watched were whatever played on television or the few religious and children's films they played in theatres. But once I was studying, I was totally lost, like, 'What to do, where should I go now, what next?' So, slowly, I inched towards filmmaking, because it was the closest to what I loved the most—stories and storytelling.

Was there a film that really made you want to work in the film industry?

Yes. When I was in my final year of college—which was ten to twelve years ago, I saw this IPTA [Indian People Theatre's Association] film called *Garam Hava* [M. S. Sathyu, 1973]. During the same time, I saw a lot of Kurosawa films: *Rashômon*, *Yôjinbo*, *Red Beard*, *Seven Samurais*. I was blown away. I had never seen films like these. There was this whole world out there, which I had no clue about. That's when I started watching films. I was already twenty-one then.

Was that your first experience with world cinema?

I had seen *Jurassic Park* before that. *(laughs)*

Do you feel that to be an editor you have to watch a lot of movies?

Yes. I feel I should watch as many good films as possible, and with the audiences. It really gives me a sense of where the story is working, where it's not working, where people laugh. Just be with them, and build my own audience memory, which helps me when I am editing.

What is a good film?

A film that engages me and that somehow, I am able to associate with, at some level. A film that affects me in many ways: it can make me angry, it can provoke me to do something for the society, or something for myself, be a better person.

You became an editor by chance, you wanted to be an actress.

I started doing theatre in college and I was really enjoying it. In my college, there were very few girls, so I got a lot of attention. I was the only girl in the theatre group, so I used to get all the roles. We did one play once, where they needed three women, in three different age groups. They couldn't find them. So I played the three women, with three different get-ups. I would go change, become an older woman, etc. So I thought that's what I wanted to do, theatre. But eventually, I figured that it is not something that I would be able to sustain for a longer time. I did a part in Dibakar's film called *Love, Sex aur Dhokha* [Dibakar Banerjee, 2010]. It was so tough, because I had to be fitter. He told me, 'You have to lose ten kilos if you want this part.' I started dieting and gymming, it was crazy! Once I finished the film, it was such a relief to eat pizza and pasta. That's not a life for me. I love eating, so I don't think I can be an actor. *(laughs)*

Tell us the story of how you became an editor.

Because I was doing all this theatre, I was not studying in college and I had no interest in studying the subjects I had taken up. I was studying to be an IT programmer. I worked for six months as a programmer and I discovered this is not it. I don't know how I passed, I was totally not into it. I come from an academic, orthodox sort of family, so my parents were keen that I become an engineer or take up a teaching job, something of this sort; something that brings good money and puts me in good standing. But I left that. I found a job in a graphic design studio, where they do layouts for books, book covers and small ads. There, I discovered that I have this flair for writing. Then, I landed this job with NDTV. There's this French show called *Guignols*, they did the same kind of show here, with puppets as politicians. I was a production assistant for that show. I learnt a lot there. I was doing a little bit of sound mixing and I was really fascinated by it. But at one point, television really bored me. Because it's so cyclical: it's the same things that happen in cycles. After the first initial high was over—that there will be deadlines, cool people, cool office—I got over all that. I got used to the freedom of working in a media house and I really started feeling suffocated there. That's when I applied to film school and incidentally, I got through. I wanted to do sound, but eventually I ended up doing editing, because for sound, you needed to be a physics graduate. Going to film school really changed things for me. It just completely opened my world up. I saw so many films that I had never seen, never heard of. It was like a second life for me.

Why did you choose to apply to the Satyajit Ray Film School in Calcutta and not to FTII [Film and Television Institute of India] in Pune?

When I applied to film school, I was already twenty-three and my parents were pushing me to get married, because for them it was the right age to get married. The Pune exam was the year after. I couldn't buy one more year from my parents. They just couldn't believe it. Why would I want to leave all my education, my academics and do something so bizarre? They were like: 'Who studies films? And why?' So later, when people would ask them what their daughter was doing, they would say, 'multimedia', just because they were so embarrassed to say that it is films.

Are they still embarrassed?

No, not at all. They are very happy. I used to keep telling them that if I am happy, it will all work out. Of course, they had their reservations. But it was the first time I was living in a hostel, so they started missing me after a point and they became okay. I was also tired of doing the kind of jobs I was doing and they knew I was tired. But I am so glad I went to Calcutta, because not just films, but the whole Bengali culture opened up in front of me.

What are your fondest memories of film school?

The editing department was superb there. Their focus was not really on the techniques of editing. It was more on storytelling. As editors, you are storytellers, you are not just putting things together. You have to take responsibilities for the director. So they used to tell us we were the second director on a film and that we had to have that attitude also, which I think is very good for learning editing—because it's an open field and you can create the story that you want to.

How difficult was it to get a job after film school?

I was very nervous in the last one year. I could visualize my parents standing at the gate asking me to get married again, even before I could step out. So I needed something to start my life. I started editing four-five documentaries while I was in film school. I think it built my confidence. Those films did quite well in festivals and Dibakar Banerjee saw one of those films, *I Am The Very Beautiful* [Shyamal Karmakar, 2008], which was about this relationship between a character—a cabaret singer—and a filmmaker, and how mutually exploitative it is. Dibakar then contacted me for the edit of *Oye Lucky! Lucky Oye!* We met and clicked. I was damn lucky.

You said in an interview that most editors in the world are women. Do you think being a woman brings something special to your work as an editor?

The very conventional way of looking at it is to say that men are the directors, the hunters and the gatherers and women are the cooks and the editors. I don't know if that really has to do with gender, but I feel we are more affectionate and more patient. If I like my director, I just give everything I have. It's really like a relationship for me. In that sense, I don't know if men feel the same way. I feel really protective towards my directors. I want to give them my best, I want their vision to be executed in the best possible way. I don't know if I feel like that because I am a woman, or because that's the way I am. Maybe a woman is not as aggressive as a man is and there's a certain amount of persistence that goes into editing, we keep doing and undoing. Initially I think it must have started with the practical aspect that you don't have to go out there, be in the field, and carry things around physically. It's more about being confined in a space, and doing things very patiently with a lot of love and affection. But today, it just seems incorrect to say that I am an editor because I am a woman.

And in other fields?

There are fewer women in photography and sound. In photography, maybe it has more to do with people having confidence, like directors, because it's a very physical job, so people still have some sorts of bias against women.

Have you ever been treated differently because you are a woman?

No, never. In fact, I think I am paid quite at par with the men. There's no difference at all.

What do you think of the image of women in Indian cinema?

We are still stuck in that whole patriarchal system, where women are supposed to be a certain way, to suit the convenience of the society. We really need to change—especially in advertising, the way the item numbers are done, how films are advertised as a place where you can see semi-clad women, where they do sexy things. Men can also do these things. We really need to address it. I find it so deeply ingrained. A woman who sleeps around, like what happens in *Cocktail* [Homi Adajania, 2012] is not the one who's finally chosen. You have advertising which says that you are a good woman if you dress up well for your husband. You have creams to lighten up or tighten up your vagina. You have popular item numbers where if the woman says, 'I'm like a *chicken tikka*, you can have me with alcohol', it becomes the biggest hit of the year. You're giving out wrong signals to the people who are watching these films. There has to be a certain amount of social responsibility. We are just reinforcing the same old beliefs, that women may be liberated—by liberated, I mean they go out to work, they earn money, they probably have friends of their own, a life of their own—but still at home, the man is the boss. You can never reach a point of equality like that. There are very few people who want to change that image. Men want to hear that because it reinforces their beliefs that they are superior to women and that they can look at women in a sexually-perverted way. I am glad there are so many women in filmmaking now, because somehow it is inching towards a fairer world. If I have kids tomorrow, I'll tell them that there is no difference between men and women. You have to respect women as human beings. We are all human beings first, not men, or women, or a certain caste. When I started working at [Yash] Raj, which is one of the biggest studios here, I was practically the only woman on the whole floor, but now there are so many. It's really a good sign, because all of them want things to change.

What do these women do at Yash Raj?

They are directors, photographers, producers, editors, lots of writers. But it's a very slow and small change, and to reach the actual audience is going to be a really tough task.

Which audience are we talking about? The one that wants to watch movies like *Cocktail*?

It's a very urban audience who made it such a huge success. It's a scary thought. But I feel a little confident when a film like *Kahaani* [Sujoy Ghosh, 2012] works, which is about a single woman who's travelling on her own, calling the shots, manipulating her way around. Whatever audience you're catering to, whether it's the educated, uneducated—because we have a huge audience that is uneducated—if it's an engaging story told well, they are willing to buy it. Of course, they'll have their reservations. In *LSD* [*Love, Sex aur Dhokha*], there was this whole debate that opened up, because in the second story, the girl is a dark girl and she's the one who ends up being exploited. A lot of my friends had an objection to that. 'Why did you choose a dark girl to be exploited?' I don't think it was a conscious decision. It was not the message. For me, I want to see that this girl has been able to make a life for herself despite whatever has happened to her. So even if a lot of people think that *Kahaani* is jingoistic and unrealistic, I am really happy if a lot of men have gone to watch it and liked it. It's a scratch on the surface if nothing else.

Who went to see *Kahaani*?

It did well in all circuits, like educated, uneducated, urban. It did very well in rural Bengal. In fact it broke some kind of record. But Bengal maybe has this tradition of women being stronger. The woman is the one who wears the pants there. We need more of them in the northern parts of India, where patriarchy is a way of life. Even women think it's the way of life and that's how they bring up their sons. The cycle continues, because mothers, more than fathers, believe that this is the role that they have to play.

How do you choose the movies you work on? Which kind of movies appeal to you?

I can't do films that are incorrect. Some of these films have become very popular, but I'm so glad I wasn't [a] part of them. But then, there are films that don't engage me when I read the script. I have to believe in the director. For me, the director is the most important person, because it's his vision that I am executing and facilitating at some level, so I have to be totally in harmony with him.

Is it important for an editor to know the director on a personal level?

I am telling his story. I am the medium here. So if I understand this person or I connect with him or I have some kind of respect and affection for this person, I will be more sincere, or I will make more effort to do my job well. The first film I did, I just came out of film school. I was very fresh, I thought I knew everything so I started suggesting things to the director. He got really irritated with it, and at one point he just exploded and burst out. He told me, 'This is my film, not your film, and I will make it the way I want to make it.' It was a very big shock for me, because somewhere I knew what he was saying was right, but I wasn't sure at what point I forgot that. And of course he threw me out of the film, somebody else completed it. I think it was the most amazing thing that happened to me, because I thought about it a lot. Another editor once said that the editor is like a psychologist to the director, you can't judge him, you can't say that this is the only way it can be, but you have to understand him and then move forward with him. Then there will be a point when he will start trusting you and maybe give you total freedom. That has happened to me. Most of the directors I've worked with I've worked with them again and I think it is because I completely believe in them. Then whatever arguments happen, happen to make it better. There are times when I am proven wrong, I regret certain decisions later. In *Kahaani*, there was a lot of debate about a lot of scenes. Most of them I won, but for one of the scenes I was wrong. I know it now. I apologized to the director, and he's happy that I have apologized.

What was the debate about?

I removed a scene because I thought it was probably not needed. There's a section where you take a flashback and you discover that the heroine was executing her own revenge. There was a scene where she goes to that guy and says I want to learn to become an agent. I thought it's too expositional, why should she say it like that? That's why I took it out. But now I feel if it was there, it could have added to her character.

You've worked on a different kind of cinema than the typical Bollywood. Is it because that's what you want to do or is it just a coincidence?

Mostly, I think there is a kind of understanding that I have with these directors and working with them always adds value to me as a person, because the stories that they tell affect me as a human being. That's why I like working with them. With Dibakar, I feel with every film we push ourselves, we try to do something different and somewhere there seems to be some kind of social relevance to it. There's a certain record of the times we are in. Also, he knows a lot about a lot of things. So I learn a lot from him. He's like an encyclopaedia on cinema. There's always this rush of doing something that has not been done before. He pushes me in that direction, and he never renounces, which is also a very good thing. It keeps me on my toes. He's never happy with what I have done, we keep working and fighting. It really adds to my craft. With Maneesh [Sharma], I get a lot of freedom to explore the story in a different way. In *Band Baaja Baraat* [Maneesh Sharma, 2010], I had those two characters, those two good actors at work. We did a lot in the edit, to make them more flesh, more creative. These directors gave me that respect, that time and space which I like. Also, I am not a fit for films which are really mainstream, because at some point I lose interest. I like watching them but I can't spend six months of my life with them, creating only entertainment for someone.

What about *Jab Tak Hai Jaan* [Yash Chopra, 2012], which you edited?

I did that film only because of Yash*ji* [Yash Chopra]. He was doing his last film, and he asked me if I wanted to do it. It was a dream for me to work with him. I discovered that I am probably not the kind of audience for this film. I accepted it at some point and I worked with that spirit. He also gave me a lot of space. Of course we had arguments: I asked Aditya [Yash Chopra's son] why Katrina [Kaif]'s character can't be married, because it adds another layer to the film and it makes it more interesting for somebody like me. Her dilemma could be now that she's married and she comes face to face with the man that she really loves. But they were making the film for the lowest common denominator and there was a certain kind of history they were catering to, because Yash*ji* has a certain name. So I had to go with their vision. I had fun doing the film because it was not the kind of film that I had done before. But I don't know how much in sync I was with the story. Maybe it shows in the film. I saw *Jab Tak Hai Jaan* with my brother in Bangalore, in a very huge place. People were booing and going crazy, and my brother was feeling bad for me. It's good to see films with audiences, be connected to reality and know that what you've done is not working with them.

Do you want to do more movies like *Jab Tak Hai Jaan*?

No, I don't think so. I have to empathize, associate with the character, with the director, with the vision of the story. In *Oye Lucky!* I was totally empathetic towards Lucky.

How different is it to work on a Bollywood movie?

There is more money because there are bigger stars and the film is made for a wider audience. So you cut it keeping that in mind. If there are ten people in the audience, *Jab Tak Hai Jaan* caters to all ten, and Dibakar caters to three out of ten. So you can have a slightly more arrogant way of looking at your film. I don't mean arrogant in a negative way, but in a more 'author' way. 'This is the story I want to tell, this is the way I want to tell it, and out of ten, only three people are going to listen to the story because only they are interested.' But in *Jab Tak Hai Jaan*, it's like ten people want to see a film like this, so let's make a film to cater to them. It's the opposite. Less freedom. Also it is more expensive. The focus is not on being super efficient. It is about being more celebratory, about cinema, about life, about love, everything is slightly over the top, even the editing. You don't really try to condense and make it super compact. You are trying to be easy with it. If an actress is smiling, keep the smile, for longer than usual, because that's what people have come for. If she's just dancing in a saree, you keep it. Even if it's not adding to the story, or taking the story forward, you do it. Because it's more like a variety show. You have dancers, you have songs, you have comedy, you have love, which makes it a package.

It's easier in some ways to work on a Bollywood movie, because it has been done for a while now, so there is a set formula that you can follow. But times are changing and not everybody can connect to a *Jab Tak Hai Jaan* anymore. People have become more selfish, they don't really connect to expensive ideas about love anymore. They don't want to see sacrificial love, especially the younger generation. There's so much more about individuality and sex over love. These films need to change and they are changing.

Working with Shah Rukh Khan was a dream for you.

Shah Rukh Khan has been the most consistent man in my life, because it started when I was ten years old. When I got the Filmfare and he gave it to me, it went on TV. My mother called me and she said, 'Why are you falling all over him? Does it look nice? What are you doing?' I hugged him first, then he hugged me back, then we hugged again, it happened quite a few times. Saif [Ali Khan] was also there and Shah Rukh said, 'She got that award for *Kahaani*, but she also edited *Jab Tak Hai Jaan*.' Saif said, 'No, nobody edited that film!' *(laughs)*

You are in your early thirties and you've won eight awards. How do you feel about them?

Awards are always good. When you get them, it means that some people value your work. But I don't want to take them very seriously. I got awards, what does that mean? Do I have to be good all the time? I want to feel free when I work. And now I am quite cool about it. When I got my first award, I was really stressed. I had just started working on *Kahaani*, and I thought I have to do a really good job, otherwise maybe they'll take my award back. *(laughs)* Now I really enjoy that moment, but I don't feel that it is what is defining me. If a director works with me again and again and I keep getting calls to work on films, I feel happy.

Do you dream of a less lonely job at one point, like direction?

It's not crystallized as yet. I think that's the next step of storytelling for me. But I don't think about it, it's not like a plan for me, like after two years I have to do this. It has to happen organically. That seed has come to my mind now, which was not there earlier. And it's not just because editing is a lonely job, but also because at one point it saturates you. In the sense that I need to feel challenged all the time and not every movie challenges you, maybe because you've done something like that before, or because you know the space better. I need to be in that space of panic, like 'I have to do this better, what can I do, what new things can I do?' And I don't know how much space editing has for that and for how long.

Would you be a director who edits her own films?

No, because one more person adds his value to the film. That person's brain is also becoming a part of my film. I think as a director I would want contribution from everyone. Of course I may not take it eventually but I'd want that option.

Are you involved in the production process?

We tried that in *LSD*, but it was not very fruitful. Also because I was acting in it, so it became really tedious, being on the set and being on the edit, because there were such hectic deadlines. It really took a lot out of me physically. I would also want to take a break. What ends up happening is one day you're on the shoot and the next day you're editing. I was on the shoot of *Jab Tak Hai Jaan*, but it was not so hectic. I played Scrabble with Shah Rukh, I danced with him, so I thought, 'Okay, now I can die in peace.' *(laughs)*

Indian cinema uses very different techniques from Western cinema, like repetitive shots of the star from different angles.

Indian movies are driven by stars, by actors, like a Shah Rukh Khan or a Salman Khan. It's like advertising, to make you feel this guy is so important; he's the one who's going to change my life. This is done more and more to reinforce the whole image of stardom. There is so much history attached to it and it's also part of our social set-up. I really enjoyed *Dabangg* [Abhinav Kashyap, 2010]. I saw it in a single-screen theatre, with people screaming and dancing and you see the power those actors have over people. Salman is *bhai* [brother]. When we used to go for tuition classes, there used to be those boys following us, eve-teasing, not in a malicious or harmful way, but to ask us to go out for a coffee. They would wear tight jeans, they would have a comb sticking out of their back pocket and they would pretty much all look the same. They would have Akshay Kumar's hair and we used to call them 'Tommy Deols', because they would wear those fake Tommy Hilfiger shirts that are really tight and they had no muscles.

Are there other techniques specific to Indian cinema?

I think songs. Integrating songs has been the biggest learning for me. It's really tough. Because there are two ways to do it: the actress and the actor meet, we feel this chemistry and—cut to Greece. Both are dancing on the beach there. That's one way. The other way is they meet, feel some chemistry, spend some time and during that time the song comes. This is slightly more believable; say what a Mani Ratnam does. They are not cutting away to Greece, or to Philadelphia to do a song and then come back to Bombay. It's very difficult to interpret songs, because no story really needs songs. But in Indian films where there are no songs, the audience reduces automatically. Like in *LSD*, Ekta [Kapoor], the producer, was very keen that we have a song towards the end and Dibakar wasn't, but it really worked. We saw that people came because the song became really popular. They were very disappointed with the film, because they thought it would be a particular kind of film. So they felt duped, but it got them into theatres. People feel that songs are a five-minute break from storytelling, so they can chill while the actors dance in beautiful costumes, their hair blowing.

How do you work with the script?

I have divided the editing process in three phases. The first phase is when I am doing the scene work. It is the most tedious part for me, with the least amount of return, because I am going through the rushes, skimming, but this is the basis, the building block, where I can manipulate the performances, get the best performance, one look from there, one small movement from here. That's the micro-editing of scenes. Then comes the macro-editing which I enjoy more, because that is where it becomes more structural, more storytelling. In the third process, I have to go back to the rushes to make it even better. First, I try to be as true to the script as possible and I show the director what I feel should be cut or replaced. Then I go back to the rushes, to find if there's something to reinforce what I'm trying to do. The film where I had limited amount of rushes was *Jab Tak Hai Jaan*, because Yash*ji* shot it completely the way he wanted to. In all other films, I had lots of rushes. Maneesh [Sharma] shoots a lot. I sometimes go crazy. But I have a lot of options to work with. I enjoy this process also, because the moment I change a little expression in the beginning of the scene, the scene changes.

Do you only work on digital?

My first digital film was *LSD*, because of the politics of the film: it had to be shot on digital. *Shanghai* and Maneesh's film [*Shuddh Desi Romance*, 2013] were shot on digital by choice. *Jab Tak Hai Jaan* was shot on 35 mm. The digital directors shoot a little bit more, there's a little bit less discipline in terms of shooting but otherwise, there is no difference for me. I started learning editing on film, so I have this whole romantic idea of cutting celluloid, but it doesn't matter. It is expensive, and time-consuming. If there are more cameras set up, you give so much power to the editor somehow. I feel that digital has resulted in the editor becoming more and more important.

Which is the best edit you have ever seen?

When I was in film school, I was really enchanted by *Seven Samurais*, because for that time, it was so brilliantly done. Then there are films that really surprise me, like *Goodfellas*, though it's a long film. In India, I really look up to Renu Saluja's work. The more I read about her, the more I find she was a really interesting person also. I could never meet her because she passed away before I came to Bombay but she's done a lot of brilliant films. For me, the essence of editing cannot only be about work, you have to be interested in people and you have to be observant if you want to make a good film. You can't just be sitting in one room. It's important for me to go on a train, see people, how they interact, how they behave, and I feel this kind of connection with Renu Seluja. I feel she was like that.

NEHA PARTI MATIYANI
Director of Photography

This book couldn't have been complete without a conversation with a Director of Photography, or DOP, as the profession is casually called. In India especially, the DOP serves almost as the second in command after the director. In charge of making sure the film gets the best image and constantly behind the camera, he/she is in fact usually placed closer to the scenes being shot, while the director retracts behind the monitor. A good relationship between the filmmaker and his DOP can thus work wonders. But because this particular profession is predominantly male-dominated, it was important for me to meet an exception to the rule; and obviously, understand why women seemed to have shied away from it. The task seemed at first impossible, but since there's no such thing as impossible in India, I was fortunate enough to cross paths with Neha Parti Matiyani.

Neha, thirty-eight, met me in a Versova café. She was between shoots and though very open to the idea of speaking about her work, she started by worrying about not being very loquacious during interviews. The concern would be short-lived and Neha soon proved to be as talkative as I had hoped, especially when it came to describing her work on the field in detail. Interestingly enough, while other female interviewees for this book such as editor Namrata Rao or music composer Sneha Khanwalkar dismissed their gender as being a handicap, Neha had to admit that being a woman was not always a bed of roses.

Even if her career as an independent has just begun—her fifth feature film, *Waiting* (Anu Menon), was released in 2015—Neha is already quite experienced. After being an assistant for five years to one of the most renowned and active directors of photography in Hindi cinema, Ravi K. Chandran (forty-one films in twenty-six years), she has learned by heart all the tricks of the Bollywood industry, and loves them almost unconditionally, which feels refreshing for once.

You have worked only on big Bollywood movies. How did that happen?

When I came to Bombay, I met a DOP called Ravi K. Chandran.

One of the most renowned.

Yes. I worked with him for five years, which is when I did the seven or eight big movies you are talking about. *Ra.One* [Anubhav Sinha, 2011] was the first film I did after leaving him, as an operative camera person.

How did you start your career in films?

In my family, there are absolutely no people who are in the film industry. As I was growing up, I used to enjoy watching movies. In every Indian household, movies are a part of your lifestyle actually. But I had no intention of getting into them until I graduated from school. I knew I wanted to get into a field which meant interacting with people rather than just being in a regular desk job. So right after school, I applied to hotel management and mass communication. When I got in mass communication, one of our projects was a video project and I figured that cinematography was what I enjoyed the most. I decided to study photography. I went to FTII Pune and pursued cinematography there.

What kind of movies did you watch with your parents?

When I was growing up, it was mostly Indian cinema, and English. My exposure to world cinema started when I came to FTII Pune. Before that, it was the regular Hollywood films that would come to India.

Did your parents agree with your choice of career?

My dad was with the forces and we moved around quite a bit. So our exposure had been wide and open. They were not against it. What they were against was me moving to Bombay. When I finished FTII, I went to Delhi and I did documentaries, corporate videos. I figured that job wasn't what I liked. That's when my dad said, 'Take three months, go to Bombay, I'll finance you only for three months. If you can make it on your own, well good, else you come back.' I actually had only done a one-year course in video—they have three courses at FTII, a three-year course and a one-year course. It meant that getting a direct opening in films would have been difficult for me. So after getting to Bombay, I immediately took up certain video projects. Eight years back, video had a lot of money. I did one quick project for twenty days, made my money and decided now I was going to be what I want. I had a list of a few DOPs that I wanted to meet and Ravi K. Chandran was on top of that. Luckily for me, I met him and he took me on a few ads where he said he'll just observe if I could manage or not. Then he took me on as an assistant.

What did you learn at FTII?

When we joined FTII, the first thing they told us is 'we are not going to teach you, you are just going to learn.' Which is true, because most of the time we were not in classes, we were on our own outside. We learn most when filmmakers came to the institute to do masterclasses. Every evening, we would have a film screening. That's where I was exposed to world cinema. After that, the students would sit and discuss and dissect the film. Then of course, you have your college project: in six months, you get into every technique in the general course and the last six months you specialize in what you are into. So you get an overall exposure to what goes into making a film.

That's when you decided to choose cinematography?

No. When you enter FTII, you have to decide on your specialization. I wrote my exams for cinematography.

How was working with Ravi K. Chandran?

He is a really difficult taskmaster because you have to be on the edge when you're working with him. The best thing about him is he puts so much responsibility on you that you have to take charge of your life and dive in deep. My colleagues and I used to be like, 'What the hell!' Every other assistant we knew had such an easy life! For five years, I practically had no life, because he was working back to back. So either we were shooting movies or doing ads—prepping the film and then shooting the film—or in the middle there were days off and we were doing the post-production of the film and getting ready for another film. Now that I've become independent, I don't read as much as I used to when I was with him. It was like being in school, we had to read everything that was in the market, all the film magazines. I am lazier now that I am on my own, so I am really thankful to him for bringing me up here. When I started my first independent project, I walked onto the sets and I had no fear. I was a pro.

What kind of responsibilities would he give to you?

Any DOP usually has two assistants. Most decisions happen during the recce. If you go to a location and say this location is fine with me, you can't walk in on the day of shoot and say that the light here is not going to be fine. So sending an assistant to the recce is a big deal for Ravi K., because if I've gone and said this location is going to be fine for me and I need five lights to shoot here, he's going to land up on the day of shoot and have to shoot with those five lights. We sometimes said we would be able to manage and then he would say, 'What the hell, how could I do this with five lights?' Then, before the shoot starts, there are pre-lighting days. He would just sit and discuss what he wanted; he wouldn't tell you, 'Go and put one 10 kilowatt light here, and one 8 kilowatt light here.' So we would be on set the day prior and do the lighting up the way we understood it best. There would be days when he'd accept what we've done and then there would be days when we would be, 'Shit, I know nothing' and start from scratch again. In post, when you're colour-matching, we would do the first parts and he would come for approvals. All the way, we were pretty much managing independently. Of course, we had his guidance, but he gave us that much freedom to go and do what we felt was right and then take charge of it.

So that's why he was able to do so many things at the same time.

We all work together. When we're doing an ad, it means that we got a break from the movie. What did help is that one would do post for one film, the other would do prep for another film. On shoot, all of us would be there.

Why did you take the decision after five years to become independent?

I didn't take the decision. He decided I was good enough to get out, and he threw me out. In fact, in the industry, he's probably the only DOP with so many assistants who became independent, because a lot of DOPs have assistants that have been with them for years. People who have started when they were in their twenties, now are forty-five and are still assisting. It has to do with the way Ravi K. functions.

Was it difficult for you to find your first assignment?

There was hardly a transition period. Because we were already talking about me trying to get independent work, he had started hiring another assistant. I took a month off to get married and on the day I was coming back, I had a call to be a camera person for *Ra.One*. Unlike in Hollywood, the DOPs also operate the cameras. So I was getting a lot of exposure in terms of lighting and running a set. If there was an action sequence, a song, we'll always have multiple cameras and that's when I would operate. When there was one scene with only one camera, Ravi K. would operate. *Ra.One* was a good break for me because I did sixty-seventy days of shoot when I was on the camera physically all the time. That was the only thing that was lacking when I was working with Ravi K. and I used that film to polish it.

It actually seems there are not too many female DOPs because it's a very physical job.

It is physically tough and interestingly, the first film I did with Yash Raj [*Mujhse Fraaandship Karoge*, Nupur Asthana, 2011] had a lady director. When I met her for the first time, she said, 'I want to keep the whole film fluid' and I said it meant there would [be] a lot of handling the camera. She looked at me and said, 'Do you think we can do hand-held?' I said, 'Be rest assured that we can.' Around 80 per cent of the film was hand-held. Though it is taxing, it's not something that ever bothered me. It was never in my mind that I wouldn't be able to physically handle the job. Of course there are longer hours for the entire camera team, because you start before everyone comes in, when you start pre-lighting the scene. Then you're shooting through the day. When everyone gets a break between shots, you're the only one who doesn't because you are actually setting up the next shot. I finish as soon as the shoot finishes, but the camera assistants will check that all the footage is right, the light guys will be wrapping up. So the camera team, after the art department, is the one that works the most on set.

Is it true that you don't find that many female DOPs in the industry?

That's true. In the mainstream industry, you can probably count one or two on your fingers. In documentary, there are still a few that have ventured in. It has a lot to do with men trusting you—producers, who are mostly men—to take up such a big responsibility. Because at the end of the day, everyone's work can be reversed except the camera person's; it would mean going back to a location, paying for permission, accreditations. I don't mean to take away from any other technical job, but if you're doing a sing-song film, if there's a screw-up on sets, you can dub the film. An editor can go back and forth.

A colleague of mine and I were both with Ravi K. for five years. It was easier for him to move out and get a film before me. Initially, it was enough that we both had Ravi K.'s stamp on us. But it was easier for him because he was a guy and he was from Ravi K. Chandran's school. I didn't have too much trouble because of the production houses that I've worked with. My first film as an assistant was Yash Raj's. So Aditya Chopra knew what I could do. He in fact recommended my name to the director, saying, 'If you are planning to start, why don't you meet her?' But if you go to an absolutely new producer, you may be Ravi K.'s assistant, what can you do? It's basically the trust factor for women, which makes it difficult to break in. I've read somewhere that for a male DOP, he's not wrong until he has done something wrong; for a female DOP, she's not right until she has done something right. It's a female DOP from Hollywood who said that. Even in Hollywood, women end up doing independent films more than films with big banners. For my biggest film, which was *Yamla Pagla Deewana* [Samir Karnik, 2011], I had to meet Sunny Deol and all. They are these hardcore Punjabis and Punjabis are a community which is more male-dominated. When I went in, I was highly recommended by some people. They hesitated before deciding to meet me. After the first meeting, there was no reaction from them for about three months. One day, they called me and asked me to do it. So there is a hesitation, definitely. People will be more ready to work with a guy than a girl. Why? For my previous film, I was out of the country for three months. So I guess it's easier for men to leave than women; they have somebody to take care of everything. Luckily for me, my husband is in the same field—he's an editor. So there's a certain understanding and it doesn't alter our relationship. But otherwise for women, it may be difficult. A commercial film sometimes means you're out for three months, six months at a stretch. And then, when you have babies, it's difficult to be away for so long. So there are all these factors; it is not just the physical aspect.

Do you know why they finally chose you for *Yamla Pagla Deewana*?

Initially, I had met them for another film, which has not taken off yet. It was an out-and-out action film. When I was working with Ravi K., I had shot some action scenes, so I showed them my work. Obviously, they looked at my size and wondered if I'd be able to handle an action film. After this, I got to know that they did background checks on me. Then they eventually called me and had a long run meeting with me, where they asked me technical questions. They didn't put it out that bluntly, but I figured what was going on. It was like, 'We know that you can handle a set, but do you know your technicalities?' That one conversation that they had with me, I think that's what convinced them.

Could you describe your work as a DOP? How do you collaborate with the director?

In Hollywood, there's a director of photography. True to his word, he's the director of *photography*, so he's the one who overlooks the entire job. The lighting will be handled by a gaffer, the camera will be operated by operative camera people, and then there will be a team of assistants who are the people who will be managing the camera. Unlike that system, in India, the title remains director of photography, but you're involved in the lighting, as in you will have to be on set when the lighting is happening, which is something Ravi K. gave us the freedom to do. Eventually, when I have a team of people that I have stayed with for so long, I'll be able to do that. As of now, I am there on my pre-lighting days as well. I am also shooting, operating the camera on set. On post, even abroad, you give the references to your colourist, who grades it. Basically, it's the on-set responsibility that differs between Hollywood and Bollywood, because there, they will pretty much be having all the discussion with the director behind the monitor. Here, the DOP is behind the camera. So discussions with the director are happening between shots.

How much can you discuss with the director?

In the pre-prod[uction], of course the director has a vision. He or she may know that they want their film to look a certain way—a sunny bright look as opposed to a cold feel. All these discussions happen at pre-prod stage. How I function is when I meet a director and we are working together for a film, after reading the script, the director will show me some references in terms of what he has in his mind. I may also have some things in my mind: I take still images, paintings, or clips from films. I have done two films with one director, whom I made my first film with, so we have this way going where we absolutely break down the scenes, like shot-wise, way before we are on sets. We do a look table where we put all we want, how we want every scene to look, whether it is an intimate scene and we want to treat it in close-up. After these discussions, we have our pre-recce. For one location, you see three or four options. You shortlist one option, then you go for your tech recce. That's when we go with our script in hand and we break it down to the teeth. Unless it's a big actor and if the actor trusts the director, he will follow the breakdown that we planned: 'Here, we want you to enter, come in, we need 30 shots for this scene.' Then on set, in terms of lensing and how I want the light up, it's pretty much something that I do, while the director is spending time with the actors. Obviously, there will be certain times when I have set up the scene in a certain way and the director may feel that she or he needs to be closer to it, or that I am too close and we need to move away. Or as the actor is speaking, he feels like there's a need to move in to the actor. Those are things that you sort of improvise on set, but that's how I worked with this director, Nupur Asthana.

On *Yamla Pagla Deewana*, unfortunately, we were different departments. On these other two films I am talking about, we had costume meetings, art meetings. When I said I wanted a scene to look like this, I discussed colours of the props with the art director, with the costume designer. We'd discuss things like we are not touching this colour until we transition into this part of the film—like there is no red in the first ten minutes of the film. On *Yamla Pagla Deewana*, we were all different departments. We had one meeting where we discussed that this film just needs to look glossy. So every department did what they needed for the film to look glossy. *Yamla Pagla Deewana* was an out-and-out comedy, we wanted the actors to look good, so we were talking bright colours. There are four different bright colours in the film! On *Mujhse Fraaandship Karoge* and on this film that I am working on right now, everything is colour-coordinated. Different things work for different films.

What do you mean when you say an actor might influence the breakdown of a film?

The look of the film will remain the same, in terms of colour tone or emotion play. But at the technical recce, if we decide that we want somebody to enter through a door, come and sit somewhere, newer actors will come, enter from the door and sit where we had planned him to. Slightly more established and experienced actors have a great understanding of the script because they have been doing it for so long. So when they feel they don't want to enter in the scene but be seated at the beginning of that scene, that changes everything for us. You have to keep improvising. It's a creative job, everyone has their interpretation of what they've read, how they've experienced life. Sometimes we're doing a scene and we've actually planned it out, we want full movement, we want the actor to bang the table at this point, get up and move around. But the actor can feel like, 'I am not going to move, I am just going to stare at the other person's eyes.'

Isn't it difficult to work with so many visions of the film?

No. At the end of the day, the director is the captain of the ship. So all final decisions, good or bad, remain with the director. I may make a suggestion, I may feel that a shot is absolutely not working the way the director is doing it, but the final call remains with the director. The director may take an option shot and in the edit keep the option shot. There are times when the director, the DOP and the actor disagree on the way things have to be done, but it's something you take ten minutes off to figure your way around and move on.

It's a common saying that in Bollywood, actors...

… rule. It's actually still true. But we are not talking about on-set decisions. These decisions are very little, this is when you will have a discussion on set and decide. When we say it's actor-dominated, it is mostly because your schedules and your shoot timings have to be worked around the actors, also at a production level. What happens now is that most actors want profit-sharing in the film. But on set, when you're there, everyone is an equal. You can agree, disagree, take a call and move on.

How do you choose the movies you want to work on?

Let me be truthful. I've just signed my fifth film. My fifth film is the first film I am choosing on the basis of having read the script. Before that, my first film was a Yash Raj film. Without even reading the script or knowing the story, I said yes. I went with an open mind, thinking whether they pay me peanuts, whether they give me all the equipment I want or not, it's a great break. What happens, unfortunately, is that a lot of independent films get made, but they don't get released. Before I did my YRF film, I had signed a film where six days before we were supposed to shoot, the producers pulled out. If it's a Yash Raj film, it's going to get made and it's going to release. So there was no question asked. Luckily for me, it turned out to be a really good film. My second film was a really small film which didn't see the light of day. After that, I did *Yamla Pagla Deewana*, which again was a really big film. My fourth film I did again with my first director. No questions asked. She had signed my dates way before I went to the *Yamla Pagla Deewana* shoot. Luckily again, it was a good script, so things have worked in my favour. My next film is a film with Dharma Productions and now I've decided that I want to take a call on the basis of liking or not liking a script. So before I said yes to them, I read the script.

Are you working in mainstream cinema by choice?

I am an out-and-out Bollywood fan, I love the song-and-dance routine. The director I made my first and fourth film with is a commercial person, but she's more realistic than a commercial person. If I have an actress coming in, I like to shoot her hair blowing in the wind. She would just want the actress to walk in and sit down with the guy. We differ in that way, she pulls me back because that's her style of filmmaking. But I had an awesome time on *Yamla Pagla Deewana*, because when the actress was walking, I could have a fan blowing her hair around! So, yes, working in mainstream cinema was a deliberate choice because initially, when I got out of film school, I tried my hand at documentaries and it wasn't my calling.

What do you like best on a Bollywood shoot?

In documentaries, you're mostly capturing what exists. Of course you beautify it a little bit, you put your little light when you need to see the person's face. I've chosen the commercial line particularly because

I like to create everything from scratch. It's what keeps me going, irrespective of long hours. Everything is how you imagine it to look like. Right now, in Indian cinema, there's an out-and-out commercial zone which is the fairy land, the world that actually doesn't exist, but we make believe; and then, there is more realistic cinema. I would love to do realistic cinema, it's just that nothing has come my way. I wanted to do my four first films to make a mark, and now I am going to start choosing projects that I want to do.

When you are talking about realistic cinema, which recent movies would you have liked to be a part of?

I would have liked to be part of *Gangs of Wasseypur* [Anurag Kashyap, 2012].

Do you agree with people who say that the fantasy world of Bollywood should come to an end?

I think independent cinema and Bollywood should co-exist. As much as I enjoy independent cinema, I also really enjoy the song-and-dance routine that exists in our commercial films and I wouldn't like that to go away. What is happening now is that a lot of commercial cinema is without songs, or with only background music. The film that I am working on right now only has four songs. Only one is picturized as a song-and-dance routine, the rest of the songs take the film forward, like montage songs.

Why is that song-and-dance routine disappearing?

It's not going away, it's moving to a more real zone. It still exists; people still go to dreamland for one song. But instead of having an absolute cut away, it's embedded in the storyline which takes the film forward.

On which movie did you have the most fun?

In the whole making process, I have enjoyed *Yamla Pagla Deewana* the most, for a lot of reasons. One, because it was my first big film as an independent. Unfortunately, the film didn't do well. But it was a large canvas for me to play around with, it was a huge responsibility. Also, the whole process of making it was great because there were amazing people on set and we had a great time filming. Technically, I've enjoyed working on *Mujhse Fraaandship* and the film that I'm working on now because you notice my work in that. *Yamla Pagla Deewana* is just a film that is nice and colourful, anyone could have shot it. In my first and fourth films which are technically good, there's a semblance of thought and when you look at it, you might ask who shot it. There are certain films which bring you name and others that you just enjoy making.

Would you collaborate again with the directors you worked with as Ravi K. Chandran's assistant?

Absolutely. I'd love to work with Sanjay Leela Bhansali, because his films, whether they've worked or not, are all visual delights. They all look different, because Bhansali has always chosen greats DOPs, so the DOPs have their inputs to enhance his vision. When we were on *Saawariya* [Sanjay Leela Bhansali, 2007], there were times when we'd do one shot a day, sometimes nothing because if the colour of the wall was not how he imagined it, he would be ripping the wall down and sit all day. It's really great to work with a person like that, he's crazy actually! *(laughs)* When we were assistants, we were like, 'What is he doing?' But I have to say that *Saawariya* was the film that I loved the most because what happens is, as assistants, you end up mostly running around and doing what you're asked. On *Saawariya*, we would light up and have the whole day to sit and look around at what we've done. That way, it was a great learning experience. See, there's no set formula that works. We put in so much in *Saawariya* and *Saawariya* didn't work. Right after, I did *Ghajini* [A. R. Murugadoss, 2008] and there were no attention to details. The film is visually strong, but you'll see hair flying, paper on the road, it's not like a perfect world film. But it worked for the film and it was a huge hit. We finished *Saawariya* and three days later, we were shooting *Ghajini*. When the heroine's hair would come on her face, it would bother me. Because we were just on a film where if there was a strand loose, we'll do fifty retakes. So I'd love to work with Sanjay Leela Bhansali because of his precision. He gives everyone the scope to improve their work.

Do you have special techniques that you use to make this fantasy world so beautiful?

The colours that we use, the costumes and locations. It is just that. You've probably not seen that in world cinema or Hollywood films, because they work with a lot of muted colours, browns, blacks and whites, which they incorporate in their sets and costumes. In commercial cinema, all departments work independently, so the costume person will put the maximum colours, the art director too. So eventually, when these two things come together, whichever way you may light up, the colours are going to pop—unless you've decided on a look, such as *Saawariya*. There was a joke that it was a blue film, because everything was blue in that film. There were only blues, blacks and whites in that film. But that was intentional. There are very few films which work in colour tones that would not look like any other film you watch. *Black* is all black and white. Blue also, but the sets were not blue, so it doesn't look like a blue film. If you take two commercial films, you won't be able to tell one from the other, which is not such a good thing, but that's how it is—and it is the reason why they all look nice, colourful and glossy. It's not intentional, it's just how the industry functions.

What about the sets? Were most of the movies you worked on made in studios?

As an assistant, most of the movies I worked on were made in studios. As a DOP, all films were shot in real locations. In terms of control, being on set is more interesting. Like I said, I like the whole process of starting from scratch and having the film looking exactly the way I want it to look. When you're shooting outdoors, you're directed by how the sun is going to move through the day. And unless you're working with a director like Sanjay Leela Bhansali—who will say if he wants backlight in this entire scene with this building, we will shoot it over five days—you have to finish a one-page scene in a day and the sun moves from one direction to another through the day. The audience might not see that difference, because you've colour-corrected and you made it match, but there's an obvious difference. Still, I enjoy the thrill of being on a real location, having to do everything in a stipulated time. When we shot *Yamla Pagla Deewana*, it was in the worst weather conditions in London. It was transitioning from autumn right into winter. So we had longish days when we started and then by the time we were on the last month of our shoot, we would be back by four. When we shot the climax of the film, we started on a sunny day, the next day it was cloudy, the day after it was foggy and then it rained. One day, we stopped the shoot but the producer said, 'You can't do this, let's think of a way.' So in the middle of the climax, suddenly Sunny Deol shouts and there's lightening and then, it's all fog and rain. When you put it together, nobody can tell what happened but there are limitations on a real location. On a set, everything will be perfect for the scene whenever the actor moves. On real location, I may sometimes be on the thirteenth floor and won't be able to get light from the outside. You need to work your way around.

Is commercial cinema being mostly shot on real locations now?

It's really what the script demands. What they do is they shoot in real locations and then, they do songs on sets.

Why are there more people on a Bollywood set?

Obviously, we have more manpower here because it's cheaper. We have no patience on our sets. If I want something done, I want it done now. So what one guy would do in five minutes, two guys will do in three minutes, simply because it's physical labour. When we go for outdoor shoots, we'd probably take two guys from India, hire four guys there, whichever part in the world we are in. So, you have six guys on set—I am just talking about my department, it differs in every department. As opposed to that, I have twelve in India. In India, I want my job done in three months. When I am there, since we are talking about fewer guys, I am also giving them more time, so producers will say, 'When you are in the United States, you shoot with six guys, why do you want twelve guys here now?' They don't understand that everyone's patience level[s] go down when you are in India. When we shoot with the Jimmy Jib, we have four guys: there's a Jimmy Jib operator, there's the guy who operates the booth, there's the guy on the trolley and there's an assistant who will run around. When we went to the United States, we had only one guy at the Jimmy Jib. But it didn't mean he was alone. All our guys were helping him set up, because we wanted it to be done in record time. Otherwise, you need to plan so well that you have to tell him the shot in the morning for him to lay out the tracks and set up his camera. That's not how we function. Which is why we have more people on sets: we don't have the patience to give every department time to do their work. Six guys can light up a set in three days. We have twelve hours here. We can equate it with the number of people.

What are the work schedules?

Way before I came to the industry, actors chose not to work on Sundays. Now, because actors are doing so much, they are ready to shoot whenever you call them to shoot because they have to distribute their time between two films a day or between ads and films—one of the reasons we say that the industry is actor-dominated. Now, there are no certain days off. I understand sometimes you have to work on Sundays because you have to shoot in an office location which you will only get on a Sunday. Otherwise I hate that. We have unions, and we are not supposed to work over twelve hours but nobody follows that. If a company gives out its equipment, they've given it for the day—from the time that you start the shoot until the time you finish it. One day doesn't mean twelve hours per equipment. It means twelve hours for the lighting guys, the art crew. Most Heads of Departments are on a contract basis. Their number of hours doesn't matter. But their crews, like my assistants, will charge for twelve hours a day. So if we extend the days of shoot, it's equal to an extra day they would have to pay for the equipment. Hence it's easier for the studio to pay overtime to people than to have one full extra day of shoot. But even if they are paid overtime, they can't go over three or four hours, and sometimes, you'll have someone from the lighting department who has made a call—you won't know who's done it—and somebody from the lighting union will be there to say it's time to pack up. On bigger films which are actor-dominated, if the actor says, 'I won't shoot beyond twelve hours', you don't shoot beyond twelve hours.

What are the qualities of Indian cinema? Its flaws?

The worst is that all departments function on their own, mostly because people are working back-to-back. I finish a project and I have a twenty-day transition before the new project. I have time to do my homework only and not to coordinate with the art department or the costume designer who's doing two other films. That I find unfortunate. I would any day exchange that for having a planned shoot.

Where do you see yourself in a few years?

Being able to choose what I want to do, space it out, give enough time to do justice to every project that I take. If I ever go abroad, I don't want to do what we call B-grade films here, something that I wouldn't do here, just for the heck of it.

THE YOUNG ACTRESSES OF HINDI CINEMA

KALKI KOECHLIN
Actress

In Indian mythology, Kalki is the last avatar of Vishnu—and mostly, a masculine name. As far as the name 'Koechlin' goes, it's perfectly French and has a few celebrities attached to it. The mystery of Kalki Koechlin is still not unveiled: born to French parents who moved to India in the 1970s to a place near Pondicherry; a thick English accent when she speaks French; perfect Hindi with a touch of musicality to it; an ex-husband who loves France—filmmaker Anurag Kashyap—and an atypical body, European for sure, but on which the saree fits like a glove.

Kalki, thirty-seven, has succeeded where only the Australian actress Fearless Nadia had (and that too, in the 1930s): if her white skin was definitely a plus in an extremely colour-conscious industry (to the point of racism), her strong French features were a definite no-no in an industry where European girls are only asked to look pretty and dance well behind the Indian heroine. But perseverance, luck, and admittedly, a great dose of talent slowly raised Kalki to stardom. She can now be seen everywhere: shooting relentlessly (as supporting cast or lead role, she's not picky as long as the movie engages her), going back to theatre, her first love, as soon as she gets free time, writing and directing plays, walking the ramp in fashion shows, she even finds time for the causes she believes in. A strong feminist, she has participated in multiple campaigns to denounce the violence against women in Indian society.

Kalki says she is Indian, but she is actually undefinable, so multicultural that you couldn't confine her to a category: as an actress, she is renowned for her dramatic roles in artistic cinema since her noteworthy performance as a juvenile prostitute in *Dev-D* [Anurag Kashyap, 2009]. She got accolades (and a National Award) for her role as a handicapped girl in *Margarita with a Straw* [Shonali Bose, 2014], and opposite Naseeruddin Shah in *Waiting* [Anu Menon, 2015], but she also likes to move in and out of Bollywood—and not only for money. She does not have that boring starry air, or the debutante's insecurity. When she welcomed me into her modest home in Versova, she was wearing shorts and already on a first name basis with me—all the while laughing at herself with endearing honesty. It's impossible not to like her.

You were part of *Yeh Jawaani Hai Deewani* [Ayan Mukherjee, 2013], a Bollywood film, with big stars [Ranbir Kapoor, Deepika Padukone]. What do you like about this genre?

I always try to break the category in which I am included. If you start your career with a commercial film, you become a heroine, a Bollywood actress; if you start with 'artistic cinema', an auteur film, you're stuck in that. Trying to twist the stereotype is something I do constantly, something that is very important to me. Also, as an actress, I've acted in many films which are very serious, very dark, and it feels good to be in a comedy where my part is very funny.

Can you tell us more about this part?

I am playing the best friend of two boys, Ranbir Kapoor, the hero and Aditya Roy Kapoor, his friend. My character is a tomboy. She acts like boys, she swears a lot, she goes on trips with them, drinks, smokes. She is one of those crazy girls. The first part is a flashback into their past and the second part happens ten years later, when they've grown up. My character is more feminine, she's calmer and she's getting married. It's for her wedding that everybody gets back together again.

Are you still the foreigner in that film, the white girl?

No! It's funny because I look completely white in the film. I have blond hair, they didn't even colour my hair. Producers said, 'It's okay, we won't explain [why she has white skin]', because I think today, people know that I am born here, that I was brought up here. They accept that I am Indian, even if I don't look Indian. So, no, in that film, they didn't mention where I come from or whatever. I am just a 'Bombay girl'. Same in *Zindagi Na Milegi Dobara* [Zoya Akhtar, 2011].

How would you explain that? Is it only because people know you, because they know you speak Indian languages?

I think so, yes. At the beginning, nobody knew who I was. And in *Dev-D* [Anurag Kashyap, 2009], the part was that of a foreigner. I was often asked where I came from, if I liked India, spicy food. Every time, I had to explain that I was born and brought up here, that I know the language. I think that Bollywood, especially commercial cinema, accepts me as an Indian, because at the end it's unrealistic cinema. Nothing needs to be real. On the other hand, in small films that I do, auteur films, [scriptwriters] explain my origin: sometimes my character is half Indian, sometimes she's completely foreign.

Do you think being white prevents you from getting roles?

I shot an auteur film on a girl who has cerebral palsy [*Margarita with a Straw*, Shonali Bose, 2015], a handicap that prevents your motor capacities from working properly. It's a film where I am Indian, where my parents are Indian. I was apprehensive, I used to say to the director, 'But how will you make me look Indian, it's difficult!' She told me not to worry, that there are a lot of Punjabis who can be very fair skinned and that with dark hair, everything will be fine. They just coloured my hair. It's really an auteur film for festivals, a serious film, there are no songs. It's the first time that in a serious film, I am seen as an Indian.

So the director didn't mind it, but you did. Do you feel Indian?

I am very conscious that physically, I look French. But inside, I feel completely French. Err, Indian! Not French at all. *(laughs)* I always say, 'My skin is white, my heart is brown.'

Let's go back to the beginning of your career, before *Dev-D*. You've done theatre before movies. You studied in London.

Yes, I did theatre at school, but it's really when I went to study in London that I took it up seriously. At eighteen, I went to study at Goldsmiths, which is an arts college. I studied theatre and it's there that I realized that I was Indian, that the Western culture was not mine. I was missing India and my family. I had stories to tell which were very Indian, culturally different in one way or the other. One of our classes was a scriptwriting one. I wrote a story that they loved, very Indian, that took place in a village of South India. That's when I understood that it was this culture that inspired me. Funny that this realization came in London.

How do you explain that you feel so Indian while your parents are French?

I went to France twice in my childhood, once at nine, once at fifteen. At nine, it was the first time I was leaving India. I was a real jungle girl. I had no shoes, I would climb trees, and my parents, especially my mother, were very interested in Indian culture. My mother is an intellectual, she has written a lot of articles and she used to teach at the French school in Pondicherry. She always made me read Indian philosophy, on Hinduism. I grew up with Indians. I was in an international school but it was not the French school. Of course, because of my parents, I also have a French culture, I saw a lot of French films while growing up, I speak French and my mother taught me French cooking. But around me, everything else was Indian; I grew up going to the temple instead of going to church. I went to Hindu weddings and we would dance to Bollywood songs. It was very different, growing up like this. It was not an expat context at all, in which I would have been surrounded by expats and lived like in Europe, but in a sunny environment.

How does it feel though, being white in a country where that automatically means you are different?

It's very frustrating, but it's something against which I will have to fight my whole life. Indians will always believe that I am not from here and I will always have to explain it. At the same time, when I go to France, I don't feel French enough. I feel like a mix of everything, but at the same time, it gives me a kind of freedom, because I have more choices. I speak several languages, I can go where I want and I feel at ease in England, in France. Being exposed to all those cultures opened a lot of doors for me.

While in London, you never thought of working in Western theatre or cinema?

No, I wanted to come back. I worked with a company called The Theatre Relativity and I went to Scotland for the French Festival. I toured England with several plays. I loved the experience and I grew up a lot because I was alone. I had to sustain myself through acting—it was not easy—but I had always planned to come back and after four years in London, I did, in 2006.

Did you come back to India to pursue a career in acting?

Yes, but I was not thinking of Bollywood. I never dreamed of Bollywood. I am quite realistic and I thought that with my fair skin, I couldn't possibly consider it as a serious career option. But I was passionate about theatre. I moved to Bombay almost immediately and I started doing theatre with The Company Theatre. I acted in a play called *Casanova*, then in *Hair*. But I had to earn money and that's when I started auditioning. I gave my portfolio to a lot of production companies. I went to Aram Nagar for auditions almost every week to find an ad.

So now you were thinking about a career in Bollywood?

Yes. I first went to Bangalore when I came back from London and I stayed for six months with my brother. Then I decided that if I really wanted to pursue an artistic career, I had to live in Bombay, because not much was happening in Bangalore. I found a flat with a friend in Bandra and was auditioning for absolutely anything, just so I could pay my rent every week because Bombay is an expensive city! I got a few small ads, which obviously resurfaced when I was more famous. Fortunately, nothing really embarrassing. *(laughs)* I also auditioned for films, but it was always for parts of white women in bikinis or dancers—and I am not a dancer. Also, it didn't interest me because I had substantial parts in theatre, so I didn't want anything ordinary. My only appearance was in *Laaga Chunari Mein Daag* [Pradeep Sarkar, 2007], where you can see me for two minutes. Apart from that, there really wasn't anything until *Dev-D,* for which they had been looking for a Chandramukhi for a long time.

Were they looking for a white woman for that part?

No, they changed the part for me. They were open to it. The producer, UTV, was only particular about wanting someone hot and new, someone they could sell. When I went to the audition, Anurag [Kashyap] wasn't there and I was briefed by the casting directors, Gautam Kishanchandani and Vasan Bala, who is now a filmmaker. They gave me the Hindi script and I said, 'My Hindi is really bad, I can't do this part, sorry.' Then they gave me the English script. I played the English part and I left. Twenty minutes later, I got a call from Anurag who said, 'Oh, you can act? I just saw your screen test, come back.' So I came back. In fact, he had seen my portfolio filled with sexy photos in a bikini and he rejected it saying, 'Again, some idiot of a model, I want an actress for this role.' The casting directors didn't tell him that they were meeting me, since UTV had said I was sexy and that they had to give me a chance! They only showed my audition to Anurag later. In short, Anurag told me to learn Hindi and work on my accent. He gave me two months. One of my theatre friends taught me Hindi during those two months; then, I gave another audition after which I got the part. That's when Anurag decided to give my character a backstory with a French-Canadian mother and an Indian father.

Did you know *Devdas*? And Anurag Kashyap? Did you want to get that part?

I didn't know Anurag at all. After meeting him, I came back home, I Googled him and then I bought *Black Friday* and his other films. I had only seen one *Devdas*, Sanjay Leela Bhansali's [2002]. Everybody knows Devdas' story in India, but Anurag specifically told me not to do any research and not to copy the Chandramukhis of the past, because he wanted something different. So I didn't work on it. I only worked on my Hindi. It worked for the film, because I am really supposed to be an ingénue that doesn't know what is happening and is suddenly entering a new world without seeing it as a tragedy, but just as a new event in her life.

Dev-D is very different from the other adaptations of *Devdas* and in a way, more respectful of the book: more importance is given to Chandramukhi than Paro, Devdas is shown as a selfish loser. Did Anurag present the film like that to you?

Not when we shot the film, not at all. Anurag, today even, doesn't tell his actors anything ever. He even likes it when actors don't know the script and only know their lines. It's his way of working. He doesn't explain anything to me either. Of course when I saw the film, I really liked what he did, but we didn't plan or talk about it.

So for your very first role, the one that gave you a name in the industry, you didn't prepare anything, you went with your instinct.

Exactly, there was a lot of improvisation: the sex talk for instance, in English, in Tamil, in French. He said, 'Oh, it's a good idea, since you speak all those languages.' It was a weird process. I didn't know anything about camera angles, close-ups, establishing shots; to me, all takes were the best takes. It was a good thing, because I acted in a very honest way. When you become more conscious of the camera, you learn to manipulate it, for instance give more of yourself when it's a close-up.

Since you came from theatre and you were not interested in Bollywood, did cinema suddenly click for you with *Dev-D*? After the film, you didn't shoot for a year, a year and a half, you went back to theatre.

I adore theatre and I feel it's very important to come back to it regularly. For me, it's where an actor works on his muscles. The public's presence is very important and cannot be worked on elsewhere. But at the same time, I have no confidence in theatre's future in India. There aren't many people who experiment and above all, there's no support. So everyone who works in theatre has another job, or is very rich. I just wrote a play that I would like to put on this year or next year. But at the same time, I really like what is happening in cinema and I don't want this to stop either. Of course, there are films that I do for the money, such as *Yeh Jawaani Hai Deewani*, and it's more fun and joyful. There are films that I can't resist, on which I am paid almost nothing, such as the film I just did on cerebral palsy. When does a woman have the opportunity, especially here, to work on such a film in her career?

Were there other films that you just couldn't resist?

Above all, there are directors that I really want to work with. One of those directors was Dibakar [Banerjee]. I really liked his films so I could only say yes to *Shanghai* [Dibakar Banerjee, 2012], even before reading the script. He told me, 'Do you want...' and I said 'Yes!' As a script, I was very excited by *Shaitan* [Bejoy Nambiar, 2011]. I was doing *Yellow Boots* [*That Girl in Yellow Boots*, Anurag Kashyap, 2010] grudgingly.

Still, you co-wrote the script with Anurag.

Yes. Anurag told me the story and I told him that it was a terribly depressing, horrific story. He said, 'No, we'll do it, anyway you don't have anything to do, you're jobless.' *(laughs)* Everything started as a fight between us and then I told him, 'Ok, if I write it, I will make it something more interesting.' I wrote a very different version, with a happy ending and a cute disclosure at the end, but he said, 'No, no, it can't be like that, else people will not be shocked, it has to be disturbing.' It was a very difficult film for me, because I had a hard time incarnating a person who goes through all that and who's always depressed, tough and insensitive. For me, you have to balance hardness with comedy. Human beings need to have feelings, a little bit of happiness.

When we hear that, we feel like Anurag is more French than you are! And you are more of a Bollywood person.

Absolutely. At the same time, a French film like *Rust and Bone* is very serious, dark even, but there is a lot of comedy in the film. I am not saying either that there should always be singing and dancing! *(laughs)*

No, it would be a little weird in Audiard's film.

In *Wasseypur* [*Gangs of Wasseypur*, Anurag Kashyap, 2012]—I think Anurag discovered it a little later—there is a lot of humour, but it's a very dark story.

How did the writing of the *Yellow Boots*' script go?

Anurag had read a few articles, one about an Indian who had an incestuous relationship with his daughter. The other one talked about this priest who had advised a father to sleep with his daughter—some tantric thing. So he collected articles on incest. It's true that incest is a taboo in India. Every girl I know has been sexually abused in one way or the other. Each of them. It was something that should be debated and that was never really debated on screen. I started writing a script as if it was a play, because I didn't know how to write a movie. I wrote a theatre script. There were several people, there was lots of drama, it was only dialogue, no action. Anurag read it and said, 'You have to cut this, and this, and this … Cut, cut, cut' *(laughs)* and at the end it was boneless, as if taking the bones from a fish.

Does the final film look like what you wrote at the beginning?

Yes, a little. Dialogues with the gangster, with his friend, everything comes from what I have written. The ending was completely different, mine was a little Bollywood; the heroine was able to stop her boyfriend before he kills her father and they leave together. Anurag didn't like that. He especially added a lot of action. For instance, the scene with the gangster at the dockyard and the hand cut, obviously, that was Anurag. *(laughs)*

So after *Dev-D*, you didn't work again immediately. Making your first film with Anurag put you in a certain category.

Yes. I had some script offers, but they were all in the same genre. They thought, 'Oh, she can play a prostitute, so we'll give her the role of a prostitute.'

Was it different after *That Girl in Yellow Boots*?

At the same time as *Yellow Boots*, I did the film *Emotional Atyachar* [Akshay Shere, 2010] that nobody saw, which took place in Goa. It was a small film with very few actors, but a funny film about a burglary in a casino. Unfortunately, it didn't work well. After that, there was *Zindagi…*, *Shaitan* and *My Friend Pinto* [Raaghav Dhar, 2010]. *Shaitan* was again very dark. It was about a lost teenager, while my character in *Zindagi…* was a crazy bitch and in *My Friend Pinto*, I was an innocent and gullible heroine. As an actress, I want to be able to play everything, a horror film, an action film, play a serial killer, or a heroine like in *Gone with the Wind*. Explore everything!

But you don't work in an industry that is diverse enough to offer such roles.

I have no choice. I am from here and I do what I can with that.

Couldn't you create your own parts, since you already wrote a script?

I found it very difficult in *Yellow Boots* to write for myself and then act, because I would interrupt myself all the time when I was acting: 'Oh no, I want to change this' and Anurag would say, 'Stop, you're not the scriptwriter anymore. Shut up and listen to me, the director.' I think I don't have enough confidence in my writing. In the future, maybe I will write scripts for myself, but even the play I just wrote is for other people. Now I am starting to get enough opportunities in films. It seems like people were waiting for someone to play weird parts! *(laughs)* A girl with cerebral palsy, nobody wants it, because you have to forget about make-up or a sexy look. It's also a very daring script because you can see her explore her sexuality; yet, you never associate handicap and sexuality. Those are things that excite me. For the time being, I won't complain. Of course there are very bad scripts that I say no to and in 2013, I didn't work again for nine months because I didn't get any offers and that's when I wrote this play. Theatre helps me keep a sound mind.

Anurag was telling me that you are a hyperactive person and that you've always been scared of the future. Are you still in that state of mind? Because now, you've become quite well known in the industry.

I am well known, but even when you create a reputation for being different, you're still being stereotyped. First, people thought I could do crazy and dark parts, then that I was at ease with comedy and right now, I am limited to comedy. Whatever you do, only your last film counts. This is frustrating for me. But it happens to Anurag too. When he did *Dev-D*, everyone told him, 'Make *Dev-D 2*' because *Dev-D* worked so well. But he said that he wanted to do something different. I don't really think about box-office when I do a film, I think about the story and whether I can do something interesting with it.

Since you don't want to be the next Katrina Kaif, one would imagine you have more choices as there has been a lot happening in Indian cinema these last few years.

Yes, in that sense, I came to Bollywood at a very good time. In the 1990s, nothing would have happened for me. There are many interesting things today. Problem is, for instance, that I already said yes to five scripts and none of them has money. Those are very beautiful stories but I don't know if someone will ever make them. I am not in a position of power where I can say, 'Yes, I will bring you a producer.' It's still a fight in that sense. And it's true that I always need to do something. Right now, I am writing another play, a play on Tagore. There's always something happening in my life.

Don't you want to do Tamil cinema, since that's where you come from?

I never knew how to force things, make contacts. I can't go to parties, speak to people, say that I want to work with them. If it happens naturally, I will be very happy. I already received some Tamil scripts, but one of them doesn't have money *(laughs)* and I didn't like the others.

As an actress, what is the difference between Anurag's set and a Bollywood film's set?

At first, I despised Bollywood a little, like, 'those are not actors, those are models who would do anything for money.' Then I worked on *Zindagi* and Zoya [Akhtar] wasn't this type of director; I've read more things for her than for any other director that I worked with. It's true that Bollywood has more money and some pomposity in their cinema, and then the songs, the music, etc. But as an actor's director, it was important for Zoya to make me understand the character and not stereotype her. 'You know, it's a Bombay girl who is a little harsh, but I don't want her to be annoying. Make sure she's human, find this balance' and it was nice to work like this. It seems to me that in a commercial film, they have a better idea of what they want; the way you have to play is more 'noisy' but at the same time, there's a specific sense of rhythm and tempo. It's a challenge to make your character believable, realistic, like in *Yeh Jawaani Hai Deewani*, where I shout like a crazy person *(she shouts a line in Hindi, 'Teri Ma ki!')*. It's a challenge that I love. It is very different from working with Dibakar, with whom we never read the script, but with whom we would do a lot of workshops around the characters, where was she before, what did she do before, how did she come here, etc. It was another way of exploring. Anurag doesn't like to say anything, but he is very spontaneous, so he can change everything at the last minute. You have to be ready for this. He can say, 'Say I love you like I hate you' or 'You know what, instead of saying goodbye, say do you want vegetables?' *(laughs)* He does strange things last minute. He's like that, you need to be prepared.

As an actress, what do you like? To improvise or for someone to explain the role to you?

What I like is the research and preparation part before shooting or before going on stage. I love harassing my directors, 'Give me books to read, research, movies to watch.' I like observing people. For instance, when I did *Zindagi Na Milegi Dobara*, I went to a lot of rich people's parties. For the film on cerebral palsy, I lived with a friend who has had this handicap for six months. I spent all my time with her. She works in a center for disabled people and I learned so much about people like her; the way they think, the way they feel, how they act in public. I got drunk with her and I looked at how people would react—because here, people stare at disabled people, they have no shame. I told her, 'I have to watch you for my part.' And she was very happy that someone would make a film on this problem.

You can't like working with Anurag too much, then!

(laughs) Even if my director tells me not to prepare anything, I do it. For *Dev-D*, he didn't know that I was watching films on prostitutes, and I read articles on the Delhi MMS scandal. I can't help doing research.

Did it become a problem, working with him while being married?

Everything I did became attached to Anurag. Everybody said that he wrote my scripts, that he gave me work in Bollywood, which frustrated me. Because he's been here for fifteen years and I've only been here for a few years, it would be very easy and obvious to seek his advice all the time. But I know I'll learn better from my own mistakes. I consciously decided to work with other people, because work started to come from outside. But it doesn't mean that we won't work together anymore. If there's a film where he needs someone like me, I'll be ready. But I can't fit in a film like *Wasseypur*, it's just logic. Also I think we have done enough dark films, so I told him, 'Next time we work together, let's do a comedy for a change, no?' *(laughs)*

Is it something he also wants?

For the moment, no, but we'll see. I'd love to make a Charlie Chaplin type of a comedy. If I write a script or if we have a story that we are interested in. It has to come naturally.

But Anurag, Dibakar, you, Abhay Deol, it's a small world that always work together, don't you think?

Yes, that's why there are comments on the fact that I don't work with Anurag. Everyone who's around Anurag now says, 'She doesn't want to work with people around Anurag.' But this is not true! When I used to work with Dibakar, everyone would say, 'That's because he's friends with Anurag, that's why she got the part.'

To come back to your Bollywood experience, do you like this song-and-dance formula? You said you didn't like dancing too much.

I am the worst dancer in the world. It's a curse, really! God is laughing from above, 'I'll throw you in the middle of Bollywood even though you really can't dance!' For *Yeh Jawaani Hai Deewani*, I had to dance. It was horrible! They gave us only one day of rehearsal before shooting because the song was not ready and those two [Ranbir Kapoor and Deepika Padukone], they dance in their sleep, they understand right away. I am more like, 'What's the first step? Right, okay, got the first step, what are the next eight?' *(laughs)* I am so bad. But it is part of what I do here, so I have to work on it. In this film, I was not prepared and I had told my director Ayan [Mukherjee] several times, 'Please, give me time, I need time', but he wouldn't listen and I dance in a funny way. Luckily, it goes along with my character, because she's a tomboy, she listens to Jim Morrison.

So dancing to Bollywood music can't really be her thing.

No. I am going to do a movie in which I have to dance again and I had a serious conversation with my director, 'I won't sign the contract if I don't have five days of rehearsals for each dance, each song.'

You're not taking any dance classes?

In the past, no, because I never really needed to dance and at present, I don't have the time. But there are so many different dances. I don't know what Bollywood dance is. It's a mix of everything. People around me tell me that you only need some experience. When Katrina [Kaif] started, she didn't know how to dance. I would need to take classes, but it's not my priority since I am not going to make many films where I'll have to dance.

Who knows? You're shooting more and more for Bollywood.

Yeh Jawaani Hai Deewani was a really commercial movie, but *Zindagi* was not one hundred per cent commercial. There was a nice structure, a nice story, some kind of realism. I will always choose this path if I choose a commercial film. I need a little bit of reality. When you see *Wake Up Sid* [Ayan Mukherjee, 2009], you realize the characters had flesh, their presence was justified.

Are there any directors that you would like to work with but haven't approached you yet?

Vishal Bhardwaj. He was the producer on a film that I worked on, *Ek Thi Daayan* [Kannan Iyer, 2013]. He also wrote the script. I love his movies. Vikram[aditya Motwane], also. He's part of the group and I would like to work with him. In the South, there's Gautham Menon whom I really like. I grew up watching his films. Now he's turned to commercial industry but he made art films.

The career span of Indian actresses is not very long. Aren't you afraid of that?

I think that the films that I make anyway have nothing glamorous about them. Even when it's a commercial film, I always play the crazy, cool, different kind of girl. I don't know what is going to happen, maybe I'll completely stop, maybe I'll only do theatre. I also dream of joining a company called Complicité, in a few years. You never know what's going to happen in your life. I am not scared, because

I know I will continue to create in some way or the other. If I am not acting, I'll be writing. But I would like to act until I am an old lady, like Jeanne Moreau.

Have you ever been contacted by foreign directors and producers?

Journalists, yes, but no directors. I'd like that, but it has to come naturally. I won't act in any French film and then also, I have this little funny accent when I speak French.

It's true that your little accent is quite strange!

I learned French here, in India. I speak French with a Tamil accent. *(laughs)*

RICHA CHADHA
Actress

She was between a gym session and a shoot. Richa Chadha, thirty-two, met me on a Sunday for lunch in a Versova café, next to her home. She was wearing a very simple dress and a hat, and immediately apologized for this get-up, as if as an actress, she always has to look her best—even when I promised a very casual conversation. Still, she brightened the room with sex-appeal and confidence.

She agreed to the interview because of her affection for Dibakar Banerjee, her 'mentor', who recommended her as I was looking for young actresses doing different work than just 'coming-of-age' films or sugar-coated love stories. When I met Richa, she had just started to be highly sought-after, be it in short films, TV series or feature films. In 2017, she had no less than five releases. Richa doesn't come from a film family, she's not a model; which already makes her stand apart in the Hindi industry. She's also a so-called 'serious' actress who started her career with the secondary part of a lost girl in *Oye Lucky! Lucky Oye!* and made sure having less time on screen didn't mean she would go unnoticed. After *Gangs of Wasseypur*, where she played the dominated wife of a gangster who took care of the household with overflowing energy as strongly as a Mother India would, she was seen in the critically-acclaimed indie film *Masaan* [Neeraj Ghaywan, 2015] where she gets blackmailed by the police for having casual sex with her boyfriend, and as serial killer Charles Sobhraj's girlfriend in *Main aur Charles* [Prawaal Raman, 2015].

Richa Chadha brings a freshness to the Indian film industry that was much needed. As she chose not to dive into mainstream cinema (her only true commercial role was in Sanjay Leela Bhansali's *Ram-Leela* in 2014), she's also very vocal about the Hindi industry not being open to all types of bodies and skins (especially to actresses who look too Indian, read 'dark') and to the incredible pressure and shaming women have to face to be accepted as heroines. Richa would like to be known as someone who refuses compromises. Good for us, as her *femme fatale* presence gives a new life to the image of Indian woman on screen.

You studied history. Would you say that you come from a family that didn't want you to be an actress?

No, I chose to study history because I had to graduate in some subject before I even considered studying acting full time. So I chose the subject that I liked obviously. I kept my options open, whether I wanted to study acting or something else, because in India it's not a prerequisite in our film industry to learn acting to be an actor. I was already working with theatre companies while I was in college and I think that offered me a lot of hands-on experience. I wouldn't say my family didn't want me to be an actor—they always knew I was inclined that way, towards performing arts in any case—but after I graduated from college, they were apprehensive. It's not very easy for somebody from the outside to make it or to even try to do their own thing. Despite the fact that I came from a regular family with a middle-class upbringing and academic parents, I still had a lot of reservations and I knew I wasn't just going to do anything. It was more fear than hesitation. That said, I looked at the acting courses to learn acting professionally, but I thought that they would not help me.

Why is that?

First of all—this is sort of bitching on government institutions—they have deteriorated in their standards and in their professionalism. I could see alumni from those places, the National Institute, the Film Institute—which are government sponsored institutes—were not getting a lot of work, or that they were not necessarily very good.

I felt that if I go there, there is no guarantee that I am going to come out shining and having learnt something. At that point, I just don't think I was ready to be in one place and then wait and learn. The way that things are taught are sort of dated and I didn't want that. The National School of Drama is very good, but I didn't want to do drama, I wanted to do film. That's a distinction one needs to make, because a drama student always tends to cater to the medium of theatre, as opposed to film. So I went to work with somebody whom I respected, Barry John. I worked a little bit with him at his school in Delhi when I was in college and after moving to Bombay too. It is here that, one of Dibakar [Banerjee]'s assistant directors spotted me and asked me to audition for his film. But even after doing *Oye Lucky!* I kept doing theatre workshops every few months to keep my zone alive, to learn, to feel something. There are organizations in Bombay that are really good for professional actors. They do a week or ten days long workshops and they get faculty from all over. I remember they had people from France, from Japan, from Korea, from the south of India, Kerala, coming and teaching us very specific things. That really helped me a lot.

Then why choose films over theatre?

I feel like films have a larger reach and of course there's glamour, money, and fame associated with cinema. If I really had something to say and I wanted to get my point across, there are so many more people I can reach this way. I was kind of disillusioned with the theatre scene. The theatre scene in Bombay, Delhi and Bangalore, the three metros, is very different. People are working hard and they're putting out productions. But the rest of the country is in another time zone and people don't really go out and watch theatre as much. Unless it's an exception—there used to be a man, who passed away recently; he had a residential theatre group in a village that performed, travelled and was part of a community. When you do something like that and you dedicate your life to that, there's a lot more people that you can reach, but honestly not when you're doing plays in one city, then another city. So I felt like cinema had a larger reach. Eventually, I would like to say something with the work that I do. Make a change, or bring a change—a change in the world of arts is also a change that will influence life in one way or the other.

When did the desire to become an actress come to you?

Very early. I was about four or five. One of the first things I remember doing when I could walk is imitating my father, putting a pillow on my belly, looking up and walking like a man. According to me, the world is divided into two kinds of people; it's a very broad category, but there are actors and there are non-actors. Anybody in front of the camera or who is at-ease with people is in the actors' category, everybody else is in the non-actors' category. This waiter, who deals with a lot of people, could be in the actors' category, a politician too. You are behind the camera, so it's the non-actors' category.

Did you watch many movies as a child?

My parents used to watch movies, but not as much as I did. My movie watching stopped at an early age also. Till date, I don't think I watch many movies. But I think a lot, I read. It gives me more imagination. One of my agendas this year is to watch many more movies just to study the craft, get to know it a little bit.

You were a model for a short time. In Bollywood, models often become actresses.

The industry becomes lazy. It looks for people who are certified as good-looking people, because it's a visual medium. Models can't necessarily act. I never wanted to model; I just wanted to know how it feels to be a model, to be in front of a camera, lose inhibitions. You're actually talking to the camera. I started modelling really early and I did it very briefly because it was dull according to me. But it taught me some basic stuff, like how to suddenly get a twinkle in the eye. Because actors are widely photographed, more than models, in this country.

When *Oye Lucky!* happened, you were also auditioning for *Dev-D* [Anurag Kashyap, 2008].

Yes, I had just started and moved to Bombay. I was getting a handle on the city, the rickshaws and living on my own for the first time, trying to understand how to make my own breakfast, manage my own finances. At that time *Oye Lucky*'s auditions were happening and I just went because somebody had spotted me at that play. I was really quite hopeful. I went and I did it, but then I didn't hear from them for like three months. I didn't know they were internally squabbling over casting me as opposed to somebody more established.

Wasn't it a huge disappointment not to do *Dev-D*?

It was a huge disappointment actually because I didn't know *Oye Lucky* was around the corner. And in any case, the part in *Dev-D*, in terms of screen time, was longer and had more to do with the plot, but in retrospect I have no regrets.

Tell us about your part in *Oye Lucky*.

It was tough and I got a lot of acclaim for it. Honestly when I did it, I was too naive, too young to let anything affect me, but genuinely I didn't find it that difficult to do, because I had grown up in that milieu in Delhi. I had seen girls like that, who talk like that, with that accent, with those aspirations. I was recently looking at my older notes that I had made for that character: one of the key things was no matter what she does, that character is very fiery, but there is an undercurrent or flavour of vulnerability in her, so she is feminine, needy, wanting that love from a man. I had a lot of fun punchlines and it could have gone to caricature, which is why I kept that undercurrent.

Did you have a lot of conversations with Dibakar on that character or were you free to make it your own?

I was so new that I only met Dibakar once or twice before we started filming. I didn't know anything, I didn't know anyone, I didn't know how the industry functions and by that regard, I think I got a lot of respect from him, from his crew, from his cast. They really made me feel at ease. I was twenty or twenty-one. I was fresh out of college, I was always afraid of offending somebody, because I was working with Hindi film veterans. There was one of the biggest film stars, Abhay Deol, there was Paresh Rawal who I had been seeing since I was a kid and there was this sort of new pin-up of the time. Dibakar let me be, but he guided what developed. Even though I feel at that time I was not smart enough to consciously do it, it just happened because subconsciously, I understood the person behind the character's words.

Do you remember how it felt during the first day of the shoot?
I was [at] first very stressed with the number of people. Six or eight months prior to *Oye Lucky*, I was warming up with theatre, I was in that spirit, in that zone. I found it really difficult to stay in one place and emote, because you have to have a mark, because in film you have to cater to the needs of the camera, and the director, and the technicalities. In theatre, you have a zone of light. You can move in and out of that and the zone of light is big, the movements are big, whereas in film you've got to stay here, no matter what you feel. I was constantly distracted with that person here placing a mic, or somebody touching my hair.

How does it feel now?
I think I've become immune to it. In the middle of that activity, you have to find that centre of sanity and peace, because you have to have a great amount of concentration to be an actor. People think it's easy; at least in India, the conception is if you can't do anything else, just become an actor. It's not like that, it's multitasking at another level. You have to remember you can't move, otherwise the camera loses you or you fall out of light; you can't turn so much; you have to remember your continuity, else the editor will have a hard time. You have to remember, while you're in the emotion, while you're performing, so it's two tasks at the same time—having to connect to your internal self in order to bring out something honest because if you're acting fake, it shows. So it's like having two tracks running; one is the technical track—stand here, move there, look there, look at the continuity, dress, light—and there's the other track: what is she saying, what does she mean, how long is the pause, how will she stop. Recently, I've just been working on that. I didn't go to film school, so I feel a little daunted with those actors, because they've read up so much and they know so much. Now I've taken up ordering a lot of books online and doing my own research, because it helps. I recently won an award for

Gangs of Wasseypur and after that, people seem to think I should just put my feet up and relax. 'I'm the best actor in the country now, I don't give a damn.' But that scares me a lot more, not because of their reaction—their reaction is what they are conditioned to have—but I'm scared that I will take my job for granted and stop working every day.

How would you define yourself as an actress? Do you follow some kind of a method?

You know something very strange happens to me—which is why I feel I was born to be an actor. If I know I have to play you, a French person, brought up in France, educated there, with French as your first language, I'll read up on you a little bit. I may imitate you in my head while brushing my teeth, I may or may not do a backstory, but I'll just let you be. Then magically, when I am performing, when the camera rolls, something of you will come into me—it's like a quantum jump. I always believe that everybody has a different universe and that they coexist. Imagination is really amazing. In *Gangs of Wasseypur*, I was playing a woman who was married, much older and had not one, but four kids. I don't even like children. I found that really hard, but after a point, I just let it grow in me. I just imagined, would I walk differently if I had four children? Would my body put on weight in any particular area? Would my voice change texture? Between action and cut, so many times things happen that I can't explain, that come from the subconscious. Maybe for my character in *Gangs of Wasseypur*, they have come from my memory of my grandmother when I was ten, doing something that I probably observed for half a second, but that's how powerful the subconscious is when you're performing. I feel like if I'm getting into the matter too much, it might seem rehearsed. However, in the future, I don't mind going the whole hog and creating a method, creating a character. I'm always flexible that way.

Why was there such a huge gap between your first film, *Oye Lucky*, released in 2008, and your second, *Gangs of Wasseypur*, released in 2012?

I was too young and not ready. Also, *Oye Lucky* didn't create magic at the box-office, because it coincided with the terrible attacks we had in Mumbai. Nobody went to the theatre. I remember going and there were two or three people. Dibakar [Banerjee] was really disheartened by it. So it didn't translate into immediate work for me. Everybody said, 'She's good', but it didn't send people running to my door. I got a lot of respect really early and people started looking at me with a lot of fascination. 'Who is this? Where does she come from? How is she doing this?' Because nobody experiments like that over here. They would have rather seen me in a song-and-dance routine and then I would have probably got widespread acceptability immediately. Even though it was not a conscious choice, like to start with—*Oye Lucky* just fell into my lap—I don't regret it because it has given me a unique place in the industry today. I can dive into the mainstream if I want to, I can sing and dance if I want to and I can continue to do my own thing. Everybody should strike for a range. During that break between my two films, I knew a day would come when I would be busy and not have time. So I kept training myself. I travelled to learn, I spent time in Pondicherry to work on my voice and body. That time went well utilized. Also, *Wasseypur* took so long to make and release, because it went to all those festivals and you can't have a release if you're going there, so the break wasn't so long for me, maybe a year and a half.

Did Anurag tell you why he chose you for *Gangs of Wasseypur*?

I don't know! He didn't tell me anything, he didn't even audition me.

What did you learn on this film?

I was away for a long time, from my city, my comfort zone and my parents. I was shooting constantly, non-stop, for about eighty or ninety days. I don't think Anurag changed me necessarily as a person, but in the film I just started aging. My husband dies and my kids become victims of the violence themselves, so as a person I started becoming sadder. In retrospect, I think that's what happened, because I just wanted to go home, not be there and shake it all off. That's the only change I felt. Otherwise, I don't relate to the character. But strange things happen; if I am performing something difficult, I'm more likely to dream about it than to discuss it, or to live it.

So I always feel like my subconscious is hyperactive, doing things when I am not looking.

You said you could easily divert to Bollywood. You're actually a trained dancer.

I've been dancing since I was six. I love dancing. I did my BA in Kathak, then I left it for a long time, because in India everybody has to at some point make a choice. Otherwise, I think we'd have a lot more sports persons, dancers and musicians in this country than we do now. Everybody is supposed to have good grades, there's no way around [it]. It's really sad, but that's how it is. Even though my parents are the most liberal parents I know, I just had to make a choice because I was giving it so much time. I was tired, I couldn't cope at school. But there are more ways that apply to dance. That's something I learned recently; I used to have a grudge against the cinema that only has dances and singing because it was so fake and unnatural. But I am so classist to feel that. In the past six years, a cinema has developed that has alienated a class of Indians that has no respite, nowhere to go. Those multiplex cinemas are great for the arts, but it's terrible for my driver, because he cannot afford to buy a two hundred rupees ticket and go and sit in a movie hall to watch people have mid-life crises and existential questions, or discuss infidelity and have so many dialogues in English. He wants to see a song-and-dance movie, because it comes from a tradition where people go and watch a ridiculously simple story, where people dance and fight. That's fun, they clap and go home. A whole class of our country has now been alienated because of the city arts, the new cinema. I feel almost guilty for looking down upon that, because that's what I saw when I was young. I didn't see alternative cinema and I enjoyed that. Within that, I found things to like and many things to dislike. Right now, I don't feel I am in a position to comment on it, not until a multiplex will lower its rates to accommodate everybody and have them watch the same films, not until we stop making films where rich kids have coming of age problems, not until we stop having so many dialogues in English. I feel it's a happy coexistence of various kinds of cinemas right now. There is the genuine new Indian cinema and the wannabe new Indian cinema that tries to imitate the new Indian cinema by having lots of nudity, abuse, love-making or ridiculous things without any sense. Then there's the commercial cinema which makes one hundred or two hundred crores at the box-office, because they go to Switzerland to shoot a romantic song and people just think, 'Oh, she's so pretty, oh that is so nice, I wish I could go there.' In Hindi, we would say it's *paisa vasool* cinema, which means something that gives you satisfaction for the money you've spent.

You've acted in Sanjay Leela Bhansali's *Ram-Leela*. Bhansali is a 'commercial' director.

The film is full of dances and songs. I've also done one song in it, in which I am not singing, but I am dancing a lot, it's another experience. You do it and you enjoy it, it's like the Baz Luhrmann experience; everything is over-the-top, beautiful, velvet, chiffon and jewellery. For Bhansali, this film is an experiment and to cast me is a big deal. Contrary to what one believes about him, he's a very educated person, he knows about Indian music, dance and literature. He's a well-read person.

How different is it to work with somebody like Bhansali and Anurag Kashyap?

Anurag, Dibakar and these people are in my comfort zone. I mean they challenge me and they ask me to do my best. But they are more patient, very understanding and they stick to the real. In commercial cinema, I almost have to change the meter of my performance. Because the dialogues are so rich, in subtext and language, I almost have to change the rhythm of my speech, to fit in. I had a really hard time there. It's so expensive. Each day of shooting costs so much, I felt a lot of pressure. Because of the reputation I am also acquiring, a lot is expected of me in three takes as opposed to somebody else in thirteen, which is pissing me off because I am the same person, I am the same age that they are and just being pushed really hard.

Are there more people on a mainstream movie shoot?

On a Bhansali shoot, there are many, many, many, many more people. First of all, the floor is sixteen times the size of the space that we are sitting in right now [an average-size café]. Sixteen, twenty or twenty-five times. Then there are people taking care of each department, so there's somebody fixing the little chandelier, somebody doing the curtains, doing the flooring, somebody looking for the costumes. I was not the lead, but I had two people looking after me, dressing me up, making me look pretty and somebody was taking care of the plants. Then there are all the regular technical people: the gaffer (the light person is called the gaffer in India) who adjusts all the lights, the DOP and his assistants. There are many more people. Too many people.

Don't you feel a little lost?

Sometimes, if I get irritated, I'll just ask them to leave the set. That's an advantage of being seen as a critically-acclaimed actress. They think that I am eccentric or moody, and when I say, 'Can you get those people out', they go. *(laughs)* While actually what I want is just less noise, peace. I think it's fair, because if I am expected to deliver in three cuts, I have to find a way to sort of make sure I deliver in those three cuts.

Your character in *Oye Lucky*...

She's seen as a bad girl to the audience. They'll judge her for being a fallen woman.

You've played a lot of bad girls.

I think the industry here tends to look at women with my jaw line or sharp features as bad girls. If I was maybe rounder in the face and cuter, it could have been different. It's about the features and the laziness of people assuming that if somebody does a character well then they can stereotype them. But what I've actually done to each of them is to bring something different to the table. I don't think the woman in *Gangs of Wasseypur* was a bad woman. She was just oppressed and angry, stuck in patriarchy, married to an asshole, raising his children when he's not around and then he dies. I mean, come on! Then her son dies. She's never satisfied; sexually—emotionally, forget about it, there's no chance—and financially, always living in debt. It does something to a person, they become aggressive.

Still, it's not the typical heroine.

In *Fukrey* [Mrigdeep Singh Lamba, 2013], I would say that I am evil, just evil. There's no grey there. She is so driven by the aspirational nature of things, so materialistic. There's no undercurrent or vulnerability like in *Oye Lucky*, oppression or frustration like in *Wasseypur*, where you see the frustration coming out and you feel bad for the character. In *Wasseypur*, when she breaks down crying so many times, you have sympathy for her. In *Fukrey*, you love her because she's so black. There's no mercy. She doesn't feel anything, she only cares about her money, she says, 'I don't know who you are, what you do, I only care about my money.' She's using men to do whatever she wants, because they come to her for help. In *Tamanchey* [Navneet Behal, 2013], she's somebody who has seen a lot of deprivation and wants to move up quickly, so she uses her sexuality. She's tough, but she's so weak inside that she has this wall around her. She's that girl that has to be with somebody for financial reasons—she's indebted. There are two scenes in particular, which are very crucial to my character. There's one scene where she's reading a book. This guy comes in and wants to have sex. He's her boss also so she can't say no and by then she's already falling for somebody. So when he lays on top of her, she looks at the camera and she smiles. He goes down and she knows he's out of her vision, and her smile fades. It's that level of, 'Okay, use my body and get it over with.' Towards the end in the climax, when she sees that she has no way out, she just sits down and weeps and weeps. In *Ram-Leela*, I am not a toughie. I am a soft girl who wants everybody to be happy. She's strong and she needs to be, but you feel for her, you fall in love with her. She's so sweet.

So you're not being stereotyped.

I wouldn't allow that for myself, even though when you let yourself be stereotyped, you make pots and pots of money.

What is your take on the image of women in Indian cinema? In one of the most popular films of Indian cinema, Dilwale Dulhania Le Jayenge [Aditya Chopra, 1995], the heroine is a weak girl and it hasn't changed that much today.

In *Dilwale Dulhania Le Jayenge*, she's not a weak woman! She falls in love with somebody much against her father's wishes.

But she's going to India with her father and she's going to get married to someone else to please him.

There are just some times when you can't say no! If my father tomorrow insists that I go to Delhi and get married, I may elope with someone on the night of the wedding, but I'll still have to go. I'll chat him up for a while. Within that time, within that patriarchy, within that structure, she was a strong female character. Also that actress—Kajol—is known to pick up roles that are not ordinary. I know you may disagree.

Still, her roles are quite different from yours!

Yes, because cinema has evolved since then. The dominant representation was largely the weak woman, waiting for her husband, because it's the male fantasy. I think that women have a lot more going on today under the surface that men would never know. This is like men's obsession with big breasts. Or how they're like, 'Oh my god, she's fasting for me, I'm so great. I love her because she's fasting for me and she's waiting for me to have dinner with her. She can't do this on her own, she needs me. I need to fix her.' I think it's part of a larger Indian male fantasy, because they see their women like that, their mothers, sort of helpless—which is why after a certain age, men in their twenties, teenagers, they're just all over their mothers. I don't think it happens anywhere else. In India, there's a lot of mother obsession. Men like strong women also, but it's like a fantasy as opposed to somebody they'd want to be with. Eventually they'd want to be with somebody that they can tame and control. Which is why somebody like Anurag is an exception, because he says that he wants to be with somebody who controls him.

Do you think that your roles are showing an image of the modern Indian woman?

What I love about my characters is that I get a lot of compliments from women, of respect, which is rare. Normally if you're a heroine, all the girls will be like, 'Yes she's pretty, but don't you think she's kinda fat?' Men say nice things, 'Oh you work really hard', or 'you were really kickass', but that's about it. They wouldn't go into the depth of things and say, 'we want a woman like you.' Of all the men that I've even sort of dated, I can identify two or three maximum that are okay with equality in every sense—I am talking of my personal life—and even get used to the idea that I could be more famous than them, or more successful, or financially in a better position.

It's like that everywhere.

Is it? It is so irritating. In France, I would just think that women can earn more money.

They can, but men don't especially like it.

I want to write a story, a film on that. About this woman who keeps her earnings hidden, so that she can keep her marriage or something.

You've been really busy lately. Is the future bright for your career?

I want to do everything. I feel like I am in the right space, in the right time, in the right age for me to experiment with everything. Had I been a little older, it would have been more difficult. Even younger, I couldn't have explored my own way. I'm consciously choosing different things. In *Ishqeria* [Prerna Wadhawan, 2013], my character is a very sweet simple girl, an average Indian girl who will stand up for what she believes in, eventually. She never has an outburst in that film, but it's an interesting love story between what we think of as the perfect man and a woman who is imperfect and okay with that imperfection.

Do you refuse a lot of scripts?

I do. People think I am foolish, that I am not materialistic, that I am not concerned about making money, or building capital or buying a better car, a better house. But if I want a career, I have to wait, do the right things and be patient, as opposed to taking whatever comes my way and being complacent. In the recent past, I have turned down two films that have offered me characters that were similar to *Tamanchey* or something else. I feel I've already done that. It would be easy to do and I'd make lots of money, but what is the use of that? 'Oh, she's only good for that.' And it happens all over the world. If it happens with me here because of my performance as a bold female character, it can happen with people constantly calling you a blonde because you're pretty and blonde and making use of that. People get typecast really easily.

Does becoming famous scare you?

Yes, it does. I am even conscious now of sitting here and people thinking, 'Oh, I've seen her somewhere.' The worst thing about being an actor is the loss of one's anonymity. People are judgemental about things, like, 'oh, why is she in such a small car?' Or, 'why is she dressed like that? Why is she without make-up?' I really enjoy being in my own space, doing my own things. It gets more and more difficult. People who say, 'I don't care if people are looking at me' are lying. You know that they are looking at you, and it annoys you. How can it not?

PART 5

CENSORSHIP AND SEXUALITY: THE TABOOS OF HINDI CINEMA

How do you justify state censorship in a democracy? In India today, censorship exists across all forms of media, and rather strongly; the controversial book by Salman Rushdie, *The Satanic Verses*, is still banned in the country; it is illegal to print a map of the Indian territory that doesn't include all of the Kashmir State (though a part of it is under Pakistani control, and another under Chinese control). In 2014, under the pressure by Hindu extremists groups, Penguin Books dropped its controversial book by Wendy Doniger, *The Hindus*; in 2015, the documentary *India's Daughter* by British filmmaker Leslee Udwin, tackling the subject of the rape and murder of a young girl in Delhi, was prohibited from being shown on TV. In 2016, *Udta Punjab* [Abhishek Chaubey], a film about the drug problem in the state of Punjab came close to never being released, as too many cuts were asked for by the Central Board of Film Certification (CBFC).

It is censorship in Indian cinema that is most frequently discussed, as the censor board's puritanism seems ridiculous in the twenty-first century where the Internet makes almost everything accessible. Admittedly, this censorship is outdated. In the 1950s, India had just got freedom from its British colonizers and it did not take its new government too long to realize the strong influence of cinema in this large country completely won over by films. In 1951, the CBFC—nicknamed the 'Censor Board'—was established to take charge of attributing a certificate to each film wanting release in India. There are three certificates today: 'U' (all audiences), 'U/A' (all audiences including children below twelve years of age but under adult supervision) and 'A' (adults only). To issue a certificate, the CBFC follows a dozen ambiguous rules, for instance, banning any remark or representation that questions the territorial integrity of India.

For a long time and even today, the existence of censorship provoked a self-censorship from the artists of popular cinema. To avoid getting an 'A' certificate, filmmakers created prudish films where sexual acts were not shown directly. Actors wouldn't even kiss on screen, because a film depicting a kiss would cause a media scandal. This also meant that filmmakers often concocted symbolic and metaphoric ways to show the desire one character felt for another. This gave birth to the famous scenes of 'wet sarees', where an actress would come out of the water all dressed up, with her wet saree showing off her figure. Today, if actors and actresses of commercial cinema reluctantly agree to kiss their partners on screen or even shoot a sex scene (though under sheets and from afar), it still does not imply that Indian cinema is freed from all its previous constraints. Some subjects, especially homosexuality, are still complete taboos under the pretext that they promote vulgarity, which is against the rules of the Board. Two of the interviewees of this chapter, filmmakers Onir and Sridhar Ranghayan, explain the difficulties they face on a daily basis because of this taboo.

Admittedly, censorship has mellowed since 1952, as the ex-CEO of the CBFC, Pankaja Thakur, asserts in this chapter. It might even disappear some day, and become only an ordinary classification system. In fact, with continued and growing criticism from the media and the public, the CBFC seems to be losing more and more power. Two previously prohibited political documentaries, Anand Patwardhan's *War and Peace* (on the atomic bomb) and *Final Solution* (on Muslim massacres in Gujarat in 2002) have eventually been released in their original version. The arrest of the former CEO of CBFC, Rakesh Kumar, for corruption, didn't help restore its image. But is state censorship alone to be blamed? In a country where feelings of communalism are rampant, with extremist groups ever-ready to burn anything that displeases them, freedom of speech might sometimes be a wish in vain, or a risk that not everyone is ready to take.

PANKAJA THAKUR
Ex-CEO of the Central Board of Film Certification (CBFC)

As I was heading to the office of the famous Censor Board, located in South Mumbai, for my interview, I was aware of how prejudiced I already was. After all, France was never unaware of the problem and had its share of fights against state censorship throughout history. Back in the 1970s, depicting how French people collaborated with the Nazis during the Second World War (a fact that the president of the Republic himself, at that time, would rather ignore) could still prevent you from television broadcasting for a decade (*The Sorrow and the Pity*, Marcel Ophuls, 1969).

The term 'censorship', however, doesn't even appear in the title of this Indian governmental organization, which is under the domain of the Ministry of Information and Broadcasting. Its name simply reads: 'Central Board of Film Certification'. Interestingly, the acronym is the same in Pakistan. But there it stands for 'Central Board of Film Censors' (which was the CBFC's actual name in India until 1983). Pankaja Thakur insisted several times in the interview that her job, similar to that in Europe or in United States, was more about classifying than censoring.

Many artists who feel they are victims of the CBFC's chopping block, have solid rebuttals to her arguments. Nevertheless, I admired her discussing censoring with me so openly. In a blink of an eye,

Pankaja agreed to meet with me in the most casual manner available in a government office, and made time to answer all my questions with honesty. There was an obvious willingness and desire on her part to restore the reputation of her profession. Was that merely a marketing ploy? It was difficult not to believe that her sincerity, or maybe, her great respect and passion for cinema, may have caused Pankaja Thakur to lose her job after four years in office. She was replaced just after my interview by Rakesh Kumar, who was arrested a little later for corruption. Since 2015, the CEO of CBFC is Anurag Srivastava, who had a career in the Ministry of Information and Broadcasting. The very charming Pankaja has now completely dissociated herself from the CBFC and turned into a filmmaker, with her short film *The Guide* being presented at the Dharamshala International Film Festival in 2016. It just seemed like the next obvious step for her.

Censorship existed before India's independence in 1947. How did it work then?

It was actually done by the Law and Order Authorities during the British time, so the Police. There was a Board of course, but most of the people who were involved were obviously not artists. It was meant in a way to control the content in cinema. But after independence, when the board was finally the Central Board of Censorship, it was under the Ministry of Culture. The idea was still to have some kind of regulation on the content, but with different intentions. It started with the Cinematograph Act which was formed in 1952 and the Board was formed in 1951. It would be a lie to believe that it was not done to censor—it was also called Board of Film Censorship—but definitely, there was a vast difference in intent between what was happening in pre-independence [India] and what has happened post.

What was the intent before independence?

The intent during those times was to see to it that a certain kind of message was not spread to films: the message of independence and messages of Free India.

Pre-independence, it was possible to have certain sexual content in Indian films, like kissing, which was forbidden after.

True. Any organization is synonymous with the people who run it. Pre-independence, it was the British who were there in the board and the cultural content regulation obviously was not the idea. So you saw Himanshu Rai and Devika Rani kiss in *Karma* [John Hunt, 1933], because they thought there was nothing offensive or shocking about it. But obviously, when the people who held positions at the Board were Indians, they started functioning as per the Indian cultural norms and what they thought was the right thing to show in cinema. For them, kissing, nudity and expressive sexual content were obviously foreign things, which was not part of the Indian culture. Look at the first film, *Raja Harishchandra* [Dadasaheb Phalke, 1913], that was made in India and the first film that Americans made, *The Great Train Robbery*. You can see the huge difference in the mindset. They made a film about a train robbery and our first film was about this person who never lied in his life, who gave up everything for truth and was a keeper of the value system that the Indians think is part of their cultural ethos.

So you're saying that the fact that there was censorship during the British rule has nothing to do with the existence of Indian censorship nowadays?

It is true that in India, a lot of things—the railways, the education system, even the police and the law and order—have been largely inherited, because it worked well. It's very difficult to imagine right now, if there was no censorship during pre-independence, whether we'd still have gone ahead. But looking at things now, the way they are, every country has a classification system, which is not called censorship. If you want a particular sex scene to be shown in your film but you want a U-rated certificate, you'll have to take that scene out. Would you call taking that out censorship? I don't think so.

It is often said that censorship of sex in India is a paradox, as it is the country which gave birth to the *Kama-Sutra*.

Kama-Sutra was written long time back. India has been invaded a number of times. Some of the invaders have made India their home.

They became very much a part of Indian culture. They brought some of their own cultural values. India has become like a cultural mix, where all kinds of influences were being cooked. Even the British have brought their own system and the British are not supposed to be very liberal. So what finally came out after independence and what you see of Indian society is such a mix of so many cultures, so many traditions and so many time zones. We have gone through so much since *Kama-Sutra*.

Are those guidelines needed because of so many cultures?

Yes. Most countries have not seen the system of joint families—how four-five brothers, their children and their grandchildren, all of them live under the same roof. There's a certain code of conduct, rules that everybody follows. Those are unwritten rules, but everybody voluntarily follows them, because they know you can't have the luxury of living together and enjoying that kind of a community living, if you don't follow certain rules. The multiple cultures, multiple languages, multiple castes are what makes us such a rich and such a diverse country. But at the same time, it is true that as Indians we have to be more tolerant than a French or a German person because we have to be careful about not hurting each other. People are sensitive about the language that they speak. Some words which are benign in one language are objectionable in another language. These are the challenges that we face, because amidst all this, we are still trying to protect the freedom of expression of each filmmaker, guaranteed by the Indian constitution. It's such a tightrope walk.

Doesn't the Indian constitution guarantee freedom of expression, with 'reasonable restrictions'?

But the importance is given to freedom of expression. Even if the matter goes to the Court, the Court also tries to see if someone's freedom of expression has been curbed unnecessarily. They try to protect it until last minute, unless it's a deliberate attempt to hurt a particular community. Those are the situations when the Board or the judiciary, if someone tries to appeal to the board, look into, 'What are the intentions of the filmmaker? Is he really trying to say something or is it a deliberate attempt to hurt a particular community or to incite people to commit an offence?'

Why are films in particular submitted for censorship?

(laughs) Look at us and that will give you the answer. What influences us the most? Open a newspaper and you'll find everything, right to the fashion sense, hair style, front pages, people who have become powerful, who have become politicians, influential people and society, people you will look up to, listen to. All are from the film industry. In India, nothing influences a person as much as films do. We take our films very seriously, not another medium. It's kind of unfortunate, but everybody knows.

How do movies influence people? Do you think that a violent film can call for violence in daily life?

No. We are not saying that because one film shows a rape, or a murder, or a crime, that someone is going to try to copy that. The idea is, if in one movie, you show a particular kind of crime not being dealt with properly—such as a rape happening which is more titillating than anything else—then the disgust that the rape was supposed to generate in people's minds disappears, even more if your film is successful and everybody else copies it. Then over a period of time, desensitization does take place and you stop getting bothered by someone getting mutilated for instance. We should not blame cinema for whatever is happening in daily life; it's not because women are portrayed in a certain way that the public will be affected. Cinema shows a lot of good things too: people giving their life for their countries, messages of tolerance and friendship. Why is this not being copied? Why is it only crimes and incidents that are being copied? Is it worth stopping the movie from being released because we fear that the film might get someone to commit a crime? Especially when films are rated Adult, you feel that it is being watched by adults who are choosing their own government. They are responsible, they know what to do or not to do. If it is not an adult-rated film, if it is going to be shown to children or teenagers, with their minds more likely to get influenced, we have to be very careful of what we are showing. That's why we are more careful of what is going to be shown on television.

Why do filmmakers fight an A certificate?

Because in India, people go and watch films on weekends with their entire family. If the film is rated A, the director loses on the family audience, so commercially it affects the film. At the same time, there are some films in which content is so good that almost every adult watches that film, like *Gangs of Wasseypur* [Anurag Kashyap, 2012], *The Dirty Picture* [Milan Luthria, 2011] or *I Am* [Onir, 2012]. If your content is good, the film doesn't suffer commercially. Some directors refuse cuts and want U-rating at the same time to make more money. The moment this dishonesty comes into your mind, then there's a problem. And those are the people who make the maximum noise about the board troubling them.

An ex-member of the Bureau, Vijay Anand, said that the fact that censorship forces directors to not show any kissing on screen made them find other means to suggest love and that films became thus more vulgar. He was talking about the 1980s films.

I don't agree because the guidelines don't say that you cannot show a kiss.

True, but that's what we mostly remember about censorship in India and a lot of actors refuse to kiss on screen!

But it comes from people because for them, it was probably not something that was part of their culture, even nudity, because it is foreign influence. So it was not the right thing to show. There was this time during independence struggle, when probably they hated everything that was foreign; they wanted everything to be Indian. In their minds, kissing was foreign and that's why probably it was not allowed. If you actually see the guidelines, they are very much against vulgarity. They say that any violence against women or children should be shown only if it's required in the story. It should be kept to a minimum so that desensitization doesn't take place. But in those 1980s films, it's the hero's sisters who get raped and murdered and that's how the whole story begin; that's why the hero takes revenge. If you cut that scene, where is the motive for the hero to take revenge? The sisters were there only to get raped and killed, but those stories were being written. So you can say it was lack of imagination on the part of filmmakers and the writers who kept on repeating those kinds of stories, but you can't say it's because they were following the guidelines that they were showing vulgarity. The guidelines don't say that, 'cut out the kissing scene but it is okay to show a woman being assaulted or raped on screen.'

I thought that forbidding kisses was an unwritten guideline.

No. The people sitting in the Committee interpret the guidelines according to their own value system. While interpreting the guidelines, if it says that they should ensure that unnecessary vulgarity is not promoted, kissing was probably vulgar for them.

You see clear changes on this subject since 2005–2006.

It began a long time back. A-rated films were anyway happening. I think in *36 Chowringhee Lane* [Aparna Sen, 1981], there was a kiss and the film was rated A.

I am actually talking about commercial cinema.

Ah, the U-rated films. But kisses and sex were allowed in commercial cinema, as long as it was A-rated.

Yes, but most famous actors and actresses didn't want to do it.

Yes, during those times, it was only the so-called art cinema actresses who would kiss on screen. The mainstream women wanted to portray a very clean, very virgin image.

So, you're saying that the change is not because of the Board, but because of filmmakers who are now comfortable with showing kissing on screen.

Yes. Actually the Board, people who join the Board, are from the same society. It's Indian society itself. You're certifying on behalf of the society. You give yourself a government and you give yourself a Board. The Board has people who have the same value system. Right now the government has put a lot of artists on the Board, so that the artist point-of-view is also seen. The chairperson is a dancer. She always says that she feels bad that a film has to be cut, because she wouldn't let anyone cut her dance piece if she was performing and somebody was telling her she can't dance like that. She empathizes, she sees cinema as a form of art. There are so many people right now on the board who are storywriters and songwriters. They empathize with the cause of cinema and freedom of expression. So it's important to them that the artistic freedom of expression and integrity are maintained. People say that it's political censorship, but if the government was really interested in censorship, it wouldn't put these people on the Board who are from the industry, who are against the idea of censorship. It's the people of India who demand censorship. Here, when people go to watch a film with the whole family, they don't want to get embarrassed by nudity or explicit sexual content. So they demand that these scenes should be cut if you give a U or a U/A rating to the film. If we belong to a group and we feel that group's sentiments have been hurt, we demand censorship. Or, we will say that violence is non-Indian because we had Mahatma Gandhi and now we're spreading the culture of violence by showing films like *Gangs of Wasseypur*.

Why do you think the Bureau has such a bad reputation in the industry then?

It's sad actually. I joined three years back, so obviously I don't want to talk about what happened before because I wouldn't know. But I will tell you that in the last three years, if you speak to people who got their films certified—except for one or two, who wanted a particular rating and wanted to keep those scenes also—ninety-five per cent of the filmmakers have been extremely happy with their experience with the Board. They find us reasonable and they think the Board was very democratic in their approach. Those who are talking about what was happening in the past have nothing else to talk about; they'll come to every meeting of the Board where we invite the filmmakers and they'll keep talking about that one film, that one scene which was cut, which is not fair. We should look ahead. Is the Board on the right path? Are we becoming better to deal with? And if we're not, what are the suggestions? Obviously, you have to deal with censorship. We call it classification, but it happens everywhere, in the United States, in South-East Asian countries. We are trying to become truly global here, because our cinema is becoming global. So if a film is rated A, we hardly give any cuts to those films. We are trying to be more transparent and efficient. We don't want filmmakers to have to come and sit in this office. We want to solve maximum number of problems over the phone. We are trying to make it so that your film is released on time with minimum cuts and when you come to meet the officers, you don't feel like they're here to cut your film or question you. It's sitting together and deciding what is the best thing to do. Having said that, there's a guideline which we have to follow.

The guidelines are quite vague. Are they being interpreted in a different way nowadays?

Yes. They are open to interpretation. What is to be achieved? That's always to be kept in mind. The guideline says that as far as possible, artistic freedom of expression has to be maintained. Secondly, you have to see the context and time in which the film is made and also the people about whom the story is. People often ask me, 'Why are you certifying foreign films with the same guidelines that you certify Indian films? Shouldn't the guideline be different?' The guiding principle is that you have to keep in mind the people, the context. If a wedding takes place in a foreign film and the bride and the groom are kissing each other, we are going to give it a U-rating, because that's the most natural thing for them to do. The interpretation has to be intelligent. If it's a gangster story and there are abusive words, you cannot just cut it, because you know gangsters do use those words. It's part of their world. But if the same thing is said by a nineteen-year-old in a college situation, then we ask why, because a nineteen-year-old shouldn't be using that kind of language.

I am going to contradict you with some examples. In Sudhir Mishra's gangster movie, *Yeh Saali Zindagi* [2011], the abuses were muted. When the *Sex and the City* TV show is broadcast on Indian television, some scenes are cut even though the intent was to show sex.

We discussed with Sudhir Mishra about the utility of the abusive words in his film. Every frame had some and it was not the villain who was using these lines, but the male lead. We asked him how to deal with that. He said, 'If you want, I can decrease the decibels on the lines that caused problems.' He was open to the discussion. It's the filmmaker who has to finally take a stand where the Board members are not convinced. If you see *Gangs of Wasseypur* versus *Yeh Saali Zindagi*, Sudhir Mishra's movie is kind of semi-urban. His characters are not hardcore gangsters and criminals; it was a love story actually. *Gangs of Wasseypur* is more heartland, there is more anger. According to the members of the Board, it was not very natural for the characters of *Yeh Saali Zindagi* to use an abusive word every third line. So Sudhir Mishra said, 'In certain situations, let me work on the decibels so that it is not too audible and in some situations, I would like to keep those words because they are required.' We agreed. About *Sex and the City*, we don't censor television shows, which are under self-regulation. A TV show is supposed to be U-rated, so that even children can watch, because the digitalization process is not complete and we don't have the system of child locks. So to make the show U-rated, all those explicit references, where the sex is shown and discussed, would have been removed.

In France, we would make the parents responsible for what they let their children watch.

We are moving towards that. The government has already brought in digitalization on television and within that, you will be required to put the child lock if you don't want the child to watch those channels.

What about those anti-smoking disclaimers in films shown before and during the film?

The Board is very much against it. It fought against the stickers, but the Ministry of Health and Family Welfare is responsible for it; they feel very strongly that icons smoking on screen leads to youngsters picking up tobacco products. It is the requirement of another Ministry but because we are the ones giving the certificate, we have been given the responsibility. We are doing something that the Board didn't agree with. Now that filmmakers know, unless it's absolutely required, they won't put a cigarette in the mouth of a character just like that.

Actually, the guidelines do talk about tobacco.

Yes, the glamorization of tobacco is forbidden. When a woman is in trouble, if the hero has to save her and smokes a cigarette before going, you show tobacco as a kind of vitamin that gives you extra strength and an extra dose of altruism. In another situation, friends meet and the boy who smokes is the one who gets the girl, you feel that maybe girls like boys who smoke because it makes them more macho. The guidelines talk about those things. It's gone to extremes and now, any kind of smoking is not allowed without the warning. It looks ugly, the Board is still trying to ask ...[that filmmakers not be forced]... to put that message.

Before working for the Board, you were not working in films, but in customs.

The Board of Film Certification is an office under the Ministry of Information and Broadcasting. A government officer can work here. I applied for this post. Before this I was on a sabbatical in Singapore, where my husband was posted. There, just out of curiosity, I did a brief course in short filmmaking, so I had the qualification to apply. I had made a short film that I attached with my application, it did give me that little edge over other applicants.

Are you a movie-buff?

Yes, I do enjoy watching films. All sorts of films, foreign, Indian.

As the CEO of the board, do you have to watch a lot of films?

I wish I had the time to watch more foreign films. In fact I wish the government would send us to film festivals abroad, just to see how other countries are dealing with difficult scenes. But because my work is more administrative, everything from transferring equipment to finances, I really don't get time to watch as many films as I would like to.

Aren't you supposed to give your opinion on cuts?

No, I do. In fact, I do make it a point to watch at least one foreign film a month, an imported film, an Indian film, mostly a film which has already generated a controversy, which has been talked about because of the risky content. Because it's very important for me to know which direction we are going in. Otherwise, I talk to my officers and ask them if they're facing a particular problem, or if there's a particular scene that's very tricky. I am in touch with the Board members all the time. I have nine regions, different languages and my job is to constantly take feedback from those people, to take all the problems to the board, find a solution and then pass it on to these people. It's important that everybody is on the same page, the Board and the nine regions. I am one person who's constantly coordinating between the Board members, the officers, the media and the Ministry.

How does the Board work exactly?

We have a pool in each region. Around one hundred and fifty people are there, and they are from all walks of life. It's not like there are only film people: there are housewives, women, professors and mothers. The government pays for that, it's their job. For each film, the regional officer creates a panel where he'll put two women and two men. The five of them sit and watch, and note down, from the point of view of what certification they want to give and what cuts they want to have. Finally, at the end of the film, they call the filmmaker in and they propose their cuts. Then there's a long discussion with the filmmaker after that. He puts forwards his point of view. So it's very democratic. Sometimes, they don't agree, sometimes, the discussion goes on for hours. Sometimes, the filmmaker is able to convince the members that this scene is required, sometimes the members are able to convince the filmmaker to leave the scene. Finally, the certification is given and if there are any cuts, it's written down. But if there's no agreement, if they are all holding on to their grounds, the filmmaker has an option to take it to a higher committee, where one of the board members stays—there are around twenty-three board members now who are usually artists, or writers or journalists. With that, a bigger committee is set, with seven–eight people and a board member. The film has more chances to be cleared, because they're supposed to have a vision, to be well-travelled, to have seen world films. If the filmmaker still is not happy, he can go to the FCAT, which is the appeal tribunal. So the filmmaker has so many chances of getting his film approved without getting any cuts. Like for *Bandit Queen* [1994], Shekhar Kapur went all the way. He went to the court, and the court allowed the film to be released with all the frontal nudity. Filmmakers just have to have the time. What happens is that they always come at the last minute.

How much time does it take to get certification?

A couple of days, maximum a week.

Even if you give the film a certificate, a State can still refuse the release of the movie. It happened to *Da Vinci Code*.

A Board of Film Certification is valid throughout India, so the States cannot ban. But there is a federal structure and there are some things that the State government is responsible for, such as the law and order. To maintain law and order, the state government can do a lot of things. It can stop people from assembling in a particular area. What they do basically is that they invoke those laws to stop a film from being distributed, since a film screening constitutes people assembling in one place. They are being very smart in that. They are only using the loopholes in the system to stop a film from being released. Now, the government is looking into that issue so filmmakers don't suffer.

How do you see the future? Do you think the Board will ever disappear or change?

Yes, definitely, it will. I have a feeling that the way things are changing, what we've achieved in the last three years, we're moving away from censorship to certification. The Board will not disappear because it has a purpose, because the certification system exists in every country; actually, it's a public service. Even I want to know if I should take my children along to a movie. At the same time, I think all kinds of films should be allowed to be seen. People should become more responsible and tolerant. I might not agree with what the film is saying, I won't go and watch, but I'll let others who want to go watch that film.

How long do you think it's going to take?

It's difficult to say. It all depends on what kind of people are there on the Board. We are not permanent employees. There can be an extension. Some people have been on the Board for six, ten years. But every two years, the Board changes. The right kind of people should be on the Board for it to change.

ONIR
Director

I met Onir near his home, in the charming café Leaping Windows, in the heart of the artists' area in Versova. Onir's reputation preceded him. Since I have been writing on Indian films, his name frequently came up in my conversations about committed, personal and 'different' (for lack of a better word) cinema. In fact, Onir is one of the few Indian personalities who not only came out publicly about his homosexuality, but also built a body of work around this very controversial subject.

It was an angry and tired man with whom I was talking on that day. Onir has definitely chosen the toughest path one could ever find in the Hindi film industry: not only does he not believe in the song-and-dance Bollywood formula, but he also chooses subjects which are either taboos or not easily appealing to the Indian audience, such as child abuse or single motherhood. Even though the most important studio of India, Yash Raj, supported the distribution of his first film, *My Brother... Nikhil* [2005] and despite the success of his films abroad and the National Awards for his second film, *I Am* [2010], Onir's fight to direct the movies he believes in is still a difficult one.

Whether you like his films from a strictly artistic point of view or not is not even the question here anymore, as one can't be left unimpressed by his integrity. 2017 will see the release of his third feature, *Shab*, seven years after *I Am*. But Onir doesn't only direct films. He also has his own production company, Anticlock films, and though struggling himself, wishes to support first-time filmmakers; such as film critic Bikas Mishra with his indie feature *Chauranga* (2014) which had a decent run in international festivals. Though I was prepared to spend time chatting about the themes Onir chooses to deal with, I ended up reviewing with him the entire Hindi film industry. Here is an interview without compromises or doublespeak.

You had quite a unique childhood.

I was born in Bhutan. My parents were Bangladeshi refugees who came to India and my father was a leftist. During the Emergency in India, a lot of leftists were killed. So, my father left with my mother to go to Bhutan and became a teacher. That's where I was born and brought up. I went to school in the capital of Bhutan, Thimphu, which I feel very fortunate about because it's a very mixed community—it included people from all over the world, because of the United Nations and a few embassies. When I grew up, we didn't have television, which was good because we did a lot of reading, and outdoor sports—like trekking, fishing. So I have a very strong bond with nature, with outdoor things. My mother always wanted to be an actress but her father never gave his approval. She was very beautiful, she was interested in music, singing, dancing. My father was a political activist and not interested in all that, but he was an extremely open man. He's the one who taught my mother cooking, encouraged her to start teaching and become independent. My brother, my sister and I have grown up in an environment where all of us have always been treated equally. All of us used to take turns in helping my father or my mother in the kitchen. I feel extremely grateful that I grew up in a family where being treated as equals was not even discussed.

My mother was a very big cinema influence, because every week she would take us to watch a film—there was one theatre in Bhutan. We would pretend that we didn't want to go, because she would bribe us with sweets. When my sister first came for college to Calcutta, she would take me to film festivals. One of the first films which made an impact on me was *Junoon* [Shyam Benegal, 1979]. I was in class eight. I didn't really understand the film, but the visuals kept on coming back to me. I knew I wanted to be a part of that, not knowing how. Then, when I was in class ten, my sister took me to a film festival where I saw this film called the *French Lieutenant's Woman*. I thought this is what I want to do, nothing else. This was a more conscious step. My parents wanted me to be a doctor, so I went to a science college. But I quickly shifted to arts.

Initially, my parents were not happy, but for the very first time in my life I was doing well in my studies. As a child, while giving exams I would write just enough correct answers in maths and chemistry to pass, because it never interested me. History, physics somehow, and literature interested me. I was also someone who liked painting, dancing, be extremely active in all this. In Calcutta, when I joined the university for Comparative Literature, I was exposed to comparative arts in parallel. I was very active in the film society, getting to know about music and painting. I had some great professors who exposed me to the entire world of literature, international and classical, which was alien to me.

I got a scholarship to go to Berlin to study editing and for me it was the third most important thing in my life. Bhutan gave me my soul, Calcutta is the place that nurtured my intellect and Berlin gave me technique, discipline, respect for my instruments, for my work and taught me to be organized. This combination made me the filmmaker I am. Somehow largely my film influence has been Bengali and European cinema. Hollywood and Bollywood have been secondary. In college, we used to watch so much of European cinema, Russian cinema and Swedish cinema. I also studied European literature. So I developed a bigger inclination towards that than American history or literature.

After I came back from Berlin, I tried to work in Calcutta which was the city I liked. By then, my family once again had to shift out because Bhutan suddenly started treating Indians as second-class citizens—even though my father had been there for twenty-five years. There were a lot of atrocities against the Nepalis, some of my father's students were arrested and found hanged. My father quit.

There are all these things that the world doesn't know. There were nearly three hundred thousand refugees, a huge number that are now seeking asylum in Germany, France and Holland, but people only want to say that this is the country of happiness. Everybody talks about the atrocities against the Tibetans in China, but not about the atrocities against the Nepalis in Bhutan and against Indians in a subtle way. There was no massacre, but suddenly after twenty-five years, my father had to come to India and get a job. It affected my mother's health very badly; she was hospitalized and nearly died. I became someone who doesn't have a home. Now, if I see a film that talks about a place that one cannot go back to, I identify with it. When I came to Calcutta to study at first, though my parents were of Bengali origin, I felt like a Bhutanese. So I was like an outsider there. In Berlin, I obviously was an outsider. Also, it was during that historical phase where East and West got together and there was an element of racism. But at the same time, some of my closest friends are German. I discovered that you can have homes all over the world. Any place can be home.

Have you thought of making a movie about the situation in Bhutan?

I've thought of it, but they won't give permission in Bhutan. My film *I Am* [2012], which is set in Kashmir, is not only about Kashmir. It's about having a home, against being an outsider everywhere. Now I feel as much at home in Bombay as in Berlin, as much as I feel an outsider in Bombay and in Berlin. Ultimately, it's the people who are around you, who are close to you, who make you feel at home anywhere in the world, not the passport or identification papers. My sexuality became an even more problematic area: you feel at home where you can be open about yourself, about who you are. When I first came to India, I was thinking I had come to this huge country which was so much more advanced in terms of thinking because they were so much more exposed than I was. The first thing that shocked me was how women were treated. I am very close to my sister and I would think, 'Why are people eve-teasing her, why are they commenting, why are they so aggressive, why is there this division all the time when we have grown up together as friends?' I realized all my women friends were really troubled. Because of my upbringing, it's important for me to show how to represent women. What is often portrayed by filmmakers, commercial or non-commercial, are women affirming their sexuality in a bold manner and it is a very male perspective. It is meant in a way that pleases the male audience. I think it is very dangerous.

Unfortunately, I feel we are going through a phase where we have such poor film criticism, because there is no culture of film criticism. When you read the news, they are so superficial. We'll see this review and we'll read that this is this actress's best ever performance. You'll read that the actor has been let down by his script. If the actors feel like they have been let down, why do they charge so much money on a bad script? The standards are so low, films that are seen as progressive don't challenge anybody. And we have a very short memory. When a film like *Gangs of Wasseypur* [Anurag Kashyap, 2012] is released, we hear this is new Indian cinema. We forget that twelve years ago, we had *Satya*, by Ram Gopal Varma [1998], which is in that same space, perhaps even with a much stronger soul, experimenting, and it's a great film. People will look at *The Dirty Picture* [Milan Luthria, 2011] and forget that we had great actresses like Shabana Azmi, Smita Patil, who challenged stereotypes. Filmmakers like Shyam Benegal and Ketan Mehta were provocative. Now, which filmmaker does films that are provocative and challenge anyone's state of confidence? Everything around us is mainstream and has a certain formula with sex, humour, violence put together, which works wonders in this country. Abuse is loved, especially abuse towards mothers and sisters. No one questions the fact that you never have a woman actress calling a man 'father fucker'. Why not? This is provocative. Every other actor is saying, 'Mother fucker, sister fucker'. They are constantly reinstating very lame stereotypes and there's nothing cool about it. But it's always projected as how cool it is to be abusing every second line. When I look at what was true parallel cinema—Satyajit Ray, Ritwik Ghatak, Adoor Gopalakrishnan, Shyam Benegal, Ketan Mehta—all of them were challenging, be it the way women were portrayed, society, politics, everything. Where do we have that now? Unfortunately, because in India cinema is not under arts and culture, all these filmmakers are producing projects which are catering to taste and not challenging it. What is important is that you have to prove yourself at the box office. If you have to do that, you will not push, because you want to please your audiences. Then cinema is not an art, but a business, where value is dictated by the box office.

What you are saying about this new cinema is very different from what I have been hearing.

I am different! *(laughs)*

Is it impossible to be provocative and get success at the box office in India?

I am not saying it is impossible. It is difficult, it is challenging, because it is a lonely journey. You won't have a studio, you won't have a channel and still you have to fight it out. You name one film that is really provocative, from recent years, which was made in this country. I am not talking about outside filmmakers doing a Hollywood movie. Tell me something that really shakes people up, that questions and angers them. It's happening in regional cinema, Marathi, Bengali, Malayalam, Tamil, because their risks are lower and there is a much larger sense of being an artist than in Bollywood. There's some exciting work happening there. Unfortunately, the definition of Indian cinema is becoming Bollywood.

Don't you think that the people who are ecstatic when watching a *Gangs of Wasseypur* are just happy to see something other than just mainstream Bollywood?

When *Bombay Talkies* [Karan Johar, Zoya Akhtar, Dibakar Banerjee, Anurag Kashyap, 2013] released, every critic started saying it was the first time we saw two men kissing in Bollywood, in the mainstream space. I've been working in this space for the last seven years. So it is marketing power. The percentage of so-called non-mainstream has increased slightly. But when you watch a Buñuel, or a Godard, or the painter Dalí, they are challenging narrative forms in terms of content and style. How is this 'new cinema' challenging, either in content or style? What is it that has not been done in Indian cinema yet? Look at *The Dirty Picture* or *Dev-D* [Anurag Kashyap, 2009]: you had films like *Mandi* [Shyam Benegal, 1983], or *Arth* [Mahesh Bhatt, 1982], which were challenging in the same space, years ago. Kissing and explicit love happened in every second Bengali film and nobody was bothered by it. Here, all publicity is about the hot kiss between this one and that one. You're marketing a kiss! What's your film, what's your story, what are you talking about? Bollywood always had different films; it had Hrishikesh Mukherjee, who was not doing progressive but feel-good films. The Amitabh Bachchan phase was much more dynamic, because it was about social class struggle, like *Kaalia* [Tinnu Anand, 1981]. Today, there are very few films which are political. You have a Sudhir Mishra. These are the films which are challenging. They are not the ones we speak of, because they are questioning the system. A *Chandni Bar* [Madhur Bhandarkar, 2001] is provocative. Today, *Vicky Donor* [Shoojit Sircar, 2012] is portrayed as new wave. What is new about it? It's not because you're talking about sperm donation that your film is non-mainstream. Everything in the film conforms to the laws. I am not saying that mainstream is not good, it is okay to be mainstream. I thoroughly enjoyed a film like *Band Baaja Baaraat* [Maneesh Sharma, 2010]. But don't define something that is not new wave as new wave, or the term loses its value. Today if you start calling *English Vinglish* [Gauri Shinde, 2012] new wave, I am very worried. Because that film is very problematic. There's a lot that needs to be questioned in that film, be it the way it deals with sexuality or with women. It reinstates every male chauvinist idea that the society wants to protect.

Is there an audience in India for provocative films?

I think if there is a platform, there'll be an audience. I'd rather say there is very little platform. Today, we don't get to see Marathi films, Bengali films, because there's no place where they are shown. You don't have a theatre that shows independent films at cheaper rates. Today, if I am going to the theatre, I have to pay four hundred rupees to see an independent film. If there's a Shah Rukh Khan film, I am going to watch the Shah Rukh Khan film because I can only afford to see one. You're unable to reach out to the audience, because of the price of the ticket, because of exhibition and distribution. I started liking another kind of cinema because I was exposed to it from childhood. People are not getting exposed to it anymore. People are only getting exposed to a certain kind of cinema. Last year, *Ishaqzaade* [Habib Faisal, 2012], produced by Yash Raj Films, was portrayed as a path-breaking, new kind of film. The hero and the heroine come from different religious and political backgrounds. The boy literally molests the girl, she falls in love with him despite that—that's some way to get to a woman! He pretends to be in love with her, has sex with her and then tells her to fuck off, that he was taking revenge. So she also wants to take revenge, goes to the mother of the guy, wanting to kill the guy and the mother tells her, 'But now, he's your husband. It's your duty to turn this animal into a human being.' I wanted to throw up. Is that a new wave film? A film justifying rape and molestation? It's a film made by a responsible production house, but unfortunately when you talk about these things, you will be called arty or intellectual, which is looked down upon in this industry. I would like to believe that what I have dedicated my life to is a much more powerful instrument and not so harmless. Cinema can be used as a tool. In this country, especially in the smaller cities, youth get majorly influenced: an eight-year-old boy and girl go to see this movie with these item numbers. The boy grows up accepting the fact that a woman will be dancing in between two hundred men and he has the right to throw money at her, touch her wherever he wants to, and the girl will grow up accepting this as normal. The entire thing is almost like a prequel to a rape. That's a reality for our society. How can you justify that by saying the woman is celebrating her sexuality? It is a lie, you are feeding into only the male discourse. You don't see a guy doing it. You never call a guy an item.

It is said that thanks to the multiplexes, there is more choice today in terms of films.

This is the biggest myth of this country. Unlike in France, where it's compulsory to keep a screen for independent cinema and a part of what the film is earning is going to the cinema fund, in India, if a big film releases, it will take up as many screens as possible. As an independent filmmaker, you're pushed to morning shows, afternoon shows and nobody wants to come from office to see the film. If I want my film to be released in this or that city, they'll say that they already have two studio films. Everything is controlled by the big producers: what shows you get, which cities you can release in, etc. It has not created a space for Indian cinema; it is in a way killing independent cinema. If my film is made for one hundred rupees, it can't be priced the same way another film which was made for one thousand rupees is priced.

I've been starting this movement to save this cinema, with a petition to the government. I've been meeting the Ministry and we have sixty-two filmmakers across the country who have joined. The first success we had was that we created a slot for indie cinema with the state-run television, which will show films that have got National Awards and that were screened in sixteen big international films festivals like Cannes, Berlin and Tokyo. I've also presented this plan: in all big cities in India, you have these small theatres, one-hundred-and-fifty seaters, where you could show only independent films of all-Indian languages, with subtitles. These are tax-free, so the ticket price is less and the money is shared between the filmmaker and the state that runs the theatre. It will take time, we won't have an audience overnight, but it will become a space that people will know. They'll come to see good cinema and it will grow. Because that's how I saw good films in Calcutta, in Nandan, where anytime you'd go you could see French cinema, German cinema or Indian cinema. To create it, not only in Bombay, but in Indore, Bhopal, I have given the Minister a plan for sixty-six cities—to create a network for independent cinema, where you have spaces which are dedicated to film workshops, a small library, a cafeteria, like the Prithvi theatre out here. The minister has liked the idea and the first theatre that they are going to do is in Delhi, where there's an auditorium that they are turning into an indie cinema hall. I have a meeting again this month to say that one is not enough. You need it all over the country, because we are like a continent. That way, a Gujarati cinema, a Marathi cinema, a Bengali cinema will start prospering and we will start watching each other's movies.

I am not fighting with the mainstream, because multiplexes' owners have their logic. They have to recover their costs of air conditioning and blankets. I don't want my audience to be lying down with a blanket while watching a movie. I want them to sit straight. When you're entering a mall, everyone is trying to please you to sell their commodity. So you go with that mindset to see a film, and suddenly here you are with a film that is hitting you. It is not the place. It's like going to a night club to dance and someone starts a classical music rendition. We need a separate venue, where people who go know where they are going and are going to sit and chat with their friends about the film after watching it, or listen to the filmmaker to interact with him. My work is a work of art: it needs an exhibition space, which cannot be in a mall.

When you say 'independent', what do you mean? So many directors use this word to define their films.

There's an international definition. In India, as usual, just like we don't follow the definition of new wave, we don't follow the definition of independent. Tomorrow, if I am doing a film with a studio, it is not an independent film. I will not see the benefits, contrary to a film that is crowdfunded, which has no studio system, no big producer. For me, being independent is first about financing, but content also. A porn film can be independent too. The content has to be in some artistic space. One could say it is debatable, but it's not. You know the difference between literature and porn novels. Similarly, there are certain ways by which one knows what independent cinema is.

How do you find money to finance your films?

Today, NFDC has a certain amount of money to produce films. Unfortunately, they haven't thought of how to distribute and how to exhibit. Because originally, their policy was also to create theatres. Instead of making ten films a year, make five films and five theatres a year, so your films get released, people see them, rather than just being in a library. The other day, I was doing a workshop for Children's Film Society. One of the officials came to the workshop and said, 'We are so proud, we have two hundred films and this year we managed to release the first one.' He should be ashamed that they are making films which are just seen in festivals or in schools. Today, Children's Film Society doesn't have a place to watch movies, because bureaucrats, mostly people who don't like cinema or have no knowledge about Indian cinema, decide the future of filmmakers. They'll probably say, 'I don't watch films', so I am like, 'What are you doing here, then?' Cinema not being part of art and culture is a big setback for us. If a Nandan in Calcutta can be a self-sustaining system, I am sure all those places, once they start, will generate money of their own. That shouldn't be the only criteria. Cinema is a form of art. It needs state patronage. Be it painting, be it music, be it architecture, it always has some form of patronage. Many people don't have the opportunity to get basic education. How are they going to appreciate art? The taste of every common denomination cannot define what is good or bad. Very often, you will see film critics who say what is loved by the masses, what is a hit, is ultimately what matters. No. If you go to Rajasthan, it's extremely popular to abort the girl child. That does not mean it's a good thing.

Let's talk about your first film, My Brother... Nikhil [2005], which explored the difficult subject of AIDS in the 1980s.

My Brother... Nikhil was not exploring just AIDS, it was the first mainstream Indian film where the male protagonist was gay.

You're saying your film is mainstream!

Absolutely. There are songs and mainstream actors. That's why recently, I challenged the saying that the first mainstream Bollywood that had male kissing was *Bombay Talkies*. If you're really looking at experimental cinema, there is a film called *Gandu* [Qaushik Mukherjee, 2010]. I have never made experimental cinema. My films fall in the space of mainstream cinema, where I challenge certain notions. I don't claim to be new wave Indian cinema. There have been a couple of short films, but nothing in the Hindi mainstream, or alternate, non-mainstream space in terms of feature films where the male protagonist was gay. It was a much more provocative thing than AIDS. AIDS would still be accepted by the audience.

I came across the subject because I was editing a documentary on Dominic D'Souza, who was the first AIDS case in India. Somehow, the story just hit me, stayed with me for years. When I was trying to make my first film, every script I would write was too provocative in terms of content to get financed. So my business partner and main actor told me, 'Why don't you write something that maybe we can shoot as a TV film?' I also wrote it in the format of a documentary fiction, so that it's cheaper to shoot and it gives you a feeling that this is real, this is not all fiction. It was produced by my friends and family, all coming together because everyone refused to make a film where the male protagonist was gay. I was told to make him heterosexual or bisexual. But I didn't want to start my career in cinema with a lie. For me, it was more important to tell the story I wanted to tell than become a director. It was always my guiding force.

My Brother... Nikhil was very difficult to make, but then I realized the distribution problem. Luckily, somehow, the movie clicked with Karan [Johar] and he recommended the film to Adi[tya Chopra], at Yash Raj, who distributed it. I will always be grateful to them for that, because Yash Raj gave it a certain branding. It's only because of them that it could be released, all over India, in seventy-seven theatres. Of course, when it got good reviews, then it got accepted for its own subject. I don't mean it was a commercial success. But at the same time, because I was a nobody, I didn't have big stars in the film, all the media awards ignored my film. There was no nomination. With *I Am* [2012], it happened all over again: even though it got two National Awards, despite being the first film funded through social networks, despite the fact that each of the stories was unique in its way, it was ignored by all the industry awards.

I've travelled the world with *My Brother... Nikhil* and *I Am*: in November, I am travelling to seven universities in the United States for the hundred years of Indian cinema, where I represent Hindi cinema and LGBT cinema. Then, I'll go to Paris for a screening of *I Am* at some festival there. *My Brother... Nikhil* constantly gets screened. It was also released in France but unfortunately, I've been cheated. Because it was my first film, I didn't know the business. I was in Montreal and this French distributor called, from Antipode films. He said he wanted to distribute the film. I was thrilled, my first French distribution! We decided on the money and they said we'll meet on the technical thing before they transfer the money. I sent them my master tape. After that, they stopped communication with me. Three months later, a friend in Paris called and told me, 'Guess what, I am at the Champs Elysées, the Virgin Megastore and I can see your DVD. I am so proud of you.' They've been selling it for six years, to satellite channels, on DVD without me getting any benefits from it.

Lots of French people, especially the queer community, know this film. People relate to the film. It's very strange, because it's a very

Indian film. But people are not so stupid. I think distributors are more stupid. When you're watching a film from Iran where the woman smokes, the audience in Paris knows that it's a big deal in Iran. Similarly, if a man is kissing another man in India, we know it's a big deal, that it wasn't done twenty years ago. Unfortunately, distributors, in Europe also, are not aware of cultural context. Bollywood has become so big, that everything else gets pushed aside. *My Brother... Nikhil* is a film I've travelled with, especially abroad, to talk about, though I wish I could do it more here. I'd rather be with a film that has longevity, than thrown in the garbage after four days of box-office success. I know that *I Am* and *My Brother... Nikhil* will always remain. They are in universities abroad as a part of the curriculum and *I Am*, because of the National Awards, will always be there in the history of Indian cinema. I am glad I've done that. I've done films that are extremely precious. Different NGOs can use my film, to start dialogue, which have also meant a lot to people who identify with the stories and have supported me to make my film.

Did you face any kind of censorship?

I feel some kind of silent censorship, which is becoming more and more aggressive now. A film called *My Lover Nikhil* wouldn't have been accepted, so I put everything as a story of a brother and a sister. It's a celebrated relationship in India, so I thought, 'Let me use that as a camouflage.' In the first half no one knows, so you fall in love with the character. Then, you get to know he's gay. So it's difficult to start hating him just because he's gay. Also I didn't show any sex, but much more the emotional bonding between the two guys, because homosexuality is often seen as a relationship which is based on physicality. It was used a lot by people to come out to their families and not just in India. I was at a screening in New York and this girl came out of the theatre ten minutes before the film ended. I thought she hated the film and she said, 'No, can I just hug you? Because my brother was seventeen, he was gay and HIV positive. He shot himself. I can't watch the rest of the film. But I want to thank you.' A lot of Blacks, Hispanics, people from the margins of some communities, identify with the film. In San Francisco, there was this review that said *My Brother... Nikhil* tells us that we should not forget. Because people are forgetting AIDS, even though somewhere else, there are people dying.

Today, when one talks of human rights, one shouldn't stop talking of gay rights. Very often, the rights of the gay community are forgotten. One never gives importance to the rights of the LGBT community world over. I see a little hope over the last few years: lots of countries are being really open to the need to respect choices and the way you are. Because I don't believe that you are just born with an identity. You can make choices. You are not only born gay or heterosexual. You might just connect to someone and get physical, that doesn't change your identity. If we're more tolerant, the world would be a better place. Let people love. It doesn't matter whether it's a boy or a girl.

I got a U certificate for *My Brother... Nikhil*. They just told me to put a card saying that everything is fictional, not to say that it is based on a true life story. I agreed because I thought when people will watch, they'll know. I was lucky. Over the years, when I was making *I Am*, I thought our society was becoming more evolved, more open. After making the film I realized that as a society, we have become more intolerant. The film, despite two National Awards, has still not been shown on satellite. Their whole thing is that there is no audience for the film. I don't believe it. I think it's because of homophobia that they are not showing the film. The same satellite channel, when there is rape happening, will say, 'Oh, Bollywood, where is the responsibility, how do you portray women?' And I say, 'Do you ever question your own satellite channel?' When a film is made that is responsible, educative, they don't show it. They're worse than the censor board, because I can fight the censor board. I can't fight television, that just refuses to show the film. I am not an idiot. I know it will not have the same audience as *Dabangg* [Abhinav Kashyap, 2012]. But saying that a film which was made through crowdfunding doesn't have an audience is a lie.

I find that people who are taking that one step to make the world better are smaller. I find it more difficult to make the films with the kind of subject I want to, in terms of finance. I understand: if satellite channels refuse to show the film, how will the producers recover their cost? Similarly, I feel the space for exhibition has shrunk. I've been told by studios that it's a company policy to refuse films that show violence or sexuality. The same censor board that gives a U/A certificate to *Bombay Talkies* gives me an A certificate and tells me that I have to cut out the kiss between the two men to get a U/A certificate. So I am also wondering if the Censor Board has evolved and has become more open, or is it because it comes from a certain position of power.

Of a Karan Johar.
Media and censorship have disempowered you, because for them it's okay for children to watch violence, but it's not okay for children to see people respect each other and learn to accept people. It's important for a child to see a movie about child sexual abuse in a country where sixty-three per cent of the children are sexually abused. But they don't want to talk about it. People don't want to harm their child by letting them know what a good touch is and what a bad touch is, and what abuse is. We have a censor board that is not educated in cinema, that is not open enough. How can they say that seeing two men kissing and having a loving relationship is not good for our children? If a man and a woman can do it, it's my right in a democracy to love, to be able to love. Instead of letting cinema be a vehicle towards progress, opening up windows, you're shutting them. The minute a film ends with everyone going *Jai Ho!*, it's all okay, but a *Salaam Bombay* [Mira Nair, 1992], which shakes you up, is not doing business.

Sometimes I feel I am losing my power as a filmmaker, sometimes I feel tired. How else will I find a way to do what I want to, how will I talk to my audience? The day I stop talking about these things, I am choking myself. I would be dishonest to my own identity, to my work as a filmmaker. That would be sad. I'd rather stop making films. How, in this euphoria of this so-called new wave Indian cinema, does a filmmaker who wants to talk about gender and sexuality find space? Where is the space for someone who doesn't want to talk to please the audience, someone who wants to make films in multiple languages? When I am doing a film about a Kashmir story, I want people to talk in their language. I don't want everyone speaking in the homogenized Hindi. When the only representation of homosexuality in Bollywood is a Pinku [*Mast Kalandar*, Rahul Rawail, 1991] who wears pink suits and is laughed at by everybody, there is a problem.

You're talking about films like *Dostana* [Tarun Mansukhani, 2008], where the heroes pretend to be gay by acting in a very eccentric manner.

The next thing that comes in the so-called non-mainstream space is *Page 3* [Madhur Bhandarkar, 2005]. The gay guy steals the actress' boyfriend. Then, *Honeymoon Travels Pvt Ltd* [Reema Kagti, 2007]: the gay guy is also a husband stealer. It's a cliché, but gay guys are supposed to make very good friends for women, because they trust them. Here, it's, 'Be careful, your gay friend is going to steal your boyfriend or your husband.' You come to *Bombay Talkies*: again! And not only that: you have this guy who, on the first night he comes to your home, is hitting on your husband and the next day, he's kissing him in the office in front of everyone. This is the only representation because at the end of it, negative representation is accepted. You'll also see films where you have *hijras* represented as criminals who are murdering women and raping them, and are always comic figures. Then you have a so-called very sensitive film, that everybody celebrated, which is difficult to understand when you see how they're speaking about the gay guys: *English Vinglish*. Sridevi gives a big sermon to her friend, saying that, 'They are gay people, they also have a heart and they can fall in love.' I'd love to see two gay guys sitting and talking about heterosexual couple the same way! This whole thing about 'let's tolerate' is the worst possible thing. Have you ever heard of a minority community having to tolerate the majority? No. The minute you start going into a representation that's not stereotyped, that's when your audience starts to be uncomfortable. *My Brother… Nikhil* has been watched on DVDs, because men are more comfortable quietly watching it and dealing with their own fears and insecurities than in the public space. Women, because of being marginalized in a way, have always been strong supporters. Feminism, women's rights movement and gay rights movement have a lot in common. The kind of violence that women go through is very similar to what gay people go through. Be it from family, be it from society, from everywhere. Within the industry, they all celebrate *The Colour of Love*, or *Brokeback Mountain*, but what are they doing to films here? Rituparno [Ghosh]'s *Not Another Love Story* didn't have a DVD or a satellite release. And the entire State went into mourning when he died. If you really respect him, show his films! For a long time, Rituparno didn't speak of his identity and he became one of the most respected and loved filmmaker. Then he started changing the way he looked and the kind of films he made. People would accept it, because they already loved him so much. What I mean is people have to play these games and I am tired of it.

What about your next projects?

I don't know yet. One is an adaptation of *Hamlet*. I am struggling to get a cast, because one of the things I wanted to do is to make Hamlet a woman. I need a big actor for this. I am also working on a film called *Shab*, my first script, which I have not been able to make because it's very provocative. Right now, I am working with a French producer who does a lot of co-production. It also has a French actor in it. It's a sensuous story between a gigolo and a call-girl set in Delhi.

Is it a take on *Breakfast at Tiffany's*?

Nowhere in that space. Very dark. I think I like dark. *(laughs)* The call-girl is a girl who has a very specialized kind of prostitution. She is hired by rich businessmen and dresses up as a bride. The hotel room is made up as a bridal room and she teaches them how to make love. It's a very special film for me. Apart from that, I am also working with a German writer on a film called *The Face*. It's a love story, between a young European guy who doesn't want to go for military service and comes to work for an NGO in Kashmir, and a man who's been falsely accused of being a militant. One is coming from a society where being gay is absolutely impossible and the other from a place where the father is in the military. The world over, there are very few places where when your son is born gay, the mother says, 'Yes, let's have a party.' Everywhere, there are different levels of discrimination. This film is about those two men who find a mutual space of freedom, learning about each other's cultures and differences, trying to come to terms with their love. That also will have to be a co-production.

I want to go more and more into co-production, to find a bigger audience, a different way where I can continue making my films without pressure—towards the space of world cinema. I found partners in France and Germany who are very interested. Because the world is waking up to LGBT rights, in the next few years, there will be much more openness, even back home. When you get support, you have that strength to speak up. Rituparno and I were probably the only ones who would constantly make films in the mainstream space. Now, one voice is gone. Nobody sees Sridhar [Rangayan]'s films, except in film festivals. For me, it's much more important that my films are seen in theatres, so people have access to them.

Your production company, Anticlock films, is supporting independent filmmakers.

Right now, I have a little bit of knowledge because of the difficulties I faced, so I would like to provide a platform to work with first-time filmmakers who have no budget. We have signed up two different films. One is *Chauranga*, which means four colours, to be directed by Bikas Mishra. The flag of India has three colours, and the missing colour is that of the caste who we say is not there—the Dalit community—which is actually the largest in India. The majority which is ruled by the minority.

The story is about a fourteen-year-old Dalit boy (again, it's a real life story), who falls in love with a sixteen-year-old upper-class girl and how their entire village system is shaken up. He's the only lower-class boy who is going for higher education. So it's about how education empowers and why a lot of people have been kept away from it. It's seen as an instrument of revolt. In reality, the boy was killed in the village.

Are you optimistic about gay rights?

I think if I was not optimistic, I would have stopped making films and also migrated. My friends keep telling me to come to Germany. It's difficult to be invisible. Recently, I had written an article for *Delhi Times* where I said I was not ashamed of being gay. It's an important part of my identity. But I don't want anybody to say that I am sensitive towards homosexuals in my films because I am gay. It's not because I show women in a certain way that my films turn me into a woman.

My Brother... Nikhil is not my story; it is a story that I identify with. In Pakistan, there is this law in the sharia saying that every four days, a woman cannot refuse to have sex with her husband. A hundred women came out to protest against this law and they were stoned. And I cried. That doesn't make me a woman. But I realized that it was important that I also came out. When I wrote this article, there were people on Twitter, on the Internet saying, 'You're a shame on our culture, you should be shot dead, you're a piece of shit, you should die.' What makes people feel so much hatred, when what I am doing doesn't bother anyone? That's what makes it difficult as a gay man, in a society where article 377 is still there. Homosexuals are scared and are living a double life, which I don't want to do. I am a public person, how can I find a companion? It's not an easy thing to tell yourself that it is a part of life that is going to stay empty, because of your profession or your identity.

SRIDHAR RANGAYAN
Director of the LGBT Film Festival 'Kashish' in Mumbai

Granted, it would be an understatement to say that India is not the most progressive country in the world in terms of homosexuality. Until 2009, Section 377 of the Indian Penal Code of 1860 criminalized 'unnnatural sexual relations'—a very vague term which has been interpreted to include homosexuality (though jail sentences prescribed by the law have rarely been applied). In July 2009, the High Court of Delhi ruled that this article violated fundamental rights, which gave an immense hope to the gay community in India. This hope was short-lived, however, as the Supreme Court decided in December 2013 to overrule the Delhi judgment, making gays and lesbians feel unwelcome again. In January 2018, the Supreme Court agreed to revise its judgement and in September, it finally ruled that Section 377 was unconstitutional.

Activism in the gay community, publicly present since the 1990s and supported today by the media and many artists, was strengthened by the Delhi High Court decision. To discuss this very subject, I contacted filmmaker Sridhar Rangayan. From the publication of the first gay magazine, *Bombay Dost*, to the creation of an LGBT film festival, Kashish, that has been held successfully every year in Mumbai since 2010, Rangayan has been one of the main witnesses of the evolution of the gay cause in India. His commitment to the cause makes him travel all around the world, and take on many projects, while still being committed to his filmmaking—in 2016, he started shooting his fourth feature, *Evening Shadows*.

We met in a café in the suburbs of Mumbai in the company of fellow filmmaker Harjant Gill, who has been closely following and documenting the struggle of Indian gays from the United States. Nonetheless, there is no pain or desire to wallow in the memories of hardships in Sridhar's discourse. On the contrary, it is with resounding, communicative laughter and optimism that he tells me about his journey, in an extravagant Bollywood style that he would not disown.

What made you turn to cinema?

I started to study to become an engineer, because most of the times that's what Indian families want their sons to do—especially in South India. I belong to a small town in South India and I've grown up in a very conservative family there.

From Karnataka, right?

It is a place called Mandya, which is about two hours from Bangalore. My father made a lot of efforts to put me [in] to an engineering college, so I did my five years. It's not something where I felt I belonged. So I came to Bombay for a Masters in Visual Communication and that's when I slowly started switching tracks in terms of moving away from engineering. Basically, I was trained as a designer, and one of the subjects was filmmaking. I started working for a corporate company, designing textiles. After that, I worked with the Hearing Impaired Institute, where I was supposed to look at their publications. I set up a film department to make films on hearing and speech impairment and right from then, I started making my first film project. Then, I quit a well-paid job at that institute and my apartment in Bandra to assist a very well-know filmmaker called Sai Paranjpye and the director Kalpana Lajmi.

At that point itself, I was interested in combining social advocacy with entertainment, in some way or the other. The first film which I made was a highly-dramatized version of hearing impairment. There were songs, dances and drama. I truly think that Indian cinema being typified by a very Bollywood kind of filmmaking is a good thing. I don't want to follow European, American cinema. I'd like to retain the value of what Indian cinema is and use it to subvert the genre.

Nobody in my family is a filmmaker, they are either doctors or engineers, or businessmen. I was not forbidden to watch films, but there was no film culture in our house. So I never thought it would be my career, but it's been a natural progression from engineer to designer to filmmaker. Each thing that I've learnt has contributed to what I am. Engineering has a logical framework to what you do. For me, it's very important when I make films; I make films for an audience and I know the kind of impact I want to make. It's not that I love the aesthetics. There's a purpose.

After apprenticing with the two filmmakers, I started doing television for three years, on telefilms, forty-minute episodes, in a lot of genres: comedy, romance, thrillers. But at the same time, I was coming out as a gay man to myself.

That's when you realized it?

It was in 1990, my last year studying at IIT in Bombay. I came in touch with two very prominent gay activists in Bombay. At that time, being gay was very underground. These were the people I felt like being with. I was kind of in the closet for many years, not speaking to anybody else. As a designer, I somehow got involved with the design of the first gay magazine in India called *Bombay Dost*, in 1990. In 1994, we founded one of the first gay organizations in India called Humsafar Trust. We set up this committee-based organization to work with gay and transgender people to provide help, facilities and rights. In that sense, it has been going in parallel, me coming out as a gay man, working with the community and my filmmaking career. I realized, while I was doing mainstream television, that there was no space in any of the mainstream television programmes for anything that was non-heteronormative. I pitched a couple of ideas of nice, soft gay relationships in these romantic series that I was doing, but they said this was not for family audiences. That was around 1999–2000. That's when I finally decided to quit television totally and concentrate on doing projects that I felt we needed to address. My partner Sagar Gupta and I started this company called Solaris Pictures, in 2001. The first production we did was a short film, *The Pink Mirror* [*Gulabi Aaina*, 2003]. We put in our own money. We wanted to make a fun movie with drag queens, talk about what it means to be a drag queen or a gay man in India. We used an extremely Bollywood style of film, with dance, drama, though instead of having a man or a woman, you have drag queens at the centre. One of the reasons I wanted to do it that way is that the Bollywood genre of filmmaking or a Bollywood TV soap is understood by the masses. The format is not new; you're not doing a boring documentary, or an experimental film. I found communicating what I wanted to much easier this way, so people felt the same way with my characters that they would feel with another character. We finished the film at the end of 2002. We submitted it to a Digital Film festival in Delhi and it was submitted to the Delhi Censor Board. *Gulabi Aaina* was refused a certificate, with the reason that it was offensive and vulgar. At that point of time, I was in Italy for the world premiere. I was not present for arguing with the Bureau—I don't know if they gave even an opportunity for arguing—so it didn't screen for the festival. Then it was up to me when I came back to India to take the case and appeal. When you make a short film with your own budget, you don't have money. The appeal process took one and a half year. I asked for the certificate three times, it was refused twice and the third time I asked for a meeting. I said I needed to know why. One of the reasons they gave is that I didn't depict the community with empathy. I said, 'I am from the community, what are you talking about?' They said, 'Your characters look happy with who they are, they don't have a problem with it.' So, basically, they wanted the homosexuals to cry, to say, 'Why am I like this? I am neither a man nor a woman, why did God make me like this?' In my film, my characters celebrated their sexuality and were questioning patriarchy, since one bisexual man was the object of desire and the others were preying on him. Usually the man is sought after by a woman in India; he's the centre of things and he's in control. Here was this man who was not in control, and these two drag queens and a gay man didn't apologize for who they are. I didn't get a certificate ever. It's gone to a lot of festivals all over the world, it's used in universities, who talk about gender, sexuality. It got critically acclaimed in a lot of places. But it didn't bring money, because there was no distribution possibility. The fact is, in India, when you look at 2003 or even now, short films or independent films don't get released.

I am actually surprised that you were surprised you didn't get a certificate.

Until that point of time, I had never taken a film with homosexual content to the Censor Board. The Censor Board never said you can't talk about homosexuality. Usually what the Censor Board has a problem with is kissing scenes, nude scenes, extreme violence and extreme sexuality. None of these things are in *Gulabi Aaina*. There was no real sex, no nudity. We didn't expect that just the idea of a positive gay portrait would be a problem. It's the first time we knew that they don't want to talk about homosexuality at all.

My second film, *Yours Emotionally*, was in 2006. It was a feature film, eighty-six minutes, in English. It was produced with a friend in the United Kingdom who said he wanted to make a film on a gay love story. It was more for an international market, so it had an exotic portrayal of India, I am guilty of that. *(laughs)* I never applied for the certificate. The whole film is centred on the point of desire, how lust leads to love. A British-Indian guy is coming to India with his white friend, and falls in love with a young guy in a small town in India. That guy in the small town doesn't have any concept of what being gay is. He's just a man who has sex with other men. Ultimately, his destiny is obviously to marry a woman, and settle down, perform his karmic duties. For him, having sex with this man who is coming from United Kingdom is like having sex with anybody else. But the British guy falls in love, and he doesn't know what to do, because there are all these issues around concepts of identities, of cultural differences between the two people. Finally, the British and the white guy come back to the United Kingdom and the village guy marries a woman. Many people didn't like it because it had a sad ending, and people like happy love stories. But these two people were so different. In India, a gay man in a small town would never be able to do what he wants to do, like choose a gay partner, live a gay lifestyle, or not be married. It was very realistic, but it met [with] a lot of negative criticism from the community in India, because they really wanted my film to say that gay relationships are possible. I was trying to be true to the characters. At the same time in the film, there is this elderly gay couple, who are in their fifties, one is unmarried and has lived in the United Kingdom and come back; the other one married a woman, had children and when the children went away and the wife died, came to live with his partner. For this small town, they are just two businessmen staying together. People find their own ways to live the way they want, within the parameters of the society. We don't need to have these labels, these categories of gay, bisexual, to be put into boxes. The film talks about these boxes and categories which the West put people in. In India, you don't need to do that. It was distributed in the United States, went to a few festivals, but it didn't do a great run. It had very limited screenings in India. I didn't send it to the Censor Board, because it was so out there, it had nudity, sex, kisses, plus homosexuality and masturbation. It's a very gay film. I've been showing it around in cultural institutes, festivals, in a college in Delhi.

You can do that even if you didn't get a certificate.

If it's for a private audience, if it's not a ticketed screening, you don't need to have a certificate, unless somebody objects to it. So you can screen it at the British Institute, Alliance Française, any of the festivals that are not held in a theatre. We screened it at this college in Delhi called Ramjas College, known to be an explosive venue. It was during election time. So I was worried. But we had a good turnout of one hundred and twenty students. One of the good things is that the professors said to the students that this film will make them very uncomfortable and that they had two choices: close their eyes, leave or watch the film and question why it was making them uncomfortable. Was it because they hadn't seen two Indian men making love on screen, expressing their desires? So ninety per cent of the people did stay back and we had a two-hour conversation after that. The boys and girls started talking to each other, asking and answering. For me, it was important that the film took the dialogue and conversation into the centre of where it was needed.

The third film did that more aggressively. *68 Pages* was done in 2007. That was more of an HIV-positive film, but again with a Bollywood style. It was made to talk about marginalized communities which are affected by AIDS, to support the national AIDS programme, to talk to counsellors, to say that they shouldn't discriminate against some of the communities. The film has a sex worker, a drug user, a transgender, and a gay man, who explain how they felt, how their life changed when they became HIV-positive. They also give the message that they're not going to die tomorrow. You can live happily if you get support from family, loved ones, a counsellor, and a medical institution. I wanted to appeal to a much larger, wider, common audience, so I had to apply for a censor certificate. People loved it at the Censor Board, but they said they were going to give it an A certificate. I said it doesn't have nudity, or violence, or sex, so why? They said 'none of your characters are normal. You can't have homosexuality and transgender as one of your main themes.' The fact that you are talking about homosexuality makes it an adult film. We wanted a U/A certificate which means you can reach to audiences from sixteen years old. We were trying to reach to the counsellors of tomorrow, people who are doing their undergrad. We couldn't reach them. Also, an A certificate blocked distribution for us. When we went to a mainstream distributor, he had the same issue, he brought up the 'normal' thing. I said the main girl is a woman, she's heterosexual, she's normal. But she had gone through a broken love affair, and was not in a relationship. She's abnormal in that sense. The Censor Board is controlled by power, beyond that rule book. If you're a bigger filmmaker, bigger production company, you have bigger distribution possibilities. A small independent filmmaker doesn't stand much chance to fight the system. There are ways to fight the system when you have power; they can get away with a lot more, twist the rule book when I don't have the resources to push to do that. Even *Brokeback Mountain* was released in India. They just cut off that one tent scene.

I thought *Fire* [Deepa Mehta, 1996] was censored.

Not by the Censor Board. They released it in Mumbai and there were riots, the Shiv Sena burned down the theatre. It was then banned in Maharashtra. *Fire* had a very limited release, but with no cuts. They only asked for a change in the names of the two characters, who were called Radha and Sita. I don't think they changed the names at the end.

I can't help thinking you're a little naive!

(laughs) But my film is holier than a cow! It has nothing offensive. We did expect that they would ask for cuts, but cuts would have cut the

characters itself. The Board agrees only when gay people are represented in a very non-positive way. If you give redemption to the character, if you explain there's a reason why he's like that, if he's punished or apologetic, then they are okay. Celebration of sexuality is a problem.

So we couldn't distribute it, and because of the A certificate, it couldn't go on national television or on a satellite channel. It still reached where it had to reach, because we had screenings at colleges, clubs, everywhere in India. Plus, we worked with the AIDS organization in India and we distributed it to all the clinics.

In 2010, I participated in the Project Bolo, an Indian LGBT project which documented twenty LGBT people in twenty states of India, talking about their lives in details, to understand what it meant to grow up as a gay, lesbian or transgender person right from the early 1940s. We had people who were in their thirties to their seventies. They were talking about how they negotiate their sexuality with their family, with their career, with their friends and colleagues. Through this project, we were trying to trace the history of the Indian LGBT movement. It's an online project; we put stuff on YouTube, and got 2,50,000 views, along with comments, hate mails and positive mails. It's inspirational for a whole generation of people to see how people negotiated their sexuality in earlier times. There was no Internet, there was no formal method of meeting.

How do you reach out to an audience that is not part of the gay community?

Gulabi Aaina has not been very successful in reaching out to a wider community; it is more restricted to a film club audience, or a very gay audience. With *68 Pages*, I think we broke ground and really reached out to a lot of local NGOs who are working with various issues. The point is if a film doesn't get a certificate, it doesn't get a mass audience. It's a vicious circle. If it gets an A certificate, it doesn't get a release in theatres or a release on television; because of that, you cannot release on DVD. These are the blockages. So I depend on alternative distribution which is very limited in its reach. There is an organization in Delhi that releases DVD of documentaries and short films. Their reach is only to a set academic circle or NGOs, not the common man. This is one of the challenges. You need a bigger budget to make bigger films, and actors who are mainstream. None of us believes in the star system, but if you really want to go out there, you need a star back-up. Onir's film, *My Brother...Nikhil* [2005], had Juhi Chawla and Sanjay Suri in the lead, but again it was not going anywhere though it had prominent actors. As soon as Yash Raj backed it, it went mainstream. For me it's important, that the film can reach the audience; whether they like the film or not is the next step.

Today, in 2013, things have changed a little. But even if Dibakar Banerjee, being a star filmmaker, makes a film with completely unknown actors, it's going to be very difficult for him to release the film, reach out to the audience. You do have small independent films releasing in theatres, but they get five or six shows and nobody knows about it, apart from the people who are still connected to the film, the filmmaker or the issue.

Did you ever find any star-backing?

One of my problems is about compromising. If the star backs up a project, he or she won't want it to be a gay film only, but to be packed with other things, so that it appeals to a wider audience. If I say it's only about gay men, you'll not find anybody to either act in the film, support or endorse it.

Even somebody like Karan Johar after *Bombay Talkies*?

I feel it's tragic that people who have the power are not really joining in full force yet, and not supporting the LGBT movement. I have a big problem with *Bombay Talkies* and I talked about it on a show with Karan Johar. Karan Johar's progression of films has been most disconcerting for me. We could tolerate the comedy in *Kal Ho Naa Ho* [Nikhil Advani, 2001] for a couple of years because we knew it was a joke. But this kind of joke went on to every award show. Then we had *Dostana* [Tarun Mansukhani, 2008], which I thought was really interesting. Though lots of people hated it, I think it's a very important film in the whole scheme of things, because it normalized the word 'gay'. It didn't normalize homosexuality, but it made the whole idea of being gay kind of cool. In a large part of the film, John Abraham and Abhishek Bachchan are pretending to be gay. Everybody was talking about it in the media. The perversion about the word 'gay', the fact that being gay was associated directly with sex went away a little bit. *Dostana* was placed in Miami, the mother came from London, so that made it easier for the film. The scene between the mother and Priyanka Chopra which has been talked about a lot is truly a nice scene, very well-written, with the feeling that gay men should be accepted for who they are. Then came this horrendous film called *Student of the Year* [Karan Johar, 2012], with homo jokes between those two gorgeous men [Siddharth Malhotra and Varun Dawan], who come out of the water again and again and are showing themselves off. One gay character is played by Rishi Kapoor, who is the professor. He's in love with the sports teacher who is married, and he is violent, he throws things at his wife because he wants her to die. That's really weird. Rishi Kapoor is a nasty guy throughout the film, and shows his whole frustration as a sexual being. He's not getting the football coach, so he takes it out on his students by punishing them. At the end, there's a student abusing him, abusing homosexuals, saying 'this pathetic ugly old man who cannot get love in his life'. At the end, Rishi Kapoor dies. It is one of the most pathetic attempts at portraying a gay man. Humour is there, but again it's really sad. I am not saying gay men are not negative, but what comes out of the student's speech is that being gay is so pathetic, being homosexual deserves being out of the school, dead. That's what the filmmaker endorses, though at the end some students come and say 'oh we loved this professor'. Then you come to a film like *Bombay Talkies*, where Karan Johar basically says he is going away from all the comedies, the big dramas and is being real. And what does he show us? He takes up this really young gay guy who has problems with his father, who wants to tell everyone that he is gay, then falls in love with the husband of his best friend, Rani Mukherjee. It's okay, it happens. But you don't go to a public television studio and kiss that guy! If I liked that guy, I'd do something in private with him. Then he gets beaten for that, and does the ugliest thing: he goes and tells his best friend that her husband kissed him, during a board meeting. We had this conversation on the show, Karan [Johar] and I, and he said it's for drama. I said 'this is not drama, this is a very real film, there are some dramatic boundaries you take in a film like this.' This gay man, who's frustrated, who's angry, is a home-breaker, and at the end beats up his father. I know that out of a million, there could be two gay men like this. We really do not have strong positive portrayals. The more negative portrayals pile up, the more difficult it is for us to talk to people, especially coming from the position of power of a Karan Johar. It becomes a prototype, an icon and people relate to characters like that. Karan said, 'but the film is not about that young gay guy who has problems, the film is about this married gay man whose truth is being exposed.' But how many married gay people are coming out? How many gay celebrities are coming out and admitting the truth, including the filmmaker? If exposing the truth was the agenda, I think it should be followed by the filmmaker. Otherwise, don't talk about it like a social cause you're supporting. People could be more responsible in what they do, especially if they're choosing a particular subject that's not being dealt with too much. Be sensitive, be a little more thoughtful, maybe have some interaction with the community, to understand where things stand. That I think is still lacking in the whole Bollywood film industry, where a lot of gay men, lesbians, bisexuals are still in the closet. I am not saying they should come out, but if they are approaching the subject, they must have a bit of understanding. One of the good things about the Karan Johar's film is that they were not stereotypical characters, but he is creating a new stereotype. If you see some of the 1960s-70s American films, the whole trend was to make the gay man a bad man, a rapist, a murderer. It's a bit dangerous and people have to be more cautious, concerned, be aware that there is a larger reality. We have seen very few good portrayals like *Pyaar Ka Superhit Formula* [Parvati Balagopalan, 2003] which had a really sensitive portrait of a make-up person and his partner in a small role. The other reasonably good portrayal has been in *Honeymoon Travels Pvt Ltd* [Reema Kagti, 2007], where it's a beautiful relationship, and it's very real. Again this guy comes between a marriage, but the way it's handled is so much more real and passionate, palpable. There's also Onir's *I Am* [2011], which I had a little problem with, because again I feel like I'd like to see one happy film I can talk about. In regional cinemas, there is very little to say. Recently, there was a Malayalam film with a big super hero playing a gay cop [*Mumbai Police*, Rosshan Andrews, 2013]. I need to check the film out. It's supposed to be quite a decent portrait. There's one film called *Journey* [Ligy J. Pullappally, 2004], made in Kerala, by an Indian-American filmmaker, one of the best queer films, about a lesbian couple trying to live their relationship in Kerala. Of course, it doesn't work and one has to cut her hair, like a symbolic death. It's one of the most interesting films I've seen. We need to possibly stop looking for mainstream cinema to provide good gay films. Let's look at short, independent films, and documentaries. That's why I started Kashish. If we can't make it, we're going to show what's been made.

Coming back to the 1990s, how difficult was it for gay people in India to come out of the closet?

In the 1990s, when I started working on *Bombay Dost*, there was just one public figure who was out, the founder of *Bombay Dost*. Now, of course, there are a lot of younger people who are coming out. When we started *Bombay Dost*, we had a limited run-out, like three hundred copies. People could not carry a particular copy. A person who lived alone could have a copy, and around that person, nine people would read it. It didn't have an explicit sexual content, but because it dealt with homosexuality, it was difficult to publish it. In those days, we didn't have a computer, so we had to go to a publishing unit. The people who were editing, doing the lay-out would all snigger, some of them refused to print it. It's just the passion which kept us going. We had no outlets to sell it, so it was being sold at a *Bombay Dost* kind of office, and also in the roadside footpaths stalls. Funnily, they would either wrap the magazine in a brown paper or they would just have the front page kept. And if you wanted a copy, they were stocked far away and they would go all the way to get it because they were too scared to stock it openly.

Bombay Dost provided a connection between people across India, to say that there is a community, that there are other gay men all over the world. We'd get letters from the North-East, from small towns, even from a prison, because those people didn't know who to talk to. Everybody had fake names; most of the people were looking for sex and love. There was a lot of police violence, of blackmailing gays at that time. If someone came to know that I am gay, he could blackmail me, saying I'll tell your colleagues, your neighbours, the police or the family. At that time, gays and lesbians didn't even exist, nobody knew about them. People were very scared, they would just have these quiet affairs. They would not have places to have sex, because people in India live with their families. Most of the time the sex would happen in a public space, in a park or in a toilet, so that's when the police would come, and threaten, sometimes beat up, sometime ask them for sexual favours. It was a difficult, scary time. Our organization, the Humsafar Trust, was created in 1994 to offer a space where you could come and be yourself. We had those Friday meetings which were attended by fifty–sixty people who felt empowered coming there, talking to other gay men and also trying to find love. Then we started to talk about AIDS, which was one of the big concerns at that time because nobody was taking precautions. None of the government agencies wanted to take it up, because for them, gay men didn't exist. Some of them actually said it only exists in the mind of Ashok [Rao Kavi, founder of *Bombay Dost*]. We started going to talk shows, showing that we exist. In 1994, we had one of the first gay conferences in India, where one hundred gay men came to discuss what we needed. It was held in a secret place because we were worried about the Shiv Sena or the police disrupting. Slowly, a lot of these small organizations started across India, in Calcutta, Delhi, Bangalore. We linked the gay right movement to AIDS because that offered a kind of funding to develop programmes. There was no money for gay rights.

It has been an interesting journey these last twenty years to see change. Now we have around two hundred such organizations across India. We basically provide training and help to other groups to start their own groups so they can manage. In 2009, the Delhi High Court ruling was completely a landmark decision, in many ways, because it finally said we were not criminals. People had the confidence to come out and say they are gay, or take queer activities much more into the open, out in the public, on Facebook, Twitter. Post-2009, there has been great visibility. One of the good things in India right through the years is that the media has been extremely supportive. Especially the English-speaking media. We did not have even one really bad reporting, except in language press, where there has been a kind of sensationalized writing. One of the really key events is that in 2001 in Lucknow, four men who were distributing condoms in a public park as part of HIV-prevention work were arrested and put in prison for forty-three days without food or water. They were charged under section 377, for promoting homosexuality. When the police raided the place, they found leaflets, safe-sex videos that were seen as pornographic material because there were condoms and lubricants. There was even a penis model for condom demonstration. It was an international issue, one of the first times everybody rallied together to help these men. We can say that the community mobilization in the media in 2001, got us the ruling in 2009. Now, especially in urban cities, we see a lot more comfort felt by gay men—in smaller towns and villages, it's still challenging. Gay men still get married to women and the women are completely disempowered. They marry a gay man, without their knowledge sometimes, and they have no option out of the marriage, when the man has the option of having a partner outside the marriage. Other thing we are keen on talking about is the fact that the woman is prone to infections because of the married gay man who has multiple partners back home. In India, you are not supposed to use a condom when you are having sex with your wife. If they don't want to make their wife pregnant, they would ejaculate outside of their wife but still not use a condom. One of the questions is then: are we talking about what exists in the West or do we have an indigenous concept about sexuality, apart from the *hijras*, which can be built upon, and empowered enough to sustain? Some question the fact that we want to follow a heteronormative way of living.

Do you talk about it in the public space also?

In the public space, we are not saying that we want gay marriage. *(laughs)* Everyone is waiting for the Supreme Court Judgment to come. The Delhi Court judgment has been challenged in the Supreme Court by a bunch of religious leaders and activists, and an anti-HIV guy who is saying that HIV is a myth build by pharmaceutical companies in the West. The whole community presented nineteen parents with an affidavit saying why their children feel marginalized, stigmatized in this country, being treated as criminals, why they felt that their child has equal rights to love and be loved, and that they have no problem with their child. At the end of December, the Supreme Court is supposed to give a verdict: either they approve the Delhi verdict, slightly change it or totally reverse it. We don't know what is going to be the outcome of it. Right now, it's just a judgment; it's not even an amendment. What we are calling about now is a reading down of the section 377 which says that any unnatural, non-vaginal sex activity is criminalized. Now the new reading says that consensual sex between people, adults of the same gender in privacy is not criminal. Privacy is a big question, because most gay and lesbians don't have a private space, so what happens if it is a park or a terrace? We want to make sure that that law is not removed, because it protects the rights of the child against paedophilia. Changing the law is going to take a long time. But if the Delhi judgment stays, it's a big step forward.

So I guess you could have your festival because of the 2009 Judgment.

Yes. As a filmmaker, I show my films around the world, I have known the whole experience of screenings on big screens, sitting in the mainstream space. There have been small festivals held in India but in cultural centres, mostly for the community. With Kashish, we wanted to put gay films in the mainstream space and open it to the public. It was an initiative we started in 2010. We wanted to do it on a completely international scale. It took us a long time to convince the multiplexes to hold it, because they were scared that their theatres would be burned down. Then they saw that we had thirty per cent more than we can accommodate, the Indian filmmakers' community came to support us, like Shyam Benegal, Juhi Chawla and Rahul Bose. That played an important role because they brought an important media focus on the festival and we could reach millions of people through television, written press.

There was no negative reaction?

Only one group in Delhi actually came forward and said that we cannot have this festival because it is against the Indian morality. But there is a right wing group in Bombay who said they were very proud that an international film festival was happening in Bombay. I don't think they knew that it was a queer festival, because the word is alien to them. *(laughs)* The festival has always been well-received and there has been no threat. We also do it with full police permission and applied to the Ministry of Information and Broadcasting to get a certificate. We do it in a very transparent, organized way. It's seen as a very good initiative of the community. Kashish became a place where people came together to enjoy cinema, sitting with their boyfriends and their girlfriends watching queer films with no hesitation and fear, and being in a multiplex theatre, having popcorn like at any other film without any mask. For the non-queer community, it allows them to get a window into queer life from around the world. We are trying to destroy the myth that being gay or lesbian is all about sex. We are human beings with happiness, trauma and career choices. These films show the diversity of experiences, and for a lot of non-queer people, it's a revelation, some kind of understanding. They have never met people who are happy, proud. Thirty per cent of the people are from the mainstream audience. The response has been immense. We turned back the thirty per cent people whom we couldn't accommodate in the theatre. What is lacking is the funding support, because the government doesn't support any LGBT initiative yet. The corporates are still hesitant; brands still do not want to associate themselves with an event like this. Kashish is the only event in India that works with corporate sponsors like banks, financial institutions like Barclays. Their involvement was very important. Now we are trying to get to other companies like Google and IBM.

What about the production studios?

They don't see it as a viable market for them. They don't see much value in promoting their brand to the gays. They are seeing how things are moving and I am sure that in the next few years, things will change. Somebody like Cinemax which is a multiplex is supporting us, as part of the jury we've had extremely prominent actors and filmmakers, like Shyam Benegal, who is our best credential. Lots of people find that reassuring.

Do you have to be gay to support the movement?

The point is gays, lesbians and transgenders in the closet are the most homophobic ones. That is a tragedy. Influential people who are in the closet are actually more homophobic than the common man in the street. They would have their own coteries and circles but they would not come forward to support, though just one or two public figures coming and supporting would be a big thing. Things have changed in the last ten years, so I am not complaining. I didn't think that we are going to see this change in our lifetime. To be part of the change is gratifying. Lots of us are not calling ourselves activists, we are helping ourselves be who we are and we need visibility to help us be who we are. We are actually doing it for a very selfish cause in that sense. We want to be seen as normal. My mother asks why I speak out. According to me, speaking out helps somebody in a small town somewhere. I've been blackmailed, I've been harassed, I came out to my family, they have not been that accepting, I've come out to some of my friends, some were accepting, some not. Today at fifty, I feel very comfortable, and this has been not only my personal growth, but also changes that have happened around me. A lot of young people are coming and taking charge, and this is amazingly reassuring. My latest film is called *Purple Skies* [2014], it's a documentary on lesbians, bisexuals and transgenders, and for the first time people have come out and talked openly, about their happiness, but also the violence they face. That couldn't have happened five years ago. It's very encouraging.

Are there more LGBT Indian films being made?

Yes, a lot of short films and documentaries are being made, none of them go to the censors, but most of these films are self-funded by filmmakers who have a passion to do something, or colleges or institutes where they're doing a student project. We still do not have anybody supporting financially any queer films at this point of time. Most of us crowdfund our projects. Kashish shows these Indian queer films made all over India, gives them cash rewards, and trophies, and tries to show them at other festivals around the world, and distribute it around the world. The majority of the films are not really of good quality, because of the lack of resources. The idea is that this content has to be made, shown as much as it can, so we see the diversity of voices, not only a Karan Johar or a Madhur Bhandarkar's representation. Kashish's future would be to set up workshops for training, set up a film fund to fund minimally. Right now, what we are concentrating on is distribution and exhibition. We have DVDs of the films available on Amazon and VOD.

If the Supreme Court removes the Delhi rule, what happens to your festival?

The festival will not die down, because it's established. Gay events are not criminalized—it's the gay sexual act which is. The gay fear now is gone. I don't think it can come back. Plus, the law was never used legally. It's been mostly threats and blackmails. The whole generation that has been empowered by this decision to come out, knows how to deal with their problems. If there's a threat, even if bad reporting happens and somebody tries to be violent towards the community, there will be more protests. We have a huge counter system in place right now.

PART 6

THE FORGOTTEN GENRES: ANIMATION AND DOCUMENTARY

This book wouldn't be complete without mentioning two genres that are usually forgotten when talking about Hindi Cinema: animated films and documentaries. The predominance of the Bollywood film—or, to be more precise, of the 'formula film'—seems to have made the West oblivious to the richness and diversity of Hindi Cinema. This ignorance, however, is not due only to our superficial view. Although the genres of animation and documentary are completely different from each other, they do have one similarity: their filmmakers struggle to survive in an environment that pays no attention to them. Even the government gives them only limited support.

The documentary genre goes back a long way. The first 'film' made in India was a documentary inspired by the Lumière brothers about a wrestling match in Mumbai [*The Wrestlers*, H. S. Bhatavdekar, 1899]. The real spark, however, came years after that in two steps: first, the establishment of the documentary genre, in the 1930s by filmmakers D. G. Tendulkar (who had been Eisenstein's assistant) and K. S. Hirlekar; and second, in 1948, the creation of the Films Division, a government department devoted to the 'production and distribution of information and news films'. Over the years, the prolific Films Division produced more than eight thousand films (including animated and short films). Its productions were dubbed in five languages, and were mandatorily screened before every feature film in theatres. In 1978, the Films Division documentary *An Encounter with Faces* by Vidhu Vinod Chopra, dealing with the subject of street children in Mumbai, even won an Oscar nomination.

This golden age declined gradually after the 1970s, as state control didn't allow much creative freedom and documentaries were screened only on the national television channel, Doordarshan. The opening of India to globalization offered other opportunities: Discovery Channel entered Indian television in 1995, and National Geographic in 1998. The creation of the Mumbai International Film Festival for Documentary, Short and Animation Films in 1990 opened a new space of expression for filmmakers. However, the contemporary scene is far from idyllic: the Censor Board decision in 2003 that all films screened at the festival should be submitted for review, provoked a protest movement that led to the creation of the film collective Vikalp, Films for Freedom. The interviewee in this chapter, Nishtha Jain, also spoke of the lack of financing in India for documentaries, which often forces filmmakers to seek out international co-producers. With fascinating subjects—dealing with society, environment, sexual identity, human rights or censorship—the documentary in India is a vibrant genre and it would be a crime to set it aside.

Indian animation came in long after the documentary, with *The Banyan Deer* [1957] being the first venture of a studio formed under the aegis of Disney. The Films Division also created its 'Cartoon Unit' that launched the career of Ram Mohan, considered the father of Indian animation (the interviewee of this chapter, Gitanjali Rao, was his apprentice). Short films, feature films, TV series for children and animated ads progressively saw the light of day, but sadly, the Indian audience simply wasn't interested, and today the nation's animated cinema is unable to compete with Disney or Pixar. In this chapter, Gitanjali Rao will try to explain the reasons for this situation. It is easy to conjecture that the lack of a proactive approach or financing would be the fundamental reason for this failure, as talent and stories cannot be lacking in a country that saw the birth of one of the oldest civilizations.

GITANJALI RAO
Director

The charming Gitanjali Rao welcomed me into her house in Goregaon, next to the Film City studios. Her home is also her workplace: all through the interview, at various points, while her assistant was editing, she paused to show me the progress of her current work, the short film *True Love Story*: a love story between a flower-seller and a bar dancer. She even offered, when the conversation was over, an exclusive screening of the film, though it was not yet complete (it was later screened as a part of the Cannes Film Festival selection in May 2014).

I have known of and followed Gitanjali's work since her first short film, *Printed Rainbow*, which premiered at Cannes in 2006, won the Best Short Film Award at the Critics' Week. Her films are innovative on various levels, style-wise as well as content-wise. One could call her work minimalistic: simple, even imperfect drawings, down-to-earth stories, but with a strong sense of poetry and a beautiful combination of truly Indian, urban realism and dreamlike sequences. You couldn't hope for anything more different from the Disney universe: Gitanjali doesn't make animation films for children, and doesn't care much about the newest techniques. She chose animation to tell a story.

Animation in India is such an underdeveloped genre that had I not known Gitanjali already, she would have anyway been the go-to person in terms of this truly 'forgotten genre' of Indian cinema. France was the first country to recognize and support her work, and even today, despite the international critical acclaim she received—she is a familiar face in Cannes, where she also served as a Jury Member in 2011—she has to independently finance her films and find most of the funding abroad. Gitanjali had a lot to say about India's ignorance of animation, and the tremendous challenges she faces, but always with the loveliest of smiles. Discouragement doesn't exist in Ms Rao's philosophy of life.

What turned you into an animation filmmaker?

I have a Bachelor in Applied Arts. Back in 1994, animation wasn't known as a field. I was very fond of painting and illustrations. I was also very interested in cinema and making films. So I was hoping to study further after I completed my arts to study filmmaking. But somehow I had to start working, so I decided I might as well work in something that leads me to cinema rather than advertising which is what I was trained for. I saw some animation films in a festival, because at that time there were no DVDs and one couldn't watch international animation films on television anywhere. In the 1990s, cable TV had just come in and we didn't have it at our place. They had started this Bombay international festival which happens every two years and had this Polish animator coming down with a retrospective of his work. I had never seen that kind of animation in my life before. For some reason, I fell in love with it and I realized this is one medium where I can continue doing my paintings and my illustrations, and also enter into cinema.

There was one studio in Bombay which was accepting arts students to train them to become animators. I joined in. It was a very commercial studio, created by Mr Ramu, who was the pioneer of animation in India, in the 1970s. The Films Division made animated films and Ramu, who was part of it, realized nobody knew animation in this country because it had never been taught. So, after a few years, when they wanted to improve the quality, they decided to teach. You were made to learn the skills on the job and got a place to explore the ideas of animation. We used to watch a lot of animation films from Canada, which got me more interested in world animation. In the studio, they used to follow a very conventional kind of animation, the Disney kind and I got tired of it after two years.

After that, I went to any studio, started some freelance work and decided it was what I wanted to do.

What kind of films were you making for that studio?

Animated ad films for television mainly. They also used to do a series of ten minutes for UNICEF, made for rural Indian people. A little girl called Ninna was telling them various ways to sort problems—basically, they were social-awareness films. They didn't get too much money out of that. We also did Bollywood film titles, animated films for Channel V and MTV who had just started their studios in India, and ten or fifteen-minute short films once in a while. When I joined, they were finishing a short film. It was supposed to be a trend, but after that no more were made, because there is no funding for short films. It has to be done in your spare time, with your money.

After the UNICEF contract finished, it was all about ad films. Then, the company merged with MTV and two hundred animators started working for Fox Television USA. Now, the company is dissolved but there was this boom from around late 1990s until about 2007–2008, where studios who were going to the Philippines started coming to Bombay and Hyderabad. They very quickly set up studios, with two to three hundred animators who were taught six-month courses on basic software. The computers came in around that time. It changed very quickly. In two years, everybody was doing some kind of outsourcing and there was a lot of money coming into the country through animation. Then, they made the first feature, *Hanuman* [Milind Ukey, V. G. Samant, 2005], after which there was this false euphoria that animation makes a lot of money. There were fifteen to twenty animation movies released. Yash Raj also got into this whole scene. Some of them did make money, most of them flopped. Because people started doing their features and India became too expensive. Studios stopped the outsourced business completely and went back to Manila. Complete studios were shut down; nobody cared what would happen to the artists. After a few years, Ramu got sick of the outsource thing and went back to his own set-up, but it was never as beautiful and original as it was. Now, there are many animators around, who have a lot of talent and not enough work.

In a country with so many children, why is there no interest in animation?

Children's films are not that popular in India. People would rather go for a Hollywood animated film. Indian films are not made with the same finish as a Hollywood film, in animation especially. The stories that are being told are being told from the Hollywood perspective, like the superhero kind of films. So there is an instant comparison and Indian films totally fall short. You cannot fool children, so they'll watch something that looks better to them. Also, it has been decided that an animated film cannot make more than four crores. The cost of producing a feature film is definitely going to be more than four crores. If you make it for less than four crores, you're bringing down the quality of the film. And when you ask for a budget that is larger, there is no justification that that kind of money is going to be brought back, whereas the profits they get by importing and dubbing a film are so huge. In the 1960s, the NFDC stepped in and they decided they don't want to make profit, but just make films, which is like cinema in France. That gave a huge boost to the artistic, non-commercial cinema. That trend still continues. But in animation, we are supposed to compete with Hollywood in the hundred-crore business. It cannot start like that in animation without any history of characters having been created for kids to be interested in, like Tintin. They would want to see those characters, because they have been brought up with them. We have some mythological characters, but no visual symbolism that is taken forward by animation. So we need first to create our audience, get them to appreciate the films, then we will start to see the profits. The first profits will not come with the first ten films. But there's no space for that: here, it has to come with the first one, or the second is not made.

It's a paradox in India, where people mostly go to watch Indian live-action films, but Hollywood-animated films.

Hollywood is mainly seen in the cities in India. Animation films have never been released in rural markets at all. They don't fit in.

The characters don't belong to a particular region. In Tamil cinema, if the character is not Tamil, if the story is not Tamil, it's not going to work. So you have to decide a region and a language where your film is going to work, which narrows down your audience and you have to make your film for a city audience. The city audience is tough, because it's anyway going to see better films from Hollywood and it will tend to compare. The reason why people continue to watch Indian films started in the 1930s. Your parents have watched it, you've watched it and your kids are watching it. Everybody likes Shah Rukh Khan. They say there's a tradition of worshipping our heroes, but Shah Rukh Khan didn't become a god just like that with his first film. Where do you compete? Where does animation start? Not even ten years ago. In animation, nothing has been defined as to what you should look for, whereas in Eastern Europe, in Russia, kids are born and brought up with their own animation. The Japanese have also done it with manga comics and created their own style; they took sixty years to reach where they have reached.

Hollywood animation is inspired by fairy tales. What could be the inspiration for Indian animation?

A lot of animation films take their stories from the *Mahabharata*. We have other texts, like *Panchatantra*, or *Jatakas*. My generation is still familiar with them because our parents used to tell us those stories, but the newer one is not even being taught these stories in school. They will know a Hansel and Gretel and Snow White, but not the Indian ones. We also don't have, like the Russians, like the French, fairy tales, story books which are read to you at night, stories from your own culture, your own language. We have a very vocal tradition. It's always been someone telling you a story, because people couldn't read or write for the longest time. The folk tradition of storytelling has started disappearing. If you go back to it, one generation back, it is completely borrowed from the *Mahabharata* and the *Ramayana*, whether you're talking about storytelling, play performances, shadow puppets, dance performances, or singing performances. The *Mahabharata* has a lot of folk stories and characters from north to south of India. It would be a really great and endless thing to delve into. *Mahabharata* is bigger in terms of content of stories than any epic from another culture or language. Plus, the ending of the stories in European fairy tales is all figured out. In India, there's a lot of freedom that has been exercised. There's a very rich literature also, like Kalidasa—which does not belong to the *Mahabharata*—or other legendary writers, who have written huge bodies of work, but are accessible only to the intellectuals. Your maid servant might not know this story, because one is our tradition of intellectual storytelling and one is the folk storytelling which has similarities. Indian classical music and Indian folk music would share the same *raga*, but one is more accessible to people and the other has its finer virtue still kept intact. In the same way, you will have the *Mahabharata*, the *Ramayana*, the *Panchatantra*, the *Jatakas*, the literature of the South which is a *sangam* literature, then regionally-based movements of literature which have happened around the country. A quarter of the country will still identify with these stories. If you're working on regional cinema, I would think that these are the stories, which you should go in for. And the potential of the stories in *Mahabharata* is the freedom to contemporize them, since these stories were never set into a period. They were written in a way that it can work in any period. We don't need to come up with new stories. How to make it relevant to an audience is something that we have to work on. There's no way to know if an original story could work or not work.

The Indian hero of an Indian-animated film could be a rickshaw driver.

That also is only in Bombay and in cities. Rickshaws are not everywhere. India is like a continent: you're dealing with France, Germany and Spain at the same time. Coming out with one superhero is very tough. Italians are not going to like the French superhero or the British superhero. It's tougher, because of completely different languages and traditions. In the southern parts of India, they actually celebrate Ravana, the antagonist of *Ramayana*. If you're making a film which is the traditional North Indian way, Ram will be the hero. If you go to the South, there is this entire country impeccably ruled by Ravana, a utopia that he runs and their claim is that he never did anything to Sita. Anything can happen in India, because everybody thinks they own the *Ramayana* or the *Mahabharata*. If you show anything that is different, you lose a huge section of the crowd. They'll say, 'Don't go watch that because in that Lord Ram is not doing what he is supposed to do.' It's much easier to work on mythology in France or in the United States than in India. That's why folk stories for me are very interesting, where you don't have gods, but there are characters which people know and which have certain powers and attributes. They're very believable, very real and not magical. That's what Shilpa Ranade has done, with what is, for me, the best Indian animation feature film, *The Adventures of Goopy and Bagha* [*Goopi Gawaiya Bagha Bajaiya*, 2013].

Is it a remake of Satyajit Ray's movie?

That's the same story of the classic folk tale, but in animation, with music and in Hindi. The film is produced by the Children Film's Society and it opened in Toronto, with a budget of less than four crores. Making that film took a long time. The Children Film's Society is a government-funded institute. Their only problem is they don't know how to market films and they refuse to let anybody market their films outside. They've made and funded some of the best children's films, but nobody has seen them. I was in the jury in a festival in India two years ago and I saw ten animation films in regional languages. I wondered how come I couldn't watch them in a theatre. If the films are not distributed nationally, how are they going to make money? It's not about the quality of the film, or the appeal of the film, it's also how you promote it, something that countries like France or the United States have figured out. Here, everybody is doing their own distribution system, like everybody is doing their own directing. Some are good at it, some are not. They don't merge, especially if one is a government institute and the other one is a private. For the past three years, I've been trying to get funding for my film from various places in the country, but companies won't work with each other. So, forty per cent of my budget is French funding.

Which French funding?

The first one has been Cinémas du Monde. From the forty per cent, they got twenty. It's one-tenth of the budget, which is a huge amount.

The other one would have been CNC, but I got rejected. Arte has not picked it up, but I'll go to Canal. I am sure they can raise the funds there, but here with NFDC, it's just waiting.

What about the private studios?

I did go to some of the studios here, but they said they wouldn't want to co-produce with the French. They would put in all the money and I should do it in 3D animation, because they have a 3D animation studio in Doha. This is not working out. Here, they have the money to put in entirely, but I don't want them to do that because they won't distribute the film, they won't take it to the world.

Basically, you want to keep control over your film.

Yes, I don't want the French to have control over my film. *(laughs)* You choose your producers smartly, so aesthetically you would trust them. Business-wise, the Indians are smart but both the parties would have to trust each other. Apparently, it is very difficult for the French to trust the Indians. I don't understand why. *(laughs)*

They'd have to understand the work culture in India.

Yeah, but not everybody can spend four years here to understand it. Even after forty years of living in this country, I still don't understand it. *(laughs)*

Animation is no longer a genre that's just dedicated to children. Your first movie, *Printed Rainbow*, is actually for adults. Where do you stand? What kind of animation would you want to do and for which audience?

I am interested in animation for adults. I am not interested in doing films only for children. My new film is for fourteen-years-old and above, because it deals with prostitution and child labour. I think any child over eight could see this movie, but it still would not go to a children's section. With a film like *Printed Rainbow*, I didn't keep any age in mind. My friends showed it to their kids when they were four years old and they would watch it differently when they were eight years old. So it's not only for children, but it works with children. When I was doing a project with Walt Disney India for a feature film, I finished the story and the character, but production hadn't started because they called it off. While writing the story, the concern was that children's films for me should also appeal to adults. It was again a totally contemporized version of the *Mahabharata*. In *Mahabharata*, the heroes are sent away from their homeland for fourteen years into another place and my characters moved from Hampi to Bombay. At one level, it worked as a plot for kids to follow, with a villain, a beginning, middle and end. For the adults, it was a take on *Mahabharata*: my generation would be familiar with the stories and some details of it and these details are twisted in the sense that they are made amusing. There are eunuchs which are a form of Krishna, because in certain stories, Krishna was a man and a woman at the same time. Also, the villain is trying to create a bridge in the name of development of Karnataka so he can practise mining from the mountains. Adults would have seen another story, about migration, queer society and mining issues.

Animation is very expensive and it's very time-consuming, I wouldn't just want to finish off a film and forget about it. After watching *Printed Rainbow*, people have told me that they looked at matchboxes differently. My movies just create a sensitivity and make people look around and see. I show those migrants at the traffic signal that indifferent people pass by in their car. I show their daily lives. People who are going to come watch my films are the people who are sitting in their cars. And if they were to just look a little more carefully for one day, that's enough. I can't do more.

You were previously talking about a conventional animation technique. What are you trying to do that is different from convention?

2D animation. By itself, 2D and 3D are two completely separate fields of animation. 2D is the original animation: the Walt Disney style was drawing frame by frame on cell sheets, keeping a background, with a static 35-mm camera on top. Disney is also a conventional style: there is a text book which shows how fat or thin characters would move.

It's very important to learn this. It's like learning your ABCs, the same way that you need the basic Roman alphabet to learn French or German. I wasn't great with it and I didn't want to spend a lifetime perfecting that art. My interest was still the story and I wanted to explore whatever style the story requires. Being a designer, I know the principles of motion, but what if I applied it to a completely different medium? If there is a shadow, and you don't have 3D, then how do you move it? It's tough if you take off a dimension. So I started getting interested in Indian art, miniature painting, which is highly detailed and doesn't show any of these conventions: there is no shadow for instance. If this was to be animated, how would it look? It was pure exploration and it was a kick because each time, I had to come out with my own formula, create new languages. Then I worked with a few people like Shilpa [Ranade], who was making a film for the BBC. She also decided to do it in a different style, which was not from a Bible like the Disney book. To work with other people, to imbibe their style is actually very healthy. It makes you start thinking that there are different ways from the conventions, that you can move your characters in a different way.

My technique is very basic. I still draw and paint every frame. It's a progressive animation which I follow, which most people still do in European animation. But with computers, the good thing was the whole process became very cheap. You didn't need papers, you didn't need cells and you didn't need a camera. Instead of painting on paper, I draw on the machine, I can undo, use short cuts. But I never got into vector software like Flash, where the machine helps you do the in-betweens.

Like when a character is running, the machine is doing all the drawings?

No, you still have to make every five or six key drawings, but then the machine will fill in three or four at least. I will draw every frame. That's a really traditional, most laborious process. But that's really the appeal of *Printed Rainbow* to a lot of animators. It took me two-three years to make this fifteen-minute-long movie.

Were you doing it all by yourself?

Yes. Right now, there are three women working with me on a seventeen-minute short film, two other animators and a production designer.

How does it work? How do they imitate your style?

They have started working with me for the last two-and-a-half months. I finished six-and-a-half minutes of the film by myself and I've got them in. They worked with me for about nine months on another feature film. I spent three months training everybody in the style. The third person who is working with me has never worked in my style. She's completely the Disney-convention style, but she was free and she was ready to help. In one part of the film, I show this Bollywood film that the boy is watching: she's done the entire Bollywood animation. So although it's a little different from the rest of the film, because her style is very conventional, I wanted the Bollywood convention to come in. Plus, just by working on it, she's come closer to my style than earlier.

I used to work with twelve people and they were all doing different things. So it became team work; some of them who were strong in the style could take over and others were doing the supporting characters. Background is not difficult at all, because it's a static visual. I've done half of the backgrounds in the film. The thing is I can do everything, so it's easy for me to teach somebody to do my style, because I can almost hold their hand.

Who edits?

I don't over-animate because I can't afford it, so the film is edited from the beginning. I am working on a timeline, finishing bits and pieces and putting it there. My timeline doesn't change.

You're preparing a feature film but the one you're making right now is a short.

It started as a short, then I got an Indian producer interested in the film and I got an idea for a feature. This short became one story of three which will come together for a feature. The Indian producer loved the script and I got the French producer of *Waltz with Bachir* interested. Two years ago, I received the French funding. I finished the script, the characters, I started doing bits and pieces of animation, but the Indian producer, Guneet [Monga], from Anurag Kashyap films, didn't manage to raise any money. So I got tired of waiting. I said, 'Let me do my short film.' I had some spare money which I invested in completing the film. Then these four girls, whom I wanted to work with, were free. Now, twelve minutes are finished, so in two-and-a-half months, we'll have completed it.

How much would you have needed to make that feature and why is it so expensive, since animation doesn't need to be shot outside or a big crew?

A studio shoot lasts for about forty days, which is your maximum cost. The budget for a feature film right now would be ten crores, if it is completely produced in a place like Bombay and made over here. It's going to take eighteen to twenty months just for frame by frame animation, when I have a team of thirty people. Thirty people, who have eight to ten years of experience and whom you pay between sixty thousand rupees to one lakh a month, are the biggest cost of the film, and not software or computers. This is without taking any star voices. Then, your producer needs to have a cut and there's the director's payment—twenty-five per cent. If you get a co-production, you have to spend fifty per cent of the money in that country. If France gives you four crores, you have to spend two in France. So, if you're taking French co-production, even if they give us four crores, two crores have to be spent in France. Those two crores are not going to be able to give me as much work as two crores in Bombay. If I get two French animators, it will cost me as much as twenty Indian animators. But also, getting two French animators is not as simple as that, it has to be a bigger creative contribution. I would actually need eight crores so that everybody gets paid and that money is difficult to find. A film like *Arjun* [*Arjun: the Warrior Prince*, Arnab Chaudhuri, 2012] cost ten crores, which is not interesting for anybody, because you can make a three-crore live-action film if you're having a forty-day shoot with no stars.

My films are also expensive because they are very low-tech. If you're using 3D softwares, the cost will go more into machines than people. Here, I am paying talent. My problem with Disney was that they said animators are jobless and we could hire them for half their pay. It would be exploitation. Disney couldn't understand that.

You really don't like 3D.

I've seen good 3D films, but for me what's important is still painting, illustrations and an atmosphere that you create. A 3D imagery is very boring, too repetitive and too perfect in its form for me. When a Tim Burton is making a 3D animation, it's so hyperrealistic that I am left with nothing to imagine.

You've made a short film called *Orange* that never cleared with the Censor Board.

My paintings were nudes, and it was about love, but nothing was really happening. It's just that this woman is roaming around everywhere and she's nude. The Board said frontal nudity is not allowed on Indian screens, even if it's animated image, even if it's just a form. They asked me to cut off all the frontal nudity scenes and after that, they would give me an A certificate. One minute of the movie would have gone and it would have made no sense.

Censor certificate is only required when you publicly screen the film. But at that time, in 1998, this short-film festival for animation and documentaries decided that they wanted films with censor certificates. Even the National Awards need a censor certificate. So I couldn't send it to the National Awards.

You often say that you are more famous in France than in India and *Printed Rainbow* got the Award for Best Short Film at the Cannes Film Festival in 2006.

My sound engineer was working on my film in France and an ex-curator in Cannes saw him working on it. She said, 'This film looks nice, why don't you ask the director to send it to Cannes?' Nobody sends their films to Cannes! Then I get this letter from

Cannes Critic's Week, saying, 'We believe you're making a short film, can you send it to Cannes?' When I met this ex-curator, Cecilia, I said, 'Do you often do things like this?' *(laughs)* She said that's the only way they find talent. I was convinced that I was not going to get selected. But my film got selected, the same day I heard that it got selected in Annecy [the festival for animation films]. I was still more excited about Annecy. I went to Cannes and I couldn't believe I won there, because I thought the best films come to Cannes. For me, they must have taken pity on Indians, because I was not a known name. This was so sudden and this was before Facebook, so nobody knew about it.

Nobody talked about it in India?

Because of the prize, yes, a little bit. Anurag got to know about it, so he spread the news. I didn't know what the label of Cannes meant to a film, or to your career—it changes your life completely. I never found funding to make my next short film, because everybody was like, 'Now you're ready to make a feature film.' And I said, 'No, another animated short. Annecy! That's the place all of you should be going to.' *(laughs)* I had no producer for the film and they don't talk to talent in France. So I had a wonderful opportunity, but I didn't know how to make anything out of it. The film was going to every festival. This was 2006. Nobody knew how to send films to festivals. Before 2006, for nine years, there was not a single Indian film in Cannes. The trend has just changed now. So many Indian films are being sent.

Suddenly, the film got shortlisted for the Academy. I got that wrong also, because I should have sent it the previous year. As a single person with no producer or no agent, I was just trying to go online and check for information. The year after, the Critics' Week saw that I was working on a feature film and they asked me to look for co-production, through the Cinémas du Monde. They were inviting me for the project and I still didn't have a producer. I went alone, because I was also part of the jury in the Critics Week, having won the previous year.

In Cannes, you have to pay with your own money and it's very expensive. Cannes never invites anyway, but they give feature-film directors three days of free stay. You have to travel on your own. So I was broke, I didn't know how to do television sales and look at contracts. I got very scared, so I just went into hiding and started my new short film, for which I didn't manage to find funding. Then, this feature happened, we did four minutes of it and the company went bankrupt. Then, I was doing this thing for Disney which didn't start. Each time I was looking for funding, I approached the French. Now, I haven't made any of these films, but I have a relationship over various projects with them. *(laughs)* I am going back in January, when there is this first edition of a festival of Indian films. They've asked five directors with a carte blanche of their selection of Indian films, non-Bollywood, non-mainstream films.

What did you choose?

Pyaasa [Guru Dutt, 1957], *Garam Hava* [M. S. Sathyu, 1975], *Shahid* [Hansal Mehta, 2012] which is a new film and *The Adventures of Goopy and Bagha*. I also selected the Tamil film *Paruthiveeran* [Ameer, 2007] and a children's film, *Pasanga* [Pandiraj, 2009]. *Paruthiveeran* has been to Berlin, but I don't think it got to France. It's very symbolic of the over-the-top and shocking style of Tamil filmmaking. It's a very different form. I also chose *Utsav* [Girish Karnad, 1984], which is one of my favourite films, based on the *Kamasutra*. The French will love it! *(laughs)* Then, a Kannada film called *Accident* [Shankar Nag, 1985] and a documentary made by a woman, Saba Dewan, on the *tawaif*, the courtesans [*The Other Song*, 2009]. There is some strain of similarities in those films—the image of the woman is slightly different from the rest of Bollywood and they're not totally objectified.

We have a very different gender perception depending on which society you've lived in. For the French, it's easier to understand that there's just one way of gender discrimination. Because you have a homogeneous society. But in India, we have these strange differences, which I wanted to bring up with these films. A very interesting point is that Indian women are not so badly off that you'd think they are. There is no wage difference for us. I never felt I was treated differently as an animator because I am a woman. But I would hear French women saying that. For me it's very strange, scandalous! *(laughs)*

Which Indian movies do you like to watch?

Right now, I am very interested in the new wave in Kerala and Tamil Nadu. Malayalam and Tamil movies are getting to be very interesting.

Do you find them in Bombay?

No. Getting them with subtitles is very rare. So Bangalore is a good place. A lot of directors are putting their movies on YouTube with subtitles. I would watch all of Anurag [Kashyap]'s productions, Onir's films. But we are making three films a day in this country. How do you find time to watch them? I avoid Bollywood and even more than Bollywood, Hollywood action films. I just can't watch them. I missed MAMI [Mumbai International Film Festival] this year, but I would have loved watching French cinema on a big screen. They have a very good selection. So I still prefer going to a festival. The films are all subtitled. All the films that I've seen from the South have been in festivals. I don't really bother watching the other films.

How do you survive as an animator in Bombay and what do you think the future holds?

It's very difficult to survive. When I was doing *Printed Rainbow*, I had enough work and I was making decent money to survive and to invest in my own films. But after *Printed Rainbow*, I stopped getting work, because people started thinking, 'Oh she's a Cannes-award filmmaker, she must be doing something or the other.' Plus, each time I work on a film, I am saying no to other jobs, which has been very bad, because if you're not staying in advertising, which is a source of earning, there are ten other people who are doing your job faster and cheaper. The moment you come back, it takes six months to establish yourself by going to parties. I'd rather make a film! I've been teaching, because all the people I know who are making animation films teach, but there's no money in teaching over here either. I've been doing a lot of work virtually for clients. If I don't need to be in Bombay, I can be in a small village and work virtually. If you can't increase your income, you might as well decrease your expenditure! So I got a little piece of land in Kerala. I want to grow my vegetables and make my films there. As long as there's Internet, you can work anywhere.

NISHTHA JAIN
Documentary Filmmaker

I met Nishtha Jain at Prithvi Theatre, in Juhu, in the north of Mumbai. The setting was ideal: Prithvi Theatre is a one-of-a-kind cultural landmark in Mumbai. The interview needed to be interrupted due to lack of time, but continued a couple of months later at another original setting—the premises of Films Division, where one of Nishtha's films was being screened, as part of a documentary festival.

These two locations couldn't have fit Nishtha's personality better: in their own different ways—one being a private institution dedicated to plays and concerts, the other working with limited government funding to finance documentaries—both Prithvi Theatre and Films Division keep art distinct from business, a precious (and rare) philosophy in Mumbai. Nishtha, having chosen to struggle for her beliefs over the easy money she could have made in the commercial film industry, would obviously feel more comfortable in these settings.

With seven films to her name, directed between 2004 and 2014, Nishtha is one of the most celebrated and internationally acclaimed documentary filmmakers in Mumbai, especially since her film *Gulabi Gang* [2014] released in commercial theatres (a rare event for the genre in India). Her films have tackled subjects as diverse as the world of photo studios (*City of Photos*, 2007), the daily struggles of lower class women (*6 Yards to Democracy,* 2006), the relationship between a domestic help and her boss (*Lakshmi and Me*, 2007), the migrants' world in the Mumbai megalopolis (*At My Doorstep*, 2009) or the political commitment of Sampat Pal, the rural women's heroine in a pink saree (*Gulabi Gang*).

Convinced by her work that she was a feminist—which could only fit perfectly in my female-dominated book—or at least a social activist, given her many political statements on social media, I was slightly surprised when she refuted the label. Instead, she delighted in detailing her working methods and the interview took a different path: Nishtha sees documentary as not only a way of translating a reality into images, but creative work in its own right.

How did you become a documentary filmmaker?

I was studying in Germany in Mass Communication, which was a confusing course, because you can land up being in an academy after that, or you could become an artist, or a filmmaker, since it covered the whole range. It was also my first exposure to film production. Before that, I was a film-buff, but I had no exposure to it at all. When I left Germany in 1987, I felt I needed to learn more, so I applied for FTII but I didn't get admission. The other way to enter the film world was to become somebody's assistant. Somehow, Bollywood, industrial cinema, didn't excite me at all. Independent cinema was still quite interesting, but it was not something that fascinated me completely. So I took the next easiest thing, which was to work in Delhi. There were enough jobs around. It was the pre-boom period in television. There were only two channels and there was a great need for alternative content. *India Today*, which was a magazine, had started a video news magazine, News Track, which was the first of its kind. You could buy a VHS which contained five current affairs pieces. Some would be a hot political story, some would be a social story, one would concern art and one would definitely be on films. It was like a package, designed around BBC television documentaries and you would get it monthly. I joined as an editor and it was fairly interesting work because those were very interesting political times. It was the times when Babri Masjid was demolished; there was militancy in Kashmir; there was the anti-Mandal agitation and the Delhi massacre. It was very exciting because before that, I didn't have an exposure to my own country, to travelling. I was twenty-one, just out of college. For a moment, I stopped thinking about cinema and I was really taken with current affairs. I left News Track after a year and a half because I had a lot of political problems with their outlook. They were out-and-out casteists, which I learned with the anti-Mandal story. Because I was pro-Mandal, they thought I was a low-caste person. I left the magazine at the time when there was another news magazine that was coming up, called Eyewitness. Its director, Karan Thapar, appeared to be a much more secular and balanced person and I joined as a correspondent. I wasn't really interested in doing political stories or the kind of stories that would form the mainstay of those magazines. I did a few documentaries; one was on dyslexia, one on Sharia and one on North Plant. I liked the content part of it, but the fact that you have to put it all in one format—a fifteen or sixteen-minute format with a voice-over—was not my thing. Every story would just be reduced to the same thing at the edit. I tried my best, but I wanted to be in cinema. In the end, I think I spent four and a half years at Eyewitness and News Track combined and according to this friend of mine, I had been crying from the first day she met me, saying how much I hated this. I said, 'Really, did I not like it for four and a half years?' So I just went and resigned. I didn't know what lay ahead. I thought of going abroad to study in a film school and I was in the process of giving the TOEFL. Meanwhile, I had developed quite a reputation as an editor, so lots of people were after me to come and join their organization. I edited a couple of documentaries and I worked as an editor for Muzaffar Ali, who was doing a fifty-two-episode serial, which was quite interesting. Meanwhile, I had got through FTII where I studied film direction for three years. When I came out, it was the same problem. I still didn't want to enter the industry. It had become far worse by then. I just didn't want to be part of the kind of films that were being produced; the kind of films I wanted to be part of were not getting made. I worked for almost nine months for the art director Kumar Shahani, but it wasn't paying well. So I returned to Delhi and I started working with my brother and his wife, who are also filmmakers. Then they left. At that time, there was a new television channel that was opening up. It was going to be the first non-fiction television channel in Mumbai. I was asked if I would like to join and I spent seven months there. We were five–six commissioning editors—all women, very amazing women—and it was fun. I also directed a series over there. It was highly creative and you could do what you wanted to do. Unfortunately, the channel never took off because of some financial scam.

I was then researching for a film that I wanted to make and for which I got a little bit of a grant from IPFA—*City of Photos*. It took a long time—three years, from 2001 to 2004—to raise the small amount of money that I needed—ten thousand euros. I had to beg and borrow, and I made the film, after which everything changed, because it was highly successful and critically acclaimed. After the film, people were ready to give me money for my next one. It's still screened in a lot of universities. The film was exploring the world of photo studios, looking into the world of self-representation, aspirations and there were a lot of morbid backgrounds that people used for their photos....

Like the attacks of 9/11.

Yes. But it's a poetic, lyrical film, with some reflections on photography and some really amazing people. It's done at the point of transitions, when we are moving from analogue to digital—how the industry, especially these photographers, in small towns, who are catering to poor people, enter into this transition, but also how the traditional moves into the modern. It was a really funny, charming kind of a film.

Was it already made under the banner of your production company?

Yes. After that, I did this film called *Call it Slut*. The Kala Ghoda Festival asked me to make a film on the celebration of womanhood. Four women directors were commissioned, and we were given one thousand dollars. It was the time when dance bars were closing down and I had just met a transgender woman, Lakshmi Tripathi. There was something about her that really attracted me. We met, we hit it off and I said, 'Why don't you teach how to be a woman.' It was a wicked film about exploring yourself. Lakshmi told me to call it 'Slut'.

Then, I did this film called *6 Yards to Democracy*, which was looking at an incident that took place a year before, during the elections. Twenty-five women had died in a stampede at a place where some sarees were being distributed, for sarees which cost one hundred rupees. You can imagine how poor they must have been to die for something like that. It also reflected how easily people can be bought for votes in India. I wanted to meet these women and understand what electoral democracy stands for. I went to Lucknow where the incident took place to meet the women who survived. By the time I got the funding, it was already late, the incident was already a year old and they had moved on. But when I started to talk to a woman about sarees and how she loved sarees, a sparkle would come into her eye. So I had a starting point and then the film went somewhere else. I started looking into the lives of these women, how difficult they are and what are the other everyday problems they have. I am not too sure about this film, whether it really worked. It was nicely done, beautifully shot, the production value is there. But I needed more money to complete it and I wasn't getting it, so I closed it. Nonetheless, it got some awards, it was shown in some festivals.

That's when I learned that it's okay not to end a film, even if you started it. In documentary, you can't really predict where it's going to go. You could take a decision about closing it and not doing it. I learned that you don't have to kill yourself about not finishing. But it also taught me to be more discerning about the possibilities and the importance of trying to script a documentary. Once you're shooting, you must forget what you've imagined and go with a clean slate.

How much research do you do for a documentary?

The research may not be for a particular documentary. It's a constant process of reading and thinking, which then resolves into a film. For me, it's more of formulation, what I want to say through this film, how I want to approach it, which is the note that I want to give. The filmmaking part of it comes from a lot of experience.

Does it often happen that your documentary doesn't go in the direction you thought it would?

No. *6 Yards to Democracy* was the only time it happened. The immediacy was over. When I thought about it, I realized I didn't want to do a news film, a current affairs film, or an investigative film. What really attracted me to the idea was the saree. I should have explored what the saree means. I shouldn't have gone into the socioeconomic aspect. I should have gone into a more abstract, less realistic aspect, which was more about femininity, empowerment.

You do say in *Lakshmi and Me* that you were born a feminist.

I was always a rebel from childhood, without having any influences really. I think from the age of six or seven, I started to ask why I should be treated differently from the boys. When mum would say, 'You shouldn't sit with your legs apart', I was like, 'Why is that? What the hell?' I used to question everything. It had to be about equality with my brothers. If you're not asking them to do something, then you're not going to ask me. Over the next few years, it got really crystallized, I started reading about feminism. Lots of suffering is due to the fact that you are a woman. There was a hyper-consciousness about the fact that I don't want to be anything that a woman is supposed to be. When I say feminism, I don't mean I want to be equal to men. But why shouldn't we get the same privileges, the same rights? Still, my films don't have to deal with women, not necessarily.

But lots of them do. You mean you don't define yourself as an activist?

No. I am not an activist filmmaker. I am not a feminist filmmaker. I am a filmmaker. It doesn't mean I am not concerned about women's issues. But when I approach something, I have social concerns and, equally, artistic concerns. When I approach an idea, a theme, form is the primary concern. I don't want to get into the debate of form and content, but I think content makes sense only through the way it is shown. There are so many things that I would like to make a film about. But until I know how I am going to do it, it doesn't make sense.

Would you say that your films are made to carry a social message?

Let's talk in the context of *Lakshmi and Me*. Something in my relationship with Lakshmi who is my domestic worker, moves me. She is a beautiful woman, young, very bright and I am her boss.

I don't know if I deserve to be in that position. It's a space that I am not very comfortable with. That's where the film starts growing. I don't like the way Indians feel very entitled to having people work for them. It's in the way they talk, their gestures, their tone. I wanted to make a film about these little things, not on the bigger subject of domestic work, of feudalism. If I wanted to make a film about servitude, I could have a lot of domestic workers talk about how badly they are treated. But I've seen a hundred films of that kind. You see them, walk out and it won't affect you, because it all adds to the information that you already have. For me, it's about creating a feeling, moving something inside you that makes you think. It doesn't matter if it's a documentary or fiction. Cinema should be able to talk to you in a way that you can feel something deep inside you. I wanted to capture all the unsaid, all the little invisible things, the tensions between two people. It's a very difficult thing to do when you are yourself in the film and you're shooting yourself. It was an experiment. Lakshmi agreed to it, she said, 'Yeah, you should make a film about me.' When soap operas started in India, one achievement was that everyone thought they had a story to tell, because soap operas were about everyday life and mundane. My mum, who was leading a very ordinary housewife life, also felt that her story was so great.

Do you agree that everybody's story is interesting?

It depends. That's a risk that you take with your casting, because in documentary, you also cast.

How do you do a good casting in documentary?

It's an instinct. I had a six-year relationship with Lakshmi and I felt she would become a great protagonist for a film. I look at people and I think there's a film there.

So it's never the subject first and the casting afterwards?

No, never, because the film is going to be about people. The people themselves have to be interesting. You need a little bit of experience to cast, to know that person will be able to be himself or herself.

Because what Lakshmi is doing is acting herself. Will she be a good actress? Will she be able to portray herself?

Was she?

She's amazing. The person who inspired *At My Doorstep*, my next film, was this poet watchman. The film was written completely on him. He used to keep a diary. He wanted to be in films and he also felt that his story was worth being told. I asked him to write a script for his story, which he's reading for me in the film. So it's about the characters, it's not about the subject. *At My Doorstep* is a completely different kind of filmmaking from *Lakshmi and Me*. With *At My Doorstep*, I thought I had learned a bit about shooting and about editing. What is really a shot and how long should the shot be? When should you cut while editing, while shooting? How long should you shoot when you're shooting? Those were very basic questions that I was dealing with at the time.

Why? Was this film more difficult to make than the others?

No, each of my previous films is a dialogue with the next film. The kind of questions that I raise, by making one film, find their answers in the next one. One film in a way leads to another. It's not just coming from outside, it's coming from your own work.

Lakshmi is your maid, the building in *At My Doorstep* is your building. How important is it for you to make your presence felt in your documentaries?

The filmmaker is always in the film, whether he is physically present or not. You're present in the way you look, in the choice of the subject, the way you edit, the way you shoot. For me, the films are about the filmmmaker's mind. I can't separate the filmmaker from the film itself. I would like to be less and less physically present, but that doesn't decrease my presence. *Lakshmi and Me* wouldn't have been possible without me. If I was making a film about Lakshmi who comes to my house for one hour to work, I didn't want to hide that. I know Lakshmi because she comes to work in my house. I wanted to look at it from that point of view. I didn't want to make a film where I raise a finger, I point at other people, other employers. I wanted to talk about myself. That's why the film really works. All those who are watching it more or less are also people who have a Lakshmi working in their house. Then they become me, it transforms them and makes them uncomfortable. You may hate it, but you can't be indifferent to it.

I didn't want to put myself into *At My Doorstep*, although these are people I know. I am not really part of the film at all, either in terms of a voice, or my presence, except in one shot, where my door opens and the watchman is standing there. I just show that this is my connection, this is the people I know, but I am not important. The gaze has shifted from inside my house to outside. The style of filming is very different. It's not a single-person narrative; it's not a macro picture at all. It's not just a home, it's four–five people and these people come from somewhere else to the city of Bombay. Bombay is a city of films, of dreams. Lots of concentric circles start from this building, so the film goes out like waves. In *Lakshmi*, the movement is much more vertical. With *At My Doorstep*, I was trying to explore what you can do with the same film, but differently. If we create this little ripple, will it become an ocean? Bombay, water—so many things mixed up. The film was made out of nothing—people, the camera and the relationship between the people and the camera. In *Lakshmi*, there is a strong story, because so many things happened in her life in those two years. There is no story in *At My Doorstep*.

It's more like portraits?

It is portraits, people talking. It's more open, it's a film that is trying to find itself. What the narrative of that film was created through is intangible stuff, while *Lakshmi and Me* is treated with very tangible stuff—the precariousness of her life, her negotiation of class, gender. It's very interesting, playing with your material in a very different way.

After that, I finished a film that I made a short of earlier, called *Family Album*. It was really about people in Calcutta looking at their albums and talking about their grandmothers, mothers—lots of stories of women. Those were middle-class, rich people, the kind of people who would get themselves photographed in the 1950s and 1960s. So it's a companion piece of *City of Photos*.

Then, I did *Gulabi Gang*, inspired by the very dynamic character of Sampat Pal. Before I could get funding, this other film, *Pink Saris* [Kim Longinotto, 2010], got made, although I started earlier. The team came quickly, made the film and went away. I always feel a kind of discomfort when I watch these films made by foreigners who come to India. Not all, some of them. I sense a feeling of re-colonization. It doesn't necessarily need to have been done by a foreigner, by white people. It could very well be done by an Indian. But what I am talking about is the western gaze, very colonial ways of how you look at films, how you look at people, at circumstances. I felt that about *Pink Saris*. [Kim Longinotto] caught Sampat Pal in a very interesting phase of her life, but because of her inability to really understand the language, she fell into some very typical traps and brought a very typical story. So I decided to go ahead with my film, although I knew it was going to be difficult to market it—[Kim Longinotto] was a celebrated filmmaker and her film would be in all the festivals. My producer told me, 'You're from India, you understand the language. You'll be able to bring something to the project that maybe an outsider cannot.' I said, 'Okay, let's give it a go', since there was money. But how different could my film be? It was not like ten years had passed, that things had changed. I was doing a film on the same subject after only one year.

Could you explain what you mean by re-colonization?

I always feel that if you understand the language, if you understand the culture, it's a different gaze. There is always danger of re-colonizing through appropriating of images and coming with a certain mindset which doesn't belong to that place. The gaze could be too critical, or too exotic, especially if people don't understand the culture. I felt this story is not black and white. It's not that men are the enemies and women are the victims. It's not true. Women and men both perpetrate patriarchy. That sense is very important to bring in. You see women in both the roles in the film. You see women as part of the patriarchy as well as trying to fight it. It was important to humanize the people and not create divides between genders.

How different is your point of view?

My purpose was not to show that my point of view is different. That's not why I did the film. I wanted to do the film because I felt I was able to bring something different. My film is not centred on Sampat Pal. Of course she's the leader of the Gulabi Gang, so it would be very difficult not to have her in the film. But in my film, I also have other women and other processes, like the election process and the Gulabi Gang trying to enter the democratic system. These cases that the Gulabi Gang is trying to solve, or take up on behalf of other women, have just become a means by which you can see how the institutions work, or rather not work. There is police, there is law in India but because of corruption, they are not doing their job and it allows people to break the laws, kill women, avoid filing cases. A lot of the work of Gulabi Gang is just fighting to get justice, which the Constitution and the law have given them, but they don't get it because the system is very corrupt.

These women are pretty familiar with media attention. Did they try to use you in any way?

Everybody is trying to use their image. If I put a camera on you, you'll also be very conscious of the image you will give. You have to look at your characters as actors. Everybody is an actor. Lakshmi is an actor, the fellow in *At My Doorstep* is an actor. If you put a camera in front of me, I will also act. In that sense, this is not my concern. In fact, it was quite refreshing to see that because Sampat Pal is so used to the camera, she sometimes forgets it and she says all kinds of things which don't make her look good. She doesn't care what the other people think. She's able to be herself, which is both good, bad and ugly. She doesn't try to pretend that she is a nice lady. She gets angry, she's impulsive, she shouts and she's passionate. In that sense, the fact that those women were used to the camera maybe helped them to be themselves.

How did the Gulabi Gang change the situation of women up there?

I think the problems are very deep-rooted. At this point of time, Gulabi Gang is eight years old. It has had an impact. They are in the papers all the time in that area. Four hundred thousand women have become members. I don't have the statistics to say what exact quantified change has happened. The important thing is how women have learned to use petitions. Earlier, women would be afraid to even enter a police station, but now they go there all the time. In various villages, they would walk in knowing they are completely entitled to walk into a police station and make the police file a case. They know how the bureaucratic hierarchy works, at which level, at which point. They first will go to a block development officer and if things don't work there, they'll go to a higher officer, then the general inspector. Working with the system is very empowering for these women, when most of them are illiterate.

That's also what you show in *Six Yards to Democracy*. Were you welcome in those bureaucrats' offices with your camera?

We don't go there and ask them for permission. We just put on the camera, and we get what we get. You don't enter a police station and ask, 'Can we shoot?' They won't allow you to shoot, so you just do it quickly before they realize that this could damage their image. Some officers welcome you, because they have nothing to hide. Others are more afraid.

Why are women equally responsible for the problems in the society?

Because they internalize the system in a way, like a mother-in-law, who has been victimized and will continue the system by victimizing the daughter-in-law. Men are being aided by women to carry on patriarchy.

The situation of women in India is so ambiguous.

I think more than any other country in the world you see very powerful women in India: in business houses, in politics, as intellectuals, as goddesses. *(laughs)* They can be equally corrupt. There are amazing women's movements all over India—social workers, reformers. It's not just that women are exploited. Even personally, as a documentary filmmaker, I don't face any gender discrimination just because I am a woman. It's different in Bollywood or in television, where they promote very patriarchal, regressive, sexist views. When you really look at women, women like Lakshmi, who are working outside, they hold up their homes. They do three jobs, they take care of the children, they do house chores. Most of the time, they might be the main earning members in the family. The man may be working, but he may be gambling or drinking. So the money the woman earns is really what holds up the family and she pays for the education of the children. When I look at the women in this country, I feel that they are the ones who are holding up our nation, especially in the poorest sections. Somehow the men became easily emasculated, victims and alcoholics, because their response to the system is one of giving up. But on the other end, the women are still alive and trying to change, and that's what you see in *Gulabi Gang*. You see the men are sort of comatose. The women are the ones who are fighting and yet, while they are fighting, they are still part of the patriarchal mindset. It's going to take many years to realize their situation of power. They still feel incomplete without the man, who most probably constantly beats them. The system has been such that women are not able to think independently of themselves as a unit. Everywhere, in the rest of the world, single women are not given the same status as married women. Even the Western emancipated societies have a very patriarchal mindset. In *Gulabi Gang*, despite the terrible living conditions, Sampat has claimed that power. Nobody has given it to her. She's decided that she's not going to take this shit. She's also lower class, uneducated, has five children, she is married, but she's able to break out a bit. She's an exceptional woman. She also shows to people that because she belongs to the same system, she serves as an example to make you break out of it. Of course, for some women, it might be more difficult, because the family might be violent. Sampat was lucky because her husband was mild. But some women get killed if they try to break the rules. Which you see also in *Gulabi Gang*—a girl gets killed by her brother, because she's divorced and she takes a lover.

Looking at your work, what strikes me most is how conscious lower class people are of the injustice of their situation.

Wherever the change has come through, it has come through workers' unions, big groups of people, coming together. When people are in unions, they are still able to get some of their share, unless the union leaders are also corrupt. For example, middle-class farmers' unions are able to get much more benefits from the government. But in my films, it's mostly unorganized sectors that are shown. I feel that the change can only come through people coming together, through movements.

Through democracy?

Democracy here is just for the name, because we are not able to implement democratic institutions in this country. Now, in the times of global capitalism, the only way for a change to happen, is if millions of people start gathering together. Otherwise, it will continue like this. If you're alone, and single and lost, if you're trying to get from month to month, to feed yourself, then it's not going to happen.

What are the projects you're working on right now?

Right now, I am exploring the relationship of workers with work itself. How come for hundreds of years, people have worked in insufferable conditions? I don't understand. Why don't they come together? Why don't they protest, why do they continue to suffer? It's a very big question in my next film, where I am looking at factory workers in Bengal. I am also looking at sex workers and talking about dignity: why do sex workers want to continue the sex work even though they didn't get into it by choice, but they were forced into it? If you look at the former Untouchables—today the scheduled caste— they still continue to do the work that was prescribed for them. It's very interesting to see what options they have: could they have gone into something else? There is caste consciousness: they know they are doing this job because they belong to a certain caste—for instance, cleaning the gutters.

Would you say that you address a certain type of an audience, mostly educated?

No. I just make films for myself in a certain way. *(laughs)* I am not saying that I am the only audience for the film, but the film has to first excite me, there has to be an inquiry. Then I try to make a film in a way that it can be accessed by anyone, even an illiterate person in a village, to universalize the human experience. My attempt is not to go for the intellectual audience, but for a universal reception of the film, across continents. That's what cinema is about. Some people make a film for an Indian audience, or for just some intellectuals, or art audience. I feel that my cinema can be universally understood. I travelled everywhere with my films. Unless there's a language problem, for example unless somebody is illiterate and doesn't understand the language that is being spoken, most of the people don't have problems understanding my films.

What is the situation of the documentary genre nowadays in India? Is it more recognized?

The Films Division of India, which is a wing of the government, is also responsible for a large part of the attitude of Indians towards documentary. Films Division commissioned films that were not really well-made. Of course, some are really amazing, but they also did a lot of propaganda work for whatever government was in power. Those films used to always run before every feature film in cinema halls. So everybody has this image of documentary as a very boring thing that they had to watch before the main film. Over the years, a lot of documentaries were very interviews-based films, agenda-related films, so they were not telling human stories. Today, the new documentary is much more cinematic. It's experimenting with different forms, different kinds of storytelling. Because it's so vibrant, the audience is expanding.

Gulabi Gang was released in multiplexes, which is a victory in India for documentaries. What about your earlier films?

Somehow, there was no chance earlier. It's only in the last two or three years that PVR has started giving this option that you could release your film. But even if you release it, how do you advertise that there is a film running in the theatres? Because you don't have money for publicity.

Do you find it easier to finance your films now?

In India, there is still no money for documentaries. Most films which are big budget are mostly international co-productions. In India, we only have two funds. One is the Films Division fund, which is a very small fund, and the other one is the PSBT fund, which used to be three-and-a-half lakh rupees. Now, they have started to give nine to ten lakh rupees, but this is still very little money.

Do you still enjoy total freedom in your productions, especially when you co-produce?

I think you have to exercise your freedom. As a director, it's your duty to make the film that you want to make, although other people will try to influence you. I've been lucky that I've been able to make the films that I wanted to make. I've not been asked to cut off something, or add something. I am very much responsible for my films. They are totally independent creations.

What about censorship?

For *Gulabi Gang*, I had a U certificate, but I had to ask for a review. They tried to censor some things, some abuses. It eventually went without any deletions.

Listening to you, one could be positive about the future of documentaries in India.

Till television doesn't start producing and acquiring documentaries, it is going to be difficult. Why has documentary survived in the rest of the world? Because television has been a big stakeholder. They give money for the films as co-producers, or as pre-acquisitions, and then those films are shown on those channels. They can enter while the film is being made and then they get the rights to show the film. We don't have that in India. Even if channels don't finance the films, they are not buying them either. Earlier, when there was only one TV channel, Doordarshan, my documentaries were broadcasted. There was an audience for that. You have to cultivate the audience. If they're used to watching Bollywood, it's not going to be easy to just shift to another kind of film.

CONCLUSION

I left Mumbai in 2017. I moved to the Maximum City in 2009, attracted, like many others (though for different reasons), by the magical power of its cinema. When I first started writing on Indian cinema, I was young, hence probably very naive and definitely optimistic. Soon, I thought, India would get the worldwide recognition it deserves, and not only because of its booming economy. Soon, Indian films would be seen in the best festivals, and film critics would fight over which ten Marathi or Tamil films one should 'watch before you die'.

I can't say I wasn't slightly disappointed when I saw the programming in the movie halls in Mumbai. I was coming from the Mecca of cinema, Paris, and I became afraid Mumbai wouldn't be able to fulfil my needs. Either the theatres were empty, and the movies didn't remain on screens for more than a week, or I had to wait two or three months to watch a film that I was really interested in—one that wasn't the same old Salman Khan blockbuster. Some of my Indian friends expressed huge disdain for their hometown's movies—though admitting that they never watched any. American movies were so much better, they said. European ones too, for that matter (though most of them were invisible in India). Also, the more I tried to understand Indian cinema, the more it seemed to escape my understanding. I was told there were too many similar movies which were made each year; most of them were flops, people were not interested in them anymore. So why keep producing them?

Writing this book was a relief. I met people who were not naive. Still, they showed the same optimism I first had, and an energy which was inspiring enough. I knew these were people who had hopes and dreams for a different kind of cinema, which would be closer to art than to business; I met people with a vision, people who could honour the wonderful legacy of the likes of Guru Dutt, Raj Kapoor, Ritwik Ghatak, Rituparno Ghosh or Adoor Gopalakrishnan, but in their own way and true to the contemporary Indian society.

In the last two–three years, many filmmakers not only showed how inspired they were, but luckily for them, they also met with an audience that appreciated them. The huge success of *Sairat* —despite being a so-called 'regional film'—is an example of what the future of Indian cinema could be, when all the stars are aligned (from production to distribution, notwithstanding a real interest in showing the best Indian movies abroad, and not only the ones which will please the vision Westerners have of India). The obstacles are many, and I don't believe censorship is the biggest one. Yes, the producers of *Udta Punjab* and *Lipstick Under My Burkha* had to fight the CBFC, but their films eventually got released with minor cuts, or no cuts at all. Yes, they got an 'A' certificate, but films are classified in the US and Europe too (and the US classification system can also be ridiculously prudish).

I am not naive anymore. But I want to stay optimistic about a country where wonderful films like Raam Reddy's *Thithi* are released, watched and appreciated. Where one of the best actresses of Indian cinema, Konkona Sen Sharma, is able to direct her first feature and get it selected at the Toronto International Film Festival. I am no screenwriter or filmmaker, and Indian by heart only. I am barely capable, with my little knowledge of Indian cinema (who could have a full knowledge of such a productive industry anyway?), of understanding the complexity of making a film in India. Still, there is a call I am eager to make: dear Indian artists, please never compromise on your Indianness. Your cinema made me fall in love with India. And I can't wait for the whole world to fall in love with it too.

ACKNOWLEDGEMENTS

To Arpita Das, my publisher, for the velocity and sheer enthusiasm with which she took to this manuscript.

To Ishita Gupta, my editor, for being so thorough all through the editing work of this book.

To Dibakar Banerjee, whom I am indebted to for at least my seven next lives.

To Ananya Banerjee, Zachary Coffin, Sarah Meeran Cave and Tunali Mukherjee, who made my English sound less French just out of friendship.

To all the fantastic interviewees who reminded me of all the many reasons why I love Mumbai.

To all those whose advice, contacts, or just daily support, helped me in finishing this book: Vikas Chandra, Fatema Kagalwala, Selvaggia Velo, Saif Akhtar, Amandine d'Azevedo, Mudit Singhal, Lucie Régereau, Céline Chesné, Clément Graminiès, Ariane Beauvillard, Sarah Elkaïm, Jérémie Horowitz and Devi Boerema.

To Shah Rukh Khan, for making me come to India.

To Mumbai, the most fascinating and exhausting megalopolis in the world.

To my family, before and after everything.

ABOUT THE AUTHOR

Ophélie Wiel teaches Film Studies at the Université de la Sorbonne Nouvelle in Paris. She moved to India from France a few years ago and fell in love with Mumbai and the Hindi film industry. She is a noted film critic and a renowned specialist of Indian cinema and classic Hollywood cinema in France. Her previous publications include the book *Bollywood et les autres: Voyage au coeur du cinéma indien* (*Bollywood and Others: A Journey into Indian Cinema*), published in 2011.

Extolled for his extraordinary courage, Bhagat Singh is one of our most venerated freedom fighters. He is valourised for his martyrdom, and rightly so, but in the ensuing enthusiasm, most of us forget his contributions as an intellectual and a thinker. In the current political climate, when it has become routine to appropriate Bhagat Singh as a nationalist icon, not much is known about his nationalist vision. This book provides a corrective to this by bringing together a majority of Bhagat Singh's writings, some of which were hitherto unavailable in English.

A collection that brings together Bhagat Singh's seminal writings.

For special offers on this and other books from SAGE, write to marketing@sagepub.in

Explore our range at www.sagepub.in

Paperback
978-93-528-0837-3

Behind the seemingly ordinary life of a practising architect lies a whole host of non-professional impulses that give shape to buildings. *Stories of Storeys: Art, Architecture and the City* is about these impulses and conditions—social, literate, personal and political—which are expressed, but often ignored in architecture. Bhatia looks at the ordinary, physical, visible and tactile involvement of our urban environment and the way it affects, communicates with, or influences us.

An all-inclusive sociology of architecture through the eyes of a renowned architect

For special offers on this and other books from SAGE, write to marketing@sagepub.in

Explore our range at
www.sagepub.in

Paperback
978-93-532-8080-2

Shah is that rare writer who combines the topical energy of journalism with the reflective depth and breadth of scholarship. Her television book is, by the same token, that exceedingly rare approach to the subject that is neither superficial nor ponderous. This is a text that navigates seamlessly between reportage, social analysis and personal memoir. It brings policy debates alive and mines everyday experience for its structural significance.

William Mazzarella
*Neukom Family Professor Chair,
Department of Anthropology, University of Chicago*

A powerful book that unravels the processes by which consumerism, trivialization and exclusion invaded the Indian newsroom.

For special offers on this and other books from SAGE, write to marketing@sagepub.in

Explore our range at www.sagepub.in

**Paperback
978-93-532-8605-7**